Sorry About That

Sorry About That

The Language of Public Apology

EDWIN L. BATTISTELLA

OXFORD
UNIVERSITY PRESS

Oxford University Press is a department of the University of
Oxford. It furthers the University's objective of excellence in research,
scholarship, and education by publishing worldwide.

Oxford   New York
Auckland   Cape Town   Dar es Salaam   Hong Kong   Karachi
Kuala Lumpur   Madrid   Melbourne   Mexico City   Nairobi
New Delhi   Shanghai   Taipei   Toronto

With offices in
Argentina   Austria   Brazil   Chile   Czech Republic   France   Greece
Guatemala   Hungary   Italy   Japan   Poland   Portugal   Singapore
South Korea   Switzerland   Thailand   Turkey   Ukraine   Vietnam

Oxford is a registered trademark of Oxford University Press
in the UK and certain other countries.

Published in the United States of America by
Oxford University Press
198 Madison Avenue, New York, NY 10016

Library of Congress Cataloging-in-Publication Data

Battistella, Edwin L., author.
Sorry about that : the language of public apology / Edwin L. Battistella.
    pages cm
Includes bibliographical references and index.
ISBN 978-0-19-930091-4 (hardcover : alk. paper)   1. Linguistic analysis (Linguistics)
2. Apologizing.   I. Title.
P126.B37 2014
158.2—dc23
2013033233

9 8 7 6 5 4 3 2 1
Printed in the United States of America
on acid-free paper

Contents

Foreword

MY INTEREST IN apologies began years ago, when a friend asked me to help him write an apology letter for a direct mail piece he had sent out. "You must have to write a lot of apologies," he joked, "Maybe you can help me."

More recently, my attention was focused on apologies by politicians and public figures, and a number of them (I won't say who) are to thank for motivating me to write this book. As I experienced their apologies vicariously in the media, I became increasingly frustrated by language being used to evade responsibility and at our willingness as consumers of language to let that happen.

As it often does, frustration led to renewed curiosity, analysis, and research, and I quickly found myself immersed in an inter- and multidisciplinary exploration of sociology, linguistics and pragmatics, philosophy and psychology, rhetoric, legal studies, and history.

My training in linguistics has informed this book not just analytically but in terms of the approach. After a couple of Goldilocks-like false starts, I found that the most useful approach was descriptive and textual. Rather than describing an ideal apology and matching actual examples to that fiction, I describe what apologies try to do, how they succeed or fail, and how they blend with other language uses such as excuses or insults. So this book is example based as well as language based.

Most of the examples in this book are new. Some more-or-less classic examples of public apologies appear here that have been discussed elsewhere in the literature—they were too good or too important to omit. I hope my discussion has added new value to their understanding.

I have a number of people to thank as well—Hallie Stebbins, Brian Hurley, and Peter Ohlin of Oxford University Press for helping me to shape this in a readable way, and Jennifer Margulis for a close reading of an early proposal. A number of colleagues also contributed ideas, examples, feedback, and kibitzing—Mary Cullinan, Maureen Flanagan, Josie Wilson, Geoff Mills, Jon Lange, and Diana Maltz. Jennifer Marcellus helped prepare the index and verify many references. She also read the entire manuscript and made numerous stylistic and content suggestions. Southern Oregon University did its share as well with a President's Scholarship and Creativity grant and a timely sabbatical (is there any other kind?).

Thanks too to the scholars on whose work I have drawn—Nicholas Tavuchis, Nick Smith, Aaron Lazare, Deborah Tannen, David Tell, Janet Holmes, Brian Weiner, Robin Tolmach Lakoff, Erving Goffman, William Benoit, Keith Hearit, Timothy Maga, Jennifer Lind, J. L. Austin, John Searle, Jenny Thomas, and H. Paul Grice.

Ashland, Oregon
May 2013

Introduction

IN 2003, PUBLISHER Doubleday released a gripping book on addiction and recovery. Writer James Frey's *A Million Little Pieces* purported to be a memoir of his treatment for alcohol and drug addiction and his grueling recovery. The book was widely praised, and Frey followed up in 2005 with another book on the father-son relationship between himself and Leonard, a mobster he met in rehab. *My Friend Leonard* also became a bestseller. Then something happened.

In January of 2006, *The Smoking Gun* website published documentation suggesting that key parts of Frey's memoir were made up. Frey had exaggerated his criminal offenses and details of his tribulations: his tale of a violent arrest and eighty-seven-day jail sentence, for example, turned out to be a quiet arrest and short stay at a police station. His account of having root canal surgery without anesthetic was disputed. The existence of his suicidal girlfriend Lily was called into question. Frey conceded that he had "altered small details" for dramatic effect.

Oprah Winfrey, who had selected *A Million Little Pieces* for her book club in 2005, was particularly angry at Frey's deception. The Smoking Gun piece had appeared under the title "The Man Who Conned Oprah." Winfrey had initially defended Frey, even going so far as to call in to the *Larry King Live* program to stress that small inaccuracies were "irrelevant" to its larger message. Yet as the facts became clearer and the inaccuracies bigger, she felt she could no longer stand by Frey and his book.

Winfrey invited Frey onto her January 26, 2005, show. She began the program by apologizing to viewers for her telephone call to *Larry King Live*. "I regret that phone call," she said, "I made a mistake and I left the impression that the truth does not matter and I am deeply sorry about that. That is not what I believe." Winfrey then turned to Frey and scolded him for betraying his readers and for betraying her. Then she led him through his lies, one by one.

James Frey did not apologize on that program. He did, however, stumble through a confession. Frey told Oprah, "I have, you know, essentially admitted to...to lying." Later editions of Frey's book contained an apology in the preface:

> *A Million Little Pieces* is about my memories of my time in a drug and alcohol treatment center. As has been accurately revealed by two journalists at an Internet Web site, and subsequently acknowledged by me, during the process of writing the book, I embellished many details about my past experiences, and altered others in order to serve what I felt was the greater purpose of the book. I sincerely apologize to those readers who have been disappointed by my actions.

According to Frey, he wasn't thinking of whether the book was fiction or memoir as he wrote it—he just wanted to write "a book that would change lives." He conceded that for dramatic reasons he "altered events and details all the way through the book."

James Frey continued to be on Oprah Winfrey's mind, and she received a lot of viewer feedback about her confrontation with him. In the fall of 2008, Winfrey called Frey to apologize for shaming him on television, and she invited Frey back on the air in 2009. On that program, she explained that her anger was driven by ego and by the feeling that she was under attack as well—for initially saying that the truth of the book was irrelevant. After watching the tape of the 2005 show, she was embarrassed. "What people saw was my lack of compassion," Winfrey explained, "So I apologize for my lack of compassion." She added:

> My position and intention was "How dare you? How dare you? How dare you lie to me? How dare you lie to the viewers?" And it really was not a position of "Let me hear your story, let me hear your side," and that is what people saw. That is what the lashing was. The lashing was not the questioning, the lashing was the lack of compassion. And for that I apologize.

Frey thanked her, and as the show went to a commercial, he initiated an awkward hug.

If you have been counting, there are three apologies in the story of Oprah Winfrey and James Frey. Oprah apologized to her viewers for defending Frey's book. Frey apologized to readers who were disappointed. And Oprah apologized to Frey for her lack of compassion. Each apology is a little different in its language and effect.

In the first, Oprah *regrets* a mistake and is *deeply sorry* for the impression left with her viewers. She blends apology with explanation: her words defending Frey's book did not reflect her belief about the importance of truthfulness. In the second, Frey sincerely apologizes, but his apology contains a large of dose of excuse-making as well. He tries to minimize and transcend his lying and he directs the apology only to certain readers— those "who have been disappointed." The burden was on readers to decide if they were disappointed or not.

And in third apology, Oprah names a failing that troubled her—putting her own anger above compassion for Frey—and apologizes for that. Even more than in her earlier regretting, here we see the moral work of an apology—Oprah takes ownership for her behavior with no excuses.

We are all a bit like Oprah and James Frey. We make mistakes. We misspeak, mislead, and misbehave. We can be inconsiderate, rude, and even offensive. Some of us lie and cheat and steal. And some people kill or commit historic crimes. When we face our transgressions, we often feel the need—or are called upon—to apologize. Some of us apologize well and use language to repair relationships and restore respect. Others apologize poorly and our insincerity leaves transgressions unresolved or even causes new harm.

This book shows how apologies work. As we investigate the nature of apology—its language, philosophy, and sociology—we will see how both sincere and insincere apologies are created. We will come to better understand why we choose to apologize or not, and how our efforts to say we are sorry succeed or fail. And by studying the principles behind apology, we'll become better consumers of apologies—and better apologizers as well. Perhaps we can even become as good as Oprah Winfrey or some of the others whose stories I tell.

Whose stories? About half the examples in the book are political in nature, the stories of presidents, senators, and international affairs. Abe Lincoln, Woodrow Wilson, Franklin Roosevelt, Harry Truman, Dwight Eisenhower, John F. Kennedy, and Richard Nixon are represented, as are Jimmy Carter, Ronald Reagan, both George Bushes, Bill Clinton, and Barack Obama. We'll also look at apologies from the worlds of business, entertainment, and the media—McDonald's and Martha Stewart, Mel Gibson and Jane Fonda, Maureen Dowd and Dan Rather, and many more.

Ten chapters follow, most with three or four examples. Chapters 1 through 4 introduce the apology process and the language of apology. Chapters 5 and 6 focus on confession and excuse, while 7 and 8 deal with national and international apologies. Chapters 9 and 10 discuss the motivation for apology and the apology in popular culture. Interspersed between the chapters of the book are about forty additional freestanding examples illustrating the ways in which apology works (or doesn't).

Sorry About That

1

The Scope of Apologies

The Buck Stops Here

In December 1950, President Harry Truman was inducted as a civilian member of the Marine Corps League, the national association of active and former Marines. He got in the hard way. Three months earlier he had written an angry letter to a California congressman who had been urging that the Marines, then fighting in Korea, be represented on the Joint Chiefs of Staff. Truman's letter to Representative Gordon McDonough explained it this way: "For your information the Marine Corps is the Navy's police force and as long as I am President that is what it will remain. They have a propaganda machine almost equal to Stalin's."

McDonough read the letter into the *Congressional Record* on September 5, just days before the Marine Corps League's national convention. Truman's comments were denounced in the Senate as "shocking" and "insulting," and Clay Nixon, the commandant of the Marine Corps League, demanded an apology. On September 6, an embarrassed Truman apologized and arranged to appear in person at the League convention. Truman's letter to General Clifton Cates, the commander of the Marine Corps, began:

> Dear General Cates:
>   I sincerely regret the unfortunate choice of language which I used in my letter of August 29 to Congressman McDonough concerning the Marine Corps.

Truman went on to explain the context of his comments and to express his appreciation for the Marines' work. The president added that, while he had been "disturbed" by the lobbying for representation on the Joint Chiefs of Staff, he was "certain that the Marine Corps itself does not indulge in such propaganda." When Truman made his surprise visit to the Marine Corps League convention on September 7, he was introduced by General Cates. Truman told the group, "When I make a mistake, I try to correct it. I try to make as few as possible." Truman received a standing ovation and was able to put the matter behind him.

Reporting on the incident, the *New York Times* characterized Truman's letter and comments as an apology. Many in the Marine Corps League found it sincere and credible, no doubt because Truman went to the League convention in person to take his lumps. But what exactly was Truman apologizing for?

Dramaturgy

To answer that question, we need to consider more precisely what an apology is and is not. Our starting point is the work of Canadian-born sociologist Erving Goffman. Goffman worked for the Canadian film board during World War II before getting a PhD at the University of Chicago and becoming an ethnographer. He viewed the sociologist as a kind of detective, a hard-boiled intellectual outsider observing social relationships. Before his death at the age of sixty, Goffman wrote eleven books studying social interactions. His work demonstrated that everyday interactions should not be taken at face value.

In his 1956 book *The Presentation of Self in Everyday Life,* Goffman introduced a long-running acting metaphor. He imagined life as a series of theatrical performances. Individuals play different roles in different contexts—and set and manage the stage as well. In these performances, people advance their interests by trying to present a coherent, positive impression while also adapting to new situations. However, we can damage our positive impression—Goffman called it *face* after the Chinese concept—by acting in ways others find offensive. Maintaining positive face is necessary for self-respect. Thus, when we have offended someone, we need to repair the relationship with an apology or some other remedial strategy. Goffman proposed in *Relations in Public* that when we apologize, we figuratively divide the self in two and cast off the past self.

> Apologies represent a splitting of the self into a blameworthy part and a part that stands back and sympathizes with the blame giving, and, by implication, is worthy of being brought back into the fold.

That is the apology in a nutshell. According to Goffman, an apology, in its fullest form, has several elements. Apologizers express embarrassment and chagrin. They acknowledge the rule of conduct they have violated and sympathize with their own ostracism. They explicitly disavow their bad behavior and vilify the former self associated with it. They commit to pursuing correct behavior in the future. And they perform penance and offer restitution.

Judged by these standards, Harry Truman fell somewhat short. He was clearly chagrined, and he acknowledged the mistake of disrespecting the Marine Corps. He even offered some verbal restitution in his praise of the Marines. But Truman expressed regret only for his language. When Truman explained what he "had in mind" in the letter to Congressman McDonough, he switched to a different strategy—what Goffman calls "giving an account." Accounts are explanations and, for Goffman, they differ from apologies in the way they characterize the offense.

> In the case of apologies there is usually an admission that the offense was a serious or real act. This provides a contrast to another type of splitting, one that supports an account, not an apology, in which the actor projects the offensive act as something not taken to be literally.

What accounts and apologies have in common is that both use language to change the meaning of an offensive act. An apology blames and disavows a past self, while an account denies the actor's guilt in the offense—denying his or her responsibility, intent, foresight, competence, or mindfulness. A good account "succeeds in restructuring the initial response of the offended and appreciably reducing the fault of the actor—at least among the fair-minded." That is what Harry Truman did. Truman blended apology and account, apologizing for his words while defending his underlying policy and intentions. Neither the media nor the Marine Corps League debated whether Truman's statement was an account or not; both treated the letter and remarks as simply an apology, which the League voted to accept. This blending of accounts and apologies is quite common, and we will see it again and again. Now let us look at an example in which the change from a blameworthy self to a repentant self is central to an apology.

Not the Same Person

On February 2, 1998, a murderer named Karla Faye Tucker was put to death by lethal injection in Huntsville, Texas. Fifteen years earlier, in June of 1983, Tucker and a boyfriend had violently killed another couple while executing a burglary. Tucker was twenty-three years old at the time and already a drug-addicted prostitute. On the night of the double murder, at the end of a three-day drug and alcohol binge, Tucker and Daniel Garrett had planned to steal a motorcycle from Jerry Dean, the husband of one of Tucker's friends. When Dean woke up during the robbery, Garrett attacked him with a hammer from Dean's toolbox. Tucker also attacked Dean and his companion, Deborah Thornton, with a pick ax, striking each of them more than twenty times. Tucker left the ax in Deborah Thornton's chest and later told friends she had experienced a sexual thrill while swinging the weapon.

Within a few months, police linked the pair to the murders and arrested Tucker and Garrett. Convicted in separate trials in 1984, both were sentenced to death for murder in the course of an armed robbery. While in prison, Tucker found religion. She reported that her conversion began shortly after her arrest when a Christian ministry visited the Harris County Jail in Houston to perform a puppet show. Tucker took a Bible and began reading it in her cell. At her trial, Tucker—clean of drugs and a born-again Christian—accepted responsibility for the murders and expressed remorse for her actions. In her testimony, she said that she did not deserve mercy and that no punishment could atone for her crime.

By the time she arrived on death row, Tucker had become a counselor to other inmates and was involved in prison ministry work. In 1995, she married a prison minister named Dana Brown. She also continued to appeal her case, arguing diminished capacity. As the appeals failed and the execution date neared, her attorney made a clemency appeal to the Texas Parole Board. Tucker told the board:

> I am truly sorry for what I did. I will never harm another person again in my life, not even trying to protect myself. I pray God will help you believe all that I have shared and will help you decide to commute my sentence to life in prison.

Imagine how Erving Goffman might view Tucker's conversion. Tucker splits into two selves, one blameworthy and the other sympathizing with the punishment and therefore morally renewed. In fact, that was the way that Tucker and her attorney presented it. The earlier Karla Faye Tucker may have deserved to die for her crime, but the later Tucker was "no longer the same moral entity alleged to have committed the offense." The five-foot-three, 120-pound

Tucker also attracted some unexpected allies. Even television evangelist Pat Robertson, a death penalty proponent, supported clemency, arguing that Tucker "had a profound conversion experience." According to Robertson,

> The person who had committed those crimes really wasn't there anymore. She was like a different person, and when we interviewed her and showed her testimony on television, and others did the same thing, they found a person who was absolutely radiant.

The appeals failed, however, and Tucker was executed on February 3, 1998. As she prepared to die, Tucker said, "I would like to say to all of you—the Thornton family and Jerry Dean's family—that I am so sorry. I hope God will give you peace with this." The *Chicago Tribune* of February 4 announced, "Karla Tucker put to death in Texas: Last statement an apology to victims' families." The *Dallas Morning News* wrote, "Tucker put to death amid raging debate: Controversial murderer apologetic and calm at execution," and The Huntsville *Daily Sentinel* wrote, "Pickax killer offers quiet apology in moments before her execution."

Tucker's apparent transformation may be why her last words were widely treated as an apology. By itself, her "I am so sorry" does not include all the elements Goffman associates with the fullest apologies (acknowledging, disavowing, repenting, and offering restitution). Her final words mixed hope for closure for the victims with expressions of love and gratitude for her supporters. But understood in the context of her earlier conversion, confession, reported moral growth, expressions of remorse, and prison ministry work, her simple "I am so sorry" was sufficient for many to view it as an apology. Her prison life fit the core of Goffman's definition.

The lingering question, of course, is whether Karla Faye Tucker meant it. Would we still consider Karla Faye Tucker's statement an apology if she was merely acting for all those years? Certainly not. Sincerity is what makes an apology genuine. But what is sincerity? We gain some insight into this question by considering a necessarily insincere apology.

I Have Performed the Deeds of an Air Pirate

As a navy pilot during the Vietnam War, young John McCain was captured by the North Vietnamese and held prisoner for five and a half years. McCain's plane, a Douglas A-4 Skyhawk, was shot down by a surface-to-air missile over Hanoi in October 1967. One of McCain's legs and both his arms were fractured in the crash. During captivity, McCain was beaten and tortured repeatedly. And when McCain's father, a US admiral, was appointed commander-in-chief of the Pacific naval forces in July 1968, his captured son became a propaganda priority for the North Vietnamese. The beatings intensified in August, as interrogators tried to obtain a statement from McCain saying he was sorry for crimes against North Vietnamese people. In his 1999 memoir, McCain recounted those beatings.

> At two-to-three hour intervals, the guards returned to administer beatings…One guard would hold me while others pounded away. Most blows were directed at my shoulders, chest, and stomach. Occasionally, when I had fallen to the floor, they kicked me in the head. They cracked several of my ribs and broke a couple of teeth. My bad right leg was swollen and hurt the most of any of my injuries.

McCain held out for four days, attempting suicide at one point. Finally, he gave up and, for twelve hours, wrote and rewrote drafts as the interrogators dictated and edited. He was told to write, "I am a black criminal and I have performed the deeds of an air pirate. I almost died and the Vietnamese people saved my life." He was told to confess that he had bombed a school and to say that he was sorry for his actions.

No one would say that McCain's statement is a credible confession or a sincere apology. Any statement signed under such circumstances cannot be considered sincere. And McCain's confession is interesting from Goffman's perspective. For McCain, capitulation was a short-lived departure from his true self, not a rejection of an earlier blameworthy self. For McCain, the blameworthy self was the one that confessed and apologized: the authentic McCain was pretending; an insincere McCain was writing and signing.

Sincere and Authentic

John McCain's pretense reminds us that an apology is sincere only when the regret expressed genuinely represents the feelings of the speaker. Or, as literary critic Lionel Trilling put it in his book *Sincerity and Authenticity*, sincerity "refers primarily to a congruence between avowal and actual feeling." As a practical matter, we judge this intuitively when someone apologizes to us in person. We gauge their embarrassment, tone, gaze, affect, and posture—along with their language.

When we are not present ourselves, as is the case in most public apologies, we rely on context—both linguistic and situational—for clues. The actual language used to apologize may be as short as a phrase or as long as a speech and will often reveal one's intentions. Apologizers can be clear about the rules of conduct they have violated and explicitly disavow their behavior, or they may qualify and hedge their regret. Young John McCain found himself in a situation where insincerity was necessary, and it was reflected in his merely copying North Vietnamese phrases like "black criminal" and "air pirate." McCain confessed and apologized using language in a way calculated to show his insincerity.

Context also includes the speaker's actions, both long term and immediate. Have offenders performed penance and offered restitution? Have they shown a commitment to changed behavior? Karla Faye Tucker demonstrated sustained repentance, in both words and actions, and those who knew her seemed convinced that she was honestly sorry. Whether Harry Truman was sincere is more complicated. Truman's apology was a political act aimed at repairing his image, and Truman blended regret for his words with a defense of his intent. His audience took the apology and his presence at the national convention as an expression of shared values.

Harry Truman's apology also highlights a criticism of Erving Goffman's dramaturgy metaphor—its lack of a moral dimension. If we are actors on a stage, are we not simply pursuing our own interests when we apologize? And would not pursuing our own interests make all our apologies insincere and instrumental? Goffman was aware of this dilemma and tried to address it by saying that the members of any group are expected to "go to certain lengths to save the feelings and the face of others present." That was Harry Truman's approach. But saving the feelings and face of others is also a way of preserving one's own face, so Truman was also serving his own interests.

Goffman's idea that consideration for others is a social expectation merges self-interest and empathy. Other scholars have challenged this merger. Nicholas Tavuchis, also a sociologist, argues that a genuine apology must be fundamentally moral rather than dramaturgical. Together the offender and the offended must explore the moral basis of the transgression and potential reconciliation. Once a mutual understanding is reached, the offender puts himself or herself in a position of moral vulnerability by offering an apology. The offended party in turn judges the apology offered. In the best possible outcome, the offended party acknowledges the offender's moral worth and sincerity, and social bonds are reaffirmed.

Tavuchis (in a long footnote in his 1991 book *Mea Culpa: A Sociology of Apology and Reconciliation*) describes his approach as "clearly at odds" with Goffman's. Goffman, he says, approaches apology too much from the viewpoint of the offender, treating it as a mere linguistic device for changing the meaning of an offense. For Tavuchis, Goffman's self-splitting metaphor also undercuts the moral attachment to the offense and considerations of sorrow and regret. Philosopher Nick Smith, in his book *I Was Wrong*, agrees. It is not enough, Smith suggests, to be sorry. A person must also acknowledge wrongdoing. Smith writes, "Although Goffman agrees that the apologizer endorses the underlying principle, this image of her dividing her identity into a conforming self and a rebellious self risks stripping her of the intentionality required to accept blame." According to Smith, such "fractured moral agency" allows mere excuse and true apology to merge, and moral responsibility to be subordinated to explanations. In short, Tavuchis and Smith see apology as moral attachment to an offense, while Goffman emphasizes an apology's role as an instrumental social ritual.

But Goffman is not a mere instrumentalist. He sees apology in its "fullest form" as disavowing past bad behavior and committing to better future behavior. In fact, it is Goffman's attention to social ritual and the apology-account continuum that helps us make sense of apologies like Harry Truman's, which blend the moral and the social. Truman apologized just enough to express regret for his intemperance and to explain his larger point.

Goffman's metaphor of a self splitting into different moral agents also helps us to understand Karla Faye Tucker's apology. Given her crimes, it was only by becoming a new moral agent that she could accept blame. And self-splitting provides insight into John McCain's coerced confession—the self that apologized was merely an actor. As we look at apologies in the pages ahead, we will return again and again to Goffman's split self, looking at ways in which apologizers position themselves ethically and socially, whether owning up to or detaching themselves from their offenses. First, however, we consider a few more examples that raise some interesting questions about the nature of apology, questions that later chapters will discuss. We begin with President Bill Clinton's apology for a great moral wrong, the Tuskegee syphilis experiments; Judge Samuel Sewall's apology for his role in the Salem witch trials; cartoonist Al Capp's apology for spoofing *Gone with the Wind*; and the *Hartford Courant*'s apology to Thomas Jefferson.

Bad Blood

"The American people are sorry—for the loss, for the years of hurt. You did nothing wrong, but you were grievously wronged. I apologize and I am sorry that this apology has been so long in coming."
—PRESIDENT BILL CLINTON, *May 16, 1997*

In 1932 the US Public Health Service began a study of the effects of syphilis on African-American men. The sexually transmitted disease was common in Macon County, Alabama, and the doctors conducting the study signed up 399 African-American men who had previously contracted the disease for free medical care. The men were told they were being treated for "bad blood." The doctors never told the men they had syphilis, and the men were never treated.

The study went on for more than forty years until a whistleblower and the national press finally exposed it in 1972. By then, twenty-eight of the men had died of syphilis and one hundred had died of syphilis-related complications. Forty wives had been infected and nineteen children were born with syphilis.

In 1973, the government settled a class-action lawsuit without admitting wrongdoing, and the following year Congress passed the National Research Act requiring review boards for studies involving human subjects. The government settlement also created theTuskegee Health Benefit Program to provide lifetime medical benefits to the surviving participants. Wives, widows, and children were later added to the medical coverage.

In 1997, the Clinton administration formally apologized to the survivors and their families. President Clinton's apology, which ran about 1,500 words, was personally delivered in the East Room of the White House to several surviving subjects and family members and by satellite to an audience at Tuskegee University.

After welcoming and acknowledging the survivors and families, Clinton explained that the government had done something that was morally wrong and that the American people were sorry for their government's actions. He pointed out that the nation "failed to live up to its ideals" and "broke the trust" underlying democracy. His rhetoric was at times direct and simple, referring to the men as having been "used in research," "betrayed," and "lied to" by their government.

Clinton emphasized the need to remember the past as a way to move forward, and he reflected on the nature of apology. "An apology," he said, "is the first step," and it entails a commitment to rebuild trust and change for the better. He added, "Today, all we can do is apologize. But [only the survivors]...have the power to forgive." And his apology announced further amends, including funding for the National Center for Bioethics in Research and Health Care at Tuskegee and the establishment of bioethics fellowships for minority students.

Clinton's apology to the experiments' survivors has many of the features that Goffman associates with the "fullest form" of an apology. Clinton acknowledged the depth of the injury and apologized personally to those harmed. He explained to the nation the importance of facing up to the moral wrong and the goals of the apology itself. And by funding the Center for Bioethics, he made a commitment to build a better future.

As the highest official in the executive branch, Clinton was the strongest possible choice to deliver the nation's apology, and his delivery underscored the seriousness of the offense and the present-day values of the American people. Clinton's apology did involve the split-self metaphor: a later president blaming and seeking forgiveness for a harm done by an earlier government. We return to national apologies and the government as a split self in Chapter 7.

The Dawn of Tolerance

"Samuel Sewall...Desires to take the Blame and shame of it."
—SAMUEL SEWALL, *January 14, 1697*

In 1692, Samuel Sewall was one of the nine men appointed by Governor William Phips to the Court of Oyer and Terminer, the tribunal that judged witch trials in colonial Salem Town, just north of Boston. Born in 1652 in England, Sewall came to Massachusetts as a child, studied at Harvard, got involved in politics and publishing, and eventually became the manager of the New England colonial printing press. As an educated, wealthy, and politically prominent member of the community, he was a good choice to serve in political office. And like many people at the time, Sewall believed in witchcraft.

As the excesses of the witch trials unfolded, Sewall came to have doubts about the court's work and especially about the evidence used to convict women of witchcraft. His diaries reveal that he felt pressured by the other judges to go along with dubious evidence that was based on dreams, visions, moles, and blemishes. In the end, he had plenty of reasons to feel guilty—the Salem court convicted twenty-six women, most of whom were hanged.

The witch hysteria abated and trials in other towns ended in acquittals. In May of 1693, Governor Phips released all remaining accused witches from prison. By late 1696, in part through Sewall's efforts, the Massachusetts legislature officially recognized the tragedy and designated January 14, 1697, as a day of fasting and atonement. That was also the day Samuel Sewell made his apology. Sewell stood in his Boston church as the Reverend Samuel Willard read a short statement prepared by Sewell. In it, Sewell addressed both God and his fellow parishioners:

> Samuel Sewall, sensible of the reiterated strokes of God upon himself and family; and being sensible, that as to the Guilt contracted upon the opening of the late Commission of Oyer and Terminer at Salem (to which the order of this Day relates) he is, upon many accounts, more concerned than any that he knows of, Desires to take the Blame and shame of it, Asking pardon of men, And especially desiring prayers that God, who has an Unlimited Authority, would pardon that sin and all other his sins; personal and Relative: And according to his infinite Benignity and Sovereignty, Not Visit the sin of him, or of any other, upon himself or any of his, nor upon the Land: But that he would powerfully defend

him against all Temptations to Sin, for the future; and vouchsafe him the efficacious, saving conduct of his Word and Spirit.

Sewall had personal reasons to repent. Since the trials had ended, two of his daughters had died and his wife had given birth to a stillborn child. By Christmas of 1696, Sewall—who had just buried one daughter—was convinced that God was punishing him.

Sewall's apology does not explicitly name his offense—he does not state that he and his fellow judges gave in to hysteria and allowed false evidence to be used to convict witches. He refers instead to "the Guilt contracted upon the opening of the late commission." And Sewall's language reflects the formal apology style of his time rather than the language of the present day. He does not "apologize" or "regret" or say he is "sorry." Rather, he "desires to take the blame and shame of it." Nevertheless, Sewall's apology arose from a recognition that he had behaved unjustly, and he was one of only three judges to express regret.

Sewall was ostracized for his apology. He had asked Cotton Mather to join him in publically repenting, but Mather would go no further than conceding that mistakes had been made and innocents had suffered. Later, many colleagues avoided Sewall. But the apology was transformative for him, and he devoted much of his life from that point forward to making amends, writing in opposition to colonial treatment of Indians and slaves.

Over time, Sewall's public repentance became transformative for New England too. It came to symbolize taking public responsibility and expressing remorse for wrongdoing. Since 1942, the Massachusetts House of Representatives has displayed a mural-sized painting of Sewall's apology by painter Albert Herter. The painting is titled "Dawn of Tolerance in Massachusetts. Public Repentance of Judge Samuel Sewall for his Action in the Witchcraft Trials." We return to the witch trials later, with discussion of a twentieth-century pardon of witches.

The Code of the Hills

"Sartin parties got their feelin's hurt! Yo' gotta make it right, Mistah Capp!! It's the code o' th' hills!!"
—MAMMY YOKUM, *December 27, 1942*

Alfred Caplin lost his left leg in a trolley accident when he was nine and turned to drawing as therapy. He became a cartoonist—publishing as Al Capp—and in 1934 launched the comic strip *Li'l Abner*, which became known for both its artistic style and its satirical commentary. Li'l Abner the comic character was a simple but decent country boy who lived in Dogpatch, Kentucky, with his tough-as-nails mother and shiftless father—Mammy and Pappy Yokum. To keep things interesting, Capp often departed from his Dogpatch story line to parody other comic strips, books, or cultural icons, from Dick Tracy and Mary Worth to Elvis Presley, Frank Sinatra, and Joan Baez. One of Capp's early parodies, however, landed him in potential legal trouble, and he was forced to apologize.

In October 1942, Capp published an extended newspaper parody called *Gone wif the Wind* featuring Li'l Abner as Wreck Butler and Daisy Mae as Scallop O'Hara. Author Margaret Mitchell and her husband, advertising executive John Marsh, were offended and their pique was exacerbated after a phone conversation between Marsh and Capp.

Capp argued that the strip was a permissible parody. Marsh and Mitchell countered with a threat to sue for copyright infringement since the title *Gone wif the Wind* was perilously close to the legally protected title *Gone with the Wind*. Lawyers for the United Feature Syndicate feared losing a $75 million lawsuit—$1 for every copy of every newspaper in which the parody had appeared. So Capp apologized.

He did it in signature fashion. His December 27, 1942, Sunday strip featured a two-panel insert in which Mammy Yokum chastises Capp, explaining, "Sartin parties got their feelin's hurt! Yo' gotta make it right, Mistah Capp!! It's the code o' th' hills!!" Capp and United Feature added their own apology as well and transferred the copyright of the disputed strips to Mitchell. Capp's part of the apology, in the final panel, acknowledged the "use of characters, situations, and background" adapted from Mitchell's book and said, "We would like to apologize to Miss Mitchell for thus making unauthorized use of her property and we have taken steps to correct any infringement of the copyright that may have occurred."

Capp manages to have it both ways in his apology. He apologized under threat of a lawsuit and winked his own insincerity. Mammy Yokum moralizes about making things "right" because "it's the code o' th' hills" (both are bold-face in the original strip), but her words also poke fun at Mitchell and Marsh as overly sensitive parties who "got their feelin's hurt."

Dear Tom Jefferson

"Well, it's never too late to admit a mistake."
—*A Hartford Courant editorial on April 13, 1993*

The Hartford Courant, established in 1764 as the weekly *Connecticut Courant*, is arguably the nation's oldest newspaper. It was around during the American Revolution and in the post-colonial battles between the Federalists, whom *The Courant* supported, and the Democratic-Republican Party.

In the campaign for the hotly contested election of 1800, *The Courant's* publishers, Barzillai Hudson and George Goodwin, planted a series of letters published under the pen name of Mr. Burleigh. The letters derided Thomas Jefferson, the Unitarian who had famously proposed the separation of church and state, as anti-Christian. They characterized the former ambassador to France as a tool of the French and as a radical influenced by the Jacobins. They argued that Jefferson would ignore the Constitution, or worse: "There is scarcely a possibility that we shall escape a Civil War. Murder, robbery, rape, adultery and incest will openly be taught and practised, the air will be rent with the cries of distress, the soil soaked with blood, and the nation black with crimes." Needless to say, Connecticut's electors supported Aaron Burr in 1801.

Hudson and Goodwin kept at it after Jefferson became president. Before his first year was completed, *The Courant* called for his impeachment. And in 1806, Hudson and Goodwin published allegations that President Jefferson and the Congress had secretly voted to bribe Napoleon with $2 million. Jefferson's supporters were so incensed that a federal judge indicted the publishers for common law seditious libel. The case went to the Supreme Court, which ruled that federal courts had no constitutional authority to enforce common law crimes.

On April 13, 1993, the editors of *The Courant* apologized for the paper's treatment of the third president. They wrote, "On your 250th birthday today, it seems proper to let bygones be bygones." *The Courant* recounted its offenses against Jefferson and explained:

> Well, it's never too late to admit a mistake. We, the 1990s stewards of the nation's oldest continuously published newspaper, have the benefit of hindsight. You turned out to be a good influence on America. In fact, some would say that you were a terrific influence on the world.
>
> *The Courant's* early publishers weren't entirely off the mark, however. They were right to point out the contradiction, and hypocrisy, of your owning slaves and preaching freedom.

So you weren't perfect, Tom. But *The Courant* wishes you happy birthday anyway. And if you were around in 1992, our hunch is that we would have championed your candidacy for president.

The editorial used the form of apology—asking for forgiveness, addressing the offended, and naming the transgressions. But the modern-day editors were not really apologizing, of course, even though they addressed their editorial to Jefferson. The offenses had long been forgotten by anyone who would be offended. *The Courant*'s purpose was not to express regret but rather to celebrate the paper's long history and present-day fairness. It is the apology as self-promotion. As Chapter 9 shows, we apologize for various reasons.

2

How Apologies Succeed and Fail

THE SUCCESS OR failure of an apology depends on not only the words and intent of the person apologizing but the interests and attitudes of the other party as well. This chapter examines apology as a process involving both an apologizer's interests and the interaction between actors.

"Forgive Me and Forget My Manners"

As president of Princeton University in the early 1900s, Woodrow Wilson improved academic standards, reorganized undergraduate social life, battled the powerful dean of the graduate school, and eventually antagonized many of Princeton's trustees. He was ready for a change. Colonel George Harvey, editor of *Harper's Weekly*, persuaded New Jersey's Democratic establishment to support Wilson for governor in 1910. A conservative Democrat with ties to both Wall Street and party bosses, Harvey had long followed Wilson's career and saw in him a counterbalance to the influential Nebraskan William Jennings Bryan.

In the 1910 campaign and then as governor, Wilson turned on the state party bosses. He pushed through a progressive agenda that included direct primaries, state regulations of public utilities, worker's compensation, and school reform. His record made him a contender for the 1912 presidential nomination, though not for the reasons Colonel Harvey had hoped.

When Wilson criticized Wall Street, many conservative backers left him. But Harvey remained loyal and even ran the slogan "For President: Woodrow Wilson" above his *Harper's* editorials. Privately, however, Wilson's key advisors worried that Harvey's support was a liability. That topic came up when Wilson, Harvey, and Henry Watterson (the editor of the Louisville *Courier-Journal*) met for dinner on December 7, 1911. When Harvey brought up the slogan, Wilson mentioned that his advisors thought it was hurting his presidential chances, especially in the West.

Soon after the meeting, an angered Harvey removed the slogan from his editorials. Wilson, realizing that he had offended his long-time patron, wrote to Harvey on December 21. Wilson began by noting that he often had a one-track mind and continued:

> When…you asked me that question about the *Weekly*, I answered it simply as a matter of fact and of business, and said never a word of my sincere gratitude or of you for all your generous support, or of my hope that it might be continued. Forgive me and forget my manners.

Wilson's apology, with its tinge of excuse, didn't help. Harvey replied that since Wilson felt his support was hurting, the only solution "was to relieve you of your embarrassment…by ceasing to advocate for your nomination." A few days later, Wilson tried again:

> My dear Col. Harvey:
> Generous and cordial as was your letter written in reply to my note from the University Club, it has left me uneasy, because, in its perfect frankness, it shows that I did hurt you by what I so tactlessly said at the Knickerbocker Club. I am very much ashamed of myself, for there is nothing I am more ashamed of than hurting a true friend, however unintentional the hurt may have been.

In his letter, Wilson explained that he had tried—unsuccessfully—to visit Harvey in person. And he expressed his gratitude for Harvey's support and chastised himself for his thoughtlessness. Wilson's second apology didn't help either. *Harper's* published a statement explaining that it had removed the endorsement because Wilson felt it was harming his candidacy. The anti-Wilson press headlined the story as a sign of Wilson's ingratitude and bad character. The *Courier-Journal* wrote that a man who "would show himself so disloyal to a private friendship cannot be trusted to be loyal to anything." It also cited Wilson's "realignments and readjustments" and "selfish aims."

Faced with widespread criticism, Wilson released his correspondence with Colonel Harvey to the press, and his advisors circulated a story claiming that the real reason for the break was Wilson's refusal of a contribution from financier Thomas F. Ryan. Wilson's supporters turned the story of his supposed ingratitude into a narrative of independence from political bosses and Wall Street influence, ultimately strengthening his progressive credentials. Wilson's original intention, however, had been to repair his relationship with his old friend and supporter Harvey. He failed in that.

Why did Wilson's apology fail? It seems sincere by the standards we've looked at so far. In his second letter Wilson singles out his blameworthy action and restates his belief in the social norm ("there is nothing I am more ashamed of than hurting a true friend"). Wilson's letters contain explanation and excuse as well, but the real problem was that Colonel Harvey was not willing to accept the apology. He apparently believed that the affront was too severe and that Wilson only cared about his own interests. Harvey's animosity remained, and he supported Charles Evans Hughes in the 1916 election, writing that "the betrayal of his country for the gratification of personal ambition proves incontestably that Mr. Wilson stands for Mr. Wilson first."

The Wilson-Harvey break demonstrates a limitation of Goffman's approach mentioned in the previous chapter. We cannot just focus on the person apologizing. We must also consider the person being apologized to. The failure of Wilson's apology was not a failure of Wilson's words. It was a breakdown in the process that leads to reconciliation.

The Apology Process

For a very minor offense—a jostle, spill, or burp—it is sufficient to view an apology as an isolated remedial exchange. I bump into you and say I'm sorry, and you acknowledge my apology. But apologies for more serious offenses almost always go beyond simple social exchanges of dialogue. Nicholas Tavuchis sees apology as a three-step "moral syllogism": a call to apologize, an apology, and a response. Here is how the process works.

The *call to apologize* is the recognition by the offender and the offended of an infraction that can be reconciled by an apology. The call can arise in different ways. It can begin as a spontaneous internal realization by the person who has done something wrong, or with some external response by the person harmed—or by a third party who points out the harm to the offender. The offended must be called to the apology—he or she must understand the offense as a matter that can be potentially reconciled by an apology. Because both the offender and offended must think about the apology as a possible resolution, the call to apologize involves a mutual reunderstanding of the harm.

The apology step actually consists of two parts. The first is a *naming* aspect in which the offender acknowledges or names the transgression and shows an understanding of the harm done. The second, complementary aspect is the *literal apology*, the words with which the offender says that he or she is sorry for the transgression. It is helpful to think of the naming aspect of the apology as confessing the harm, with the offender attaching himself or herself to the offense, and the literal apology as the regretting, with the offender expressing sorrow.

The *response* to the apology is the province of the offended party (or parties, since a transgression may harm more than a single person). An apology may be accepted or rejected, of course, but those are not the only options. When an apology is inadequate in some way, further negotiation between offender and offended may be necessary. An inadequate apology may even create a new transgression or a return to the call to apology. This was the case with Woodrow Wilson's first letter, which Colonel Harvey must have seen as exacerbating the original insult and which seems to have prompted Harvey to a more public airing of differences with Wilson.

Represented as a sequence of steps, Nicholas Tavuchis's moral syllogism model looks like this:

Transgression
↓
Call to apology (a mutual understanding of the transgression)
Apology (naming the offense and making the literal apology)
Response (acceptance, rejection, or discussion)
↓
Reconciliation

Apologies can fail at any step. An apology can go wrong if the offender and offended do not see the call to apologize in the same way. An apology can also go wrong if its naming aspect is subverted and the offender tries to apologize for something other than the actual offense, or if the language of the literal apology is incomplete or ambiguous, failing to express sincere regret. And an apology can fail at the response step, when the offended person may reject it.

The exchange between Woodrow Wilson and George Harvey is just such a failed apology. Wilson and Harvey, it seems, did not have a shared understanding of the offense (things might have been different had Wilson apologized in person). And it is clear from Colonel Harvey's later comments that he did not feel that Wilson was truly sorry or that Wilson was even capable of genuine friendship.

"Articulate, Bright, Clean, Nice-looking"

The Wilson-Harvey example shows how a well-meaning apology can fail at the call and response stages. Now let's consider the process from a different perspective. Can a flawed apology succeed?

In 2007, as candidates began to jockey for the 2008 presidential nominations, Senator Joe Biden discussed other potential Democratic candidates in an interview with the *New York Observer*. Biden referred to Barack Obama as "the first sort of mainstream African-American, who is articulate and bright and clean and a nice-looking guy." Biden was attempting to indicate that Obama would be a formidable candidate, but in praising Obama, Biden had backhandedly insulted other African-American politicians and had placed the question of racial stereotypes front and center. If Obama was the first to be articulate and bright and clean and nice-looking, the implication was that earlier African-American candidates lacked these qualities. The comment also marginalized Obama himself, suggesting that his success depended on not appearing to be part of the mid-twentieth century civil rights movement but in being somehow post-racial.

Biden quickly apologized in a call to Obama and a public statement saying "I deeply regret any offense my remark in the *New York Observer* might have caused anyone. That was not my intent and I expressed that to Senator Obama." He also went on the *Daily Show* and explained that he should have used the word *fresh* rather than *clean*. And Biden also telephoned earlier candidates Jesse Jackson and Al Sharpton with apologies.

Obama at first brushed the issue off, saying that he didn't think Biden intended to offend, though "the way he constructed the statement was probably a little unfortunate." Obama later issued an acceptance of Biden's apology that he used to acknowledge previous African-American candidates. Obama said, "I didn't take Sen. Biden's comments personally, but obviously they were historically inaccurate," adding that "African-American presidential candidates like Jesse Jackson, Shirley Chisholm, Carol Moseley Braun, and Al Sharpton gave a voice to many important issues through their campaigns, and no one would call them inarticulate."

Jesse Jackson too accepted the apology, calling Biden's statement "a gaffe" and explaining that, in his opinion, "it was not an intentional racially pejorative statement. It could be interpreted that way, but that's not what he meant." Al Sharpton responded to the adjective *clean* and reported that when Biden called to apologize, "I told him I take a bath every day." And the *Washington Post*'s Eugene Robinson focused on the word *articulate*.

Robinson noted that the word was sometimes used to refer to those whose speech was free of African-American vernacular. "Articulate," Robinson wrote, was "being used to describe a black person around whom white people can be comfortable."

The discourse around Biden's gaffe quickly dissipated. His apology and responses brought a measure of closure to the public discussion. This closure seems to have served the needs of most of the principals—Biden, Obama, Jackson, and Sharpton—who saw little political purpose in continuing either the discussion of what makes a nationally electable African-American candidate or of the moral and linguistic issues involved. Biden's apology was successful in an instrumental sense. But it was not a genuine apology that named and expressed regret for a moral lapse.

Biden began by minimizing the offense, explaining to reporters that everyone knew what he meant. He also tried to clarify his language, particularly the adjective *clean*. As his various explanations failed, he moved on to his broader conditional apology: "I deeply regret any offense my remark in the *New York Observer* might have caused anyone." With the phrasings "any offense" and "might have caused anyone," along with the vagueness about what he was apologizing for, Biden offered a weak apology that separated his earlier words from his intent.

If Biden had taken his transgression seriously as a moral matter, attaching himself to the offense, what would he have apologized for? There were three offensive things about his remark. He spoke carelessly and was insensitive to the way in which historically loaded words can remind listeners of racial slights and stereotypes. He needlessly injected race into his comments about other candidates. And with his clumsy compliment to Obama, he disparaged earlier African-American candidates. Speaking carelessly is a fairly minor transgression, but insensitivity, needlessly injecting race, and disparaging colleagues are more serious. Biden's apology left all of these possible transgressions unnamed, but it succeeded anyway.

It succeeded because Biden, Obama, and others treated it as minor, as a verbal gaffe rather than a moral breach indicative of bad intentions on Biden's part. In having his apology accepted and offense minimized, Biden no doubt benefitted from his Senate record supporting civil rights. And despite an insensitive comment about Indian-Americans in 2006, this second gaffe was not taken to indicate a pattern of racism on his part.

Biden's public apology was offered and accepted instrumentally, without a full exploration of the underlying issues. It succeeded because Obama, Jackson, and Sharpton tacitly settled on the call to apologize. They choose not to tackle the larger issues and returned instead to the business of the campaign cycle.

"The Apology We Had Sought and Requested"

In July of 2006, actor Mel Gibson was stopped for driving eighty-seven miles per hour along the Pacific Coast Highway. Gibson failed a breathalyzer test, and police officers placed him under arrest. As he was being arrested, Gibson asked one of the officers if he was Jewish and then launched into an anti-Semitic tirade. Gibson's words, recorded in the arrest report, made their way in the media in unexpurgated form. The following day, Gibson's publicist released a statement that apologized to the sheriff's deputies and to "anyone else" he offended:

> ... I acted like a person completely out of control when I was arrested, and said things that I do not believe to be true and which are despicable. I am deeply ashamed of everything I said and I apologize to anyone who I have offended. Also, I take this opportunity to apologize to the deputies involved for my belligerent behavior...
>
> I apologize for any behavior unbecoming of me in my inebriated state and have already taken necessary steps to ensure my return to health.

Gibson refers to being "ashamed" and uses the word *apologize* three times: he apologizes "to anyone who I have offended," "to the deputies involved for my belligerent behavior," and "for any behavior unbecoming of me in my inebriated state." In saying that he was "out of control," Gibson attributes his words and behavior to another self—one under the influence of alcohol. But his statement merely highlights the question of whether his inebriated beliefs are more deeply held than those of his sober persona. Gibson's apology also fails by specifically apologizing only for his belligerence and for drunk driving, without naming his other offenses: it's another vague, contingent apology to "anyone I have offended" for "any behavior unbecoming of me."

Abraham Foxman, national director of the Anti-Defamation League (ADL), rejected Gibson's apology. Foxman explained that Gibson's statement was "unremorseful and insufficient," adding, "It's not a proper apology because it does not go to the essence of his bigotry and his anti-Semitism." Foxman also suggested that Gibson's drunken words revealed "his true self," and he called on Hollywood to distance itself from Gibson. It was not the first time that the ADL had expressed concerns about Gibson: his 2004 film *The Passion of the Christ* was seen by many as anti-Semitic.

Gibson made a second apology on August 1. He began by stating, "There is no excuse, nor should there be any tolerance, for anyone who thinks or expresses any kind of anti-Semitic remark. I want to apologize specifically to everyone in the Jewish community for the vitriolic and harmful words that I said to a law enforcement officer the night I was arrested on a DUI charge." Gibson added that he took personal responsibility for his words and he believed that in his heart he was not a bigot. He hoped to "meet with leaders in the Jewish community, with whom I can have a one-on-one discussion to discern the appropriate path for healing."

Gibson's second apology did a better job of naming his offense (citing his "vitriolic and harmful words"), though he still avoided fully naming the offense, proposing instead personal meetings to find "the appropriate path to healing." Nevertheless, the ADL accepted the apology and the offer of continued dialogue. "This is the apology we had sought and requested," Foxman's statement began. It went on to say, "We are glad that Mel Gibson has finally owned up to the fact that he made anti-Semitic remarks, and his apology sounds sincere. We welcome his efforts to repair the damage he has caused, to reach out to the Jewish community, and to seek help." Foxman implicitly rejected Gibson's claim that he was not a bigot, offering instead to help him overcome his "disease of prejudice."

As Gibson's statements evolved, his language increasingly emphasized personal responsibility and became more specific about naming his offenses and the associated harms. In rejecting Gibson's first apology—for being an unruly drunk—the ADL issued a call for Gibson to apologize based on the moral content of his words. Gibson's second apology attached himself to his vitriolic, hateful speech.

The success of the apology, of course, was due to the engagement of Abraham Foxman not Gibson's words alone. For Gibson, the initial call to apologize may have been the public revelation of what he had done or his morning-after recollection of the evening's events. His initial apology failed because he named just one of his transgressions (shouting at the police) and only vaguely apologized for everything else. Foxman rightly rejected this, establishing a new call for Gibson to apologize. While Gibson's second apology did better, it still contained some incongruities and tangents, including references to film and artistic license and to a world "gone mad." But Foxman judged the apology sincere enough to accept.

While the ADL accepted the apology, not all Jewish leaders did, and many in the media and entertainment industry debated its sincerity and effectiveness. That raises a new question (and one that will occupy us more in Chapter 7). When an apology is directed to an entire community, who is empowered to accept it? The ADL had some claim to this role, since it had engaged Gibson in the first place by asking for an apology. But Gibson's apology addressed "everyone in the Jewish community," leaving individuals free to determine their level of acceptance or rejection. Speaking for the ADL, Abraham Foxman chose qualified acceptance of Gibson's apology, and from that perspective Gibson's second apology was a qualified success. It began a dialogue.

The Role of the Offended Party

The three examples discussed here highlight apology as a process—call, apology, and response—and show the crucial role of the offended party in that process. We see how apologies can fail at various stages. Woodrow Wilson's apology to Colonel Harvey failed because the principals lacked a mutual understanding of the offense. Without that, Harvey was unable to trust in Wilson's sincerity. Nothing Wilson could say could convince Harvey that Wilson's behavior was not rooted in self-centeredness.

Joe Biden's apology failed in one sense and succeeded in another. It failed morally in that Biden never identified his real offense, characterizing it only as misspeaking. But his apology succeeded instrumentally because Obama and others accepted Biden's characterization of the offense and his regret. The call and response of the apology process were successful even though the literal apology was weak. Mel Gibson's apologies also had their weaknesses, and his first was summarily rejected by Foxman. That rejection established a new call to apologize, which led to a more acceptable apology.

Of the three apologies, only Biden's achieved real reconciliation, even though it was the most superficial. Perhaps that is because the bond between Biden and the other principals—Obama, Jackson, and Sharpton—was stronger than the perceived transgression. Biden's apology was Goffman-like dramaturgy, rebalancing face among the offended and offender. Wilson's and Gibson's apologies involved greater articulation of moral issues, though in both instances those receiving the apologies still had concerns about the apologizer. Colonel Harvey, who had doubly lost face in his interactions with Wilson, had simply given up on the president. And Foxman made it clear that the apology was only a first step toward reconciliation. There was further moral work to be done by Gibson.

Other apologies that failed in interesting ways even when accepted by the person offended include Alabama governor George Wallace's apology for his support of segregation, former senator Bob Kerrey's apology to candidate Barack Obama, Abe Lincoln's apology to James Shields, and golfer Fuzzy Zoeller's apology to Tiger Woods.

The Schoolhouse Door

"I did stand, with a majority of the white people, for the separation of the schools. But that was wrong, and that will never come back again."
—GEORGE C. WALLACE, *1982*

The iconic image of four-time Alabama governor George Wallace is of him standing in front of Foster Auditorium at the University of Alabama on June 11, 1963, attempting to bar students Vivian Malone and James Hood from enrolling. In the 1962 gubernatorial campaign, Wallace had vowed to stand in "the schoolhouse door" to prevent desegregation. Federal marshals and the Alabama National Guard, led by President Kennedy's deputy attorney general, confronted Wallace and he stood aside. But he had made his political statement.

Wallace began his career as a populist. But after losing the 1958 Democratic gubernatorial primary to a candidate endorsed by the Ku Klux Klan, he began to court white segregationist voters with a message of state's rights, anti-elitism, and "law and order." Wallace also found a national constituency and ran for president four times, winning ten million votes and carrying five states in his 1968 run as an independent. Campaigning in Maryland in 1972, Wallace was shot by a would-be assassin. He was paralyzed and lived the rest of his life in a wheelchair. The brush with death caused Wallace to reassess his life. In time, he began to seek forgiveness for the harm he had caused.

In 1979, he called on civil rights leader John Lewis, who had been beaten by Alabama state troopers during Wallace's first term as governor. He also spoke that year at the Dexter Avenue Baptist Church in Montgomery, saying, "I have learned what suffering means. In a way that was impossible before, I think I can understand something of the pain black people have come to endure. I know I contributed to that pain, and I can only ask your forgiveness." At a meeting of the Southern Christian Leadership Conference in 1982, he said, "I did stand, with a majority of the white people, for the separation of the schools. But that was wrong, and that will never come back again."

His public statements were weak apologies. Wallace selectively identified his transgression—standing for separation of the schools—but omitted exploring the climate of hatred and violence that his actions fostered. He presented himself as part of a group rather than an individual. And he talked of empathy rather than accepting blame. Wallace's apologies were also complicated by the fact he was preparing to run for governor in 1982, prompting speculation that expediency rather than conscience lay behind his words.

Nevertheless, many chose to see them as sincere. According to John Lewis, Wallace "poured out his soul and heart to me. It was almost a confession." When Wallace joined others in marking the thirtieth anniversary of the Selma to Montgomery civil rights marches, the Reverend Joseph Lowery, president of the Southern Christian Leadership Conference, told him, "You are a different George Wallace today." And Vivian Malone, one of the students Wallace had tried to bar from the University of Alabama, received a private apology in 1996 along with the Lurleen B. Wallace Award of Courage. Speaking to reporters, Malone reflected, "We all make mistakes."

Not everyone was willing to forgive. Judge Frank Johnson, a law school classmate of Wallace's who ruled on historic civil rights cases, had been a particular target. Wallace had denounced him as an "integratin', carpetbaggin', scalliwaggin' liar" and once suggested he be given a "barbed-wire enema." Johnson, whose mother's house was firebombed and whose son committed suicide, refused to take Wallace's call. When a mutual friend approached Johnson about hearing Wallace out, Johnson replied, "If he wanted to get forgiveness, he'd have to get it from the Lord." The success of Wallace's apologies depended on the willingness of those harmed to listen to them. For some, Wallace's apologies symbolized change and reconciliation. For others, like Frank Johnson, they held no appeal.

Dear Barack

"I am sorry for the insult."
—FORMER SENATOR BOB KERREY, *December, 2007*

Nebraska's Bob Kerrey was a Navy SEAL during the Vietnam War and a Medal of Honor winner. He was a businessman, governor, and two-term US senator. He served on the 9-11 Commission and as president of the New School. He is also prone to colorful, unedited speech.

Kerrey supported Hillary Clinton for the 2008 Democratic presidential nomination. When he endorsed Senator Clinton in December of 2007, Kerrey also commented on then-senator Barack Obama. "The fact that he's African-American is a big deal," Kerrey said, adding that if Obama were elected he would be a positive influence on "a lot of underperforming black youth today." Kerrey went on to say:

> It's probably not something that appeals to him, but I like the fact that his name is Barack Hussein Obama, and that his father was a Muslim and that his paternal grandmother is a Muslim. There's a billion people on the planet that are Muslims and I think that experience is a big deal.

The Obama campaign team was sensitive to rumors that he was secretly a Muslim who would have a covert agenda as president. Some thought that Kerrey, by emphasizing Obama's middle name and his father and grandmother's religion, was actually intending to spread the Muslim-not-Christian rumors through his apparent compliment. When his comments were challenged in the media, Kerrey made a clumsy clarification and quickly apologized to Obama, sending him a letter that began:

> Dear Barack,
>
> I want to sincerely apologize for the remarks I made on Sunday in Council Bluffs, Iowa, after an event at which I endorsed Senator Hillary Clinton's Presidential candidacy. I answered a question about your qualifications to be President in a way that has been interpreted as a backhanded insult of you. I assure you I meant to do just the opposite.

Kerrey went on to tell Obama that he was "among the two or three most talented people I have ever met in politics" and "exceptionally qualified by experience and judgment to be president." Kerrey explained that he had been trying to say that an Obama presidency would inspire African-Americans, Muslims, and others. He ended by writing, "Again, I am sorry for the insult and wish you the best on January 3 and beyond."

Kerrey is apologetic in his letter, but it is not clear what Kerrey is apologizing for. He acknowledges that his comments have been interpreted as a "backhanded insult" and reiterates that he is sorry "for the insult," using a definite article. Kerrey never explains what the insult is, saying only that he meant the comments in a positive way. And he takes no responsibility for the remarks, only regretting their misinterpretation. It is an apology with the offense unexplored and no blame accepted.

The Obama campaign released the letter to the media and issued a press statement accepting the apology. But the question remains, what was the Obama campaign accepting an apology for? As with Joe Biden's apology, here we find an expedient, superficial apology that both parties were nevertheless content with.

The Lost Townships Letter

"I had no intention of injuring your personal or private character."
—ABRAHAM LINCOLN, *1842*

Apologies can be a means of avoiding escalation of differences, but insincere apologies can backfire, as young Abraham Lincoln learned. When he was a member of the Illinois legislature in 1842, Lincoln was challenged to a duel by James Shields, the Illinois state auditor. Under a pseudonym, Lincoln had written one of a series of satirical newspaper letters about Shields in the *Sangamon Journal*. When Shields found out—from the newspaper's editor—that Lincoln was involved, he wrote an angry letter to Lincoln demanding an apology for all of the newspaper letters slandering him.

Lincoln responded by writing his own aggrieved letter asking how Shields could be sure that he had written all of the letters. This irritated Shields even further and he responded by seeking a duel, which Lincoln tried to resolve by exploiting the prevailing dueling code. Lincoln proposed that if Shields would withdraw his challenge and rephrase his question more politely and precisely, Lincoln would in turn apologize. Lincoln even previewed for Shields what his own apology would say:

> I did write the "Lost Townships" letter which appeared in the *Journal* of the 2d instant, but had no participation in any form in any other article alluding to you. I wrote that wholly for political effect—I had no intention of injuring your personal or private character or standing as a man or a gentleman; and I did not then think, and do not now think, that that article could produce or has produced that effect against you; and had I anticipated such an effect I would have forborne to write it. And I will add that your conduct toward me, so far as I know, had always been gentlemanly; and that I had no personal pique against you, and no cause for any.

Lincoln did not want to escalate the dispute, but he also did not feel he could simply apologize as a response to Shields's threat of regrettable "consequences." When Shields refused to withdraw his challenge, Lincoln agreed to the duel, choosing cavalry swords as the weapon. At six feet four, Lincoln enjoyed a decisive advantage in reach over his much shorter challenger. With the intervention of some mutual friends of both men, all the letters in the dispute were retracted, Lincoln seconded his explanation that no offense was intended, and the duel was called off.

The apology for the Lost Township letter shows both the difficulty of apology under duress—when the call to apologize comes with menace—and the role of third parties in negotiating a new call to apologize. The mutual friends of Lincoln and Shields were an indispensable part of the apology process.

Class Clown

"I didn't mean anything by it and I'm sorry if I offended anybody."
—FRANK "FUZZY" ZOELLER, *1997*

Indiana's Frank "Fuzzy" Zoeller became a professional golfer in 1973. He developed a reputation as the class clown of professional golf, often teasing other players or making jokes about the game and his own play. At the 1997 Masters Tournament, Zoeller—who finished quite poorly—directed one of his jibes at young Tiger Woods, the first person of color ever to win the tournament.

Zoeller told reporters that "that boy" was an impressive player and jokingly suggested to reporters that they "tell him not to serve fried chicken next year.... Or collard greens or whatever the hell they serve." Zoeller was referring to the fact that the defending champion selects the menu for the following year's banquet and alluding to stereotypes of African-American foods.

Zoeller was attempting to be funny, but the remark was insensitive and was delivered in Woods's absence. When it was aired a few days later by CNN, Zoeller apologized publically, saying, "I didn't mean anything by it and I'm sorry if I offended anybody. If Tiger is offended by it, I apologize to him, too. I have nothing but the utmost respect for Tiger as a person and an athlete."

The next day Zoeller was dropped by Kmart, which had been producing a line of Fuzzy Zoeller golf equipment. The retailer issued a statement calling Zoeller's comments inappropriate and insensitive. Kmart added, "Regardless of the context, [the remarks] are contrary to Kmart's longstanding policies that insure our words and deeds are without bias." A few days later, on April 24, Woods issued a statement accepting the apology:

> At first, I was shocked to hear that Fuzzy Zoeller made these unfortunate remarks. His attempt at humor was out-of-bounds, and I was disappointed by it. But having played golf with Fuzzy, I know he is a jokester; and I have concluded that no personal animosity toward me was intended.

Woods's tepid acceptance of the apology matched Zoeller's weak apology. It responded to the conditional phrasing of Zoeller's apology ("If Tiger is offended") and reported on Woods's conclusions about Zoeller's remarks and intent. But Woods did not literally accept the apology; he merely implied that he was not offended, just disappointed.

The controversy continued to receive news coverage over the next few weeks, until finally, on May 20, Woods and Zoeller had lunch at the Colonial Country Club in Fort Worth, Texas, where both were playing. Zoeller apologized again in person, and both golfers said they hoped to put the matter to rest. Woods said he had found out what he needed to know by meeting face-to-face and that he considered the matter "over."

We don't know exactly what Zoeller said in his lunch with Woods, but his initial apology was much too casual: "I didn't mean anything by it and I'm sorry if I offended anybody." Zoeller literally dismissed his insensitivity as meaningless and predicated his apology on whether Woods was offended. A more appropriate apology would have echoed Kmart's observation that words are deeds, expressed greater understanding of the offense, and demonstrated sincerity and contrition in the apology. It was only when Zoeller and Woods met face-to-face that the matter was put behind them. Once again, it is the recipient of an apology who determines its success.

3

How We Literally *Apologize*

WE HAVE LOOKED at the split self of the apologizer and the process of call, apology, and response. In this chapter and the next, we focus on the words used in apologizing. We say "I am sorry," "I regret it," and "I was wrong." We say "Forgive me," "Excuse me," or "Pardon me." We say "I apologize," the most formal of the variants. Saying "I apologize" actually does apologize. The other expressions, while often used to apologize, do not literally do so. The apologies must be inferred. *Sorry* is an adjective that indicates a subject's emotions. *Regret* is an active verb that reports a state of mind. *I was wrong* admits moral or factual error. And *Forgive me* is a request expressed as a polite command. The fact that these words primarily report or request does not prevent them from being interpreted as apologies, of course, and we shall explore that in the next chapter. We devote this chapter to looking at how the word *apologize* anchors the true performance of an apology. Our starting point is a fairly simple apology by then-vice president George H. W. Bush.

It's Freudian

In January of 1988, as George H. W. Bush was competing for the Republican presidential nomination, he was interviewed by CBS news anchor Dan Rather. Rather questioned Bush on what he knew about the Iran-Contra affair, the Reagan-era exchange of arms for hostages. The interview became heated, with Bush at one point complaining that it was unfair "to judge my whole career by a rehash on Iran." After the interview, Bush told CBS staff members just how mad he was: "Tell your goddamned network that if they want to talk to me to raise their hands at a press conference. No more Mr. Inside stuff after that."

In June of the same year, Bush was interviewed by *Nightline*-anchor Ted Koppel via a satellite link between Washington and Houston. The conversation again turned to the Iran-Contra affair and to Bush's replies during the interview with Dan Rather. At one point Koppel even played a clip of the Bush-Rather interview. As he responded to Koppel about Iran-Contra, Bush called him by the wrong name: "Yes, things went wrong. And I've admitted it. And, Dan, I'll take all the credit, all the blame—"

Koppel interrupted: "No, Dan, Dan's the other fellow." Asked whether the trial of Oliver North, one of the Iran-Contra conspirators, would hurt his electoral chances, Bush replied, "No, I don't, because, Dan, you've made a fatal error..." When Koppel again corrected him, Bush first asked, "Did I do it again?" and then remarked, "It's Freudian. Hey, listen, it's Freudian."

At the end of the interview Bush apologized, saying: "Ted, I apologize for calling you Dan. I wasn't being smart. I can't see you. I'm in Houston, and I was not trying to be provocative or amusing." Koppel accepted the apology and added a joking reference to fellow journalist Barbara Walters: "No, not at all, and I didn't take it that way. Next time, call me Barbara."

The exchange between Bush and Koppel shows a personal apology for a minor transgression. Bush misspeaks and offers a joking explanation about a Freudian slip. He recognizes that his error could be construed as disrespectful and apologizes. Koppel accepts the apology and minimizes the transgression. Both save face and the social balance is restored.

Complement Structure

Bush's choice of words provides our entrée to the grammar of the verb *apologize*, the most formal and unambiguous English word used to apologize. To understand its use, we need to briefly introduce two bits of linguistic terminology. The first is the idea of complements of a verb. Content words like verbs and nouns (and adjectives and adverbs too) have what grammarians call a complement structure. This is the grammatical frame that can be used to complete a particular word's meaning. The frame varies from word to word and both enables and limits the types of expression possible.

The possible complements of the verb *apologize* include a direct and an indirect object: you apologize *to someone for something*. And that is what George H. W. Bush did. The phrase *for calling you Dan* is a direct object (grammarians would further label it a gerund or verbal noun). It names Bush's offense. The *to someone* part is little trickier. Since Bush is speaking to Koppel, the indirect object function is filled by the name *Ted*, which identifies to whom the apology is directed.

Bush used all the grammatical resources available in the complement structure of *apologize*—a direct object and the equivalent of an indirect object. He could have said more, adding adverbs like *sincerely* or subordinating and softening the verb by adding *would like to*. He could have said less, by omitting the name *Ted* or by rephrasing his transgression more. But he neither exaggerates his apology nor understates it.

The grammatical options we have as speakers allow us to be more or less explicit in an apology and to emphasize or de-emphasize aspects of meaning. Here's an example. The direct object of *apologize* can be a gerund or a noun. When a gerund is used, as in *I apologize for calling you Dan*, the object of the verb is an action with an implied subject. The action is *calling you Dan* and the implied subject is the person apologizing (the *I*). The offense is made explicit and personalized. If Bush had said, "I apologize for the mistake" (or, slightly more personally, "I apologize for my mistake"), his apology would have been less explicit. The noun *mistake* would put distance between Bush and his action. With the gerund, there is no question what the apology is for.

That *versus* If

It is also possible to use a noun clause as the direct object of *apologize*. There are two main types. One begins with the word *that* and introduces a presumed fact (grammarians call it a factive clause). Someone might say, "I apologize that I have not gotten back to you yet," or "I apologize that I have not written in so long."

In such sentences, the subjects of the two clauses are the same (the repeated pronoun *I*). The subjects of the two clauses can also differ, as in "I apologize that the exams are not graded yet," or "We apologize that you were unable to use your card due to the renewal date." In these examples, grammar obscures the cause of the harm. In the first, the passive clause *the exams are not graded yet* hides the agent of the non-grading. In the second, *were unable* (a predicate adjective) and *due to* (an instrumental preposition) suppress the agency as well. It would be a different message to say "We apologize that we deactivated your card."

When apologizers use noun clauses, they may rename and attenuate their offenses, offering apologies for generalized mistakes or situations rather than for a speaker's actions. Thus, when then-candidate Mike Huckabee ad libbed a joke about someone aiming a gun at Barack Obama, he later explained:

I made an offhand remark that was in no way intended to offend or dis-
parage Sen. Obama. I apologize that my comments were offensive, that
was never my intention.

Huckabee dissociates himself from the offense with the phrases "offhand
remark," "in no way intended," and "not my intention." His grammatical
choice, "that my comments were offensive," similarly presents the offense as
passive happenstance rather than a blameworthy act.

The other type of noun clause complement is the conditional clause. When
if is used instead of *that*, the apology is contingent on the condition expressed
by the *if* clause. Here are two examples:

I do apologize if he's offended by that.
I apologize if my comments offended Justice Ginsberg [*sic*].

The first was from former Virginia senator George Allen after calling Indian-
American videographer S. R. Sidarth "macaca," an expression cognate with
the French word *macaque* and ultimately derived from the Bantu word for
monkey, *ma-kako*. The second was from former Kentucky senator Jim Bunning after he predicted that Justice Ruth Bader Ginsburg would die from
pancreatic cancer within nine months. Both Allen and Bunning attempted
to brush off their comments with conditional apologies, just as Fuzzy Zoeller
initially did after his inappropriate comments.

Conditionals allow speakers to qualify the act of apologizing. Rather than
mutually exploring the offense as a prelude to an apology, the apologizer
makes a unilateral conditional apology: "I apologize if you are offended." The
if clause short-circuits the process of call-apology-response and places the
onus on the offended party to say whether an offense has occurred. But what
can the offended person say in response?

Performatives and Felicity

Let's turn now to the second linguistic concept we need to explore. Why
is saying "I apologize" the most literal way to apologize? The reason is that
apologize is a performative verb. Like the verbs *promise, christen, bet, resign,*
or *accept,* the verb *apologize*—when spoken in the right circumstances—does
something by saying something. It performs.

The term *performative* was introduced by John Langshaw Austin in his
1962 book *How to Do Things with Words.* Austin was a British philosopher

at Oxford University. Trained in classics, Austin worked for MI6, the British Secret Intelligence Service during World War II, and later became one of the "ordinary language philosophers." In *How to Do Things with Words*, Austin challenged the view that all sentences have truth conditions. The term *truth conditions* is just the logician's way of talking about the real-world situations in which a sentence is true (or false). Austin argued that only sentences that are about *saying something* have truth conditions. Sentences that are about *doing something* have felicity conditions instead. Felicity conditions describe when a statement about an act really performs that act. They involve the desires, willingness, and abilities of speakers, and the beliefs of speakers and hearers.

The distinction between saying and doing is quite interesting if you've never pondered it. For example, if someone says that Grover Cleveland was the twenty-second president of the United States, the truth of the sentence can be ascertained by research about the world. (It's true, by the way, though Cleveland was also the twenty-fourth president, an interesting mathematical trick.) Now compare that statement about Grover Cleveland with a first-person sentence like "I promise to lower the deficit." Such a sentence, Austin would argue, is neither true nor false. Rather it is felicitous if the speaker intends to lower the deficit and is in a position to do so, and it is infelicitous if the speaker does not have the intent or ability to lower the deficit.

So how does felicity work in the case of a word like *apologize*? Austin himself did not discuss the verb *apologize* in much detail, but others have, including the American philosopher John Searle, who continued and extended Austin's explorations of speech acts. In Searle's view, there are four felicity conditions for an apology: (1) the statement refers to a past act done by the speaker that (2) the speaker acknowledges was harmful and (3) sincerely regrets, and (4) the speech act counts as an apology in the shared language of the speaker and hearer or hearers. (The various parts of this are known as the propositional act, the preparatory condition, the sincerity condition, and the essential condition.)

Here is how this works in our earlier example. When George H. W. Bush said, "Ted, I apologize for calling you Dan," his first-person statement referred to a past act of his. Its felicity depended on Bush's sincerity and his understanding that his past act could be viewed as disrespectful (it was a harm). Felicity also depended on Bush's and Koppel's mutual understanding that Bush's words counted as an apology. So, if Bush had been insincere or obscure, or if Koppel had misunderstood the sentence, Bush's statement would have been infelicitous.

Making Sense of Nonliteral Language

The words *I apologize* lend themselves to textbook felicitous apologies like George H. W. Bush's, but there are other grammatical options too. We can shift the verb to a less prominent position in the sentence, saying "I would like to apologize" or "I want to apologize." A literalist might object that the speaker is just liking or wanting, not apologizing. But when we speak colloquially we often depart from the most formal and literal ways of speaking. If my wife and I invite you to dinner, I might say, "We'd like you to come to dinner." It's not that I am an especially sloppy speaker unable to say what I mean. My phrasing has to do with the social fact that it is sometimes more polite to be indirect. Saying "I hereby invite you to dinner" is comically formal. When we speak naturally, we are often indirect and informal, using language that softens statements and preserves options for speakers and hearers. And when we are overly literal, we risk being uncooperative. If you respond to my dinner invitation by saying "Well, why don't you invite me?," I will probably regret the invitation.

H. Paul Grice, a British philosopher who taught at the University of California, Berkeley, developed the idea of "conversational implicatures" to talk about the ways in which we work out an intended meaning from a somewhat different literal meaning. Grice's philosophical analysis assumes that conversations are cooperative endeavors. As a result, participants in a conversation (or any other discourse) fit the literal language to the purpose of the interaction.

Grice elaborated on this cooperative principle with four generalizations he observed in effective communication. He called these maxims of conversation, and they refer to being informative (quantity), truthful (quality), relevant (relation), and clear (manner).

Here's an example. If my classroom door is open and there is a lot of hallway noise, I may say to someone near the door, "Would you get that?" The meaning both implied and inferred is the polite imperative "Please close the door." Or if I ask my department chair whether or not I can attend a meeting off campus, she may say, "Post a sign on your door, so students know you are gone." Her imperative implies assent and combines that with relevant policy guidance.

Now let's consider an apology example of conversational implicature.

Down the Memory Hole

Online retailer Amazon introduced its first-generation Kindle in 2007, allowing readers to download content from various ebook vendors through

---

GRICE'S MAXIMS OF CONVERSATION

Maxims of Quantity

1. Make your contribution to the conversation as informative as necessary.

2. Do not make your contribution to the conversation more informative than necessary.

Maxims of Quality

1. Do not say what you believe to be false.

2. Do not say that for which you lack adequate evidence.

Maxim of Relation

1. Be relevant.

Maxims of Manner

1. Avoid obscurity of expression.

2. Avoid ambiguity.

3. Be brief.

4. Be orderly.

Amazon's website. In the summer of 2009, Amazon discovered that one its vendors, publisher MobileReference, was selling books for which it did not own the US rights. Most notable among them were George Orwell's *Nineteen Eighty-four* and *Animal Farm*, high-school staples being offered for just ninety-nine cents each.

Amazon's digital rights management software enabled it to prevent users from sharing ebooks once they were purchased. It also allowed Amazon to delete content remotely, and on July 17, 2009, the offending Orwell books were purged from buyers' Kindles.

Many readers were surprised to find that Amazon could delete content remotely and some were quite inconvenienced, including a Detroit high-school student whose notes and annotations to *Nineteen Eighty-four* disappeared along with the ebook. And the irony that the deleted books were by George Orwell amplified customer anger and media interest. Amazon CEO Jeff Bezos quickly posted an apology on an Amazon customer forum:

This is an apology for the way we previously handled illegally sold copies of *1984* and other novels on Kindle. Our "solution" to the problem was stupid, thoughtless, and painfully out of line with our principles. It is wholly self-inflicted, and we deserve the criticism we've received. We will use the scar tissue from this painful mistake to help make better decisions going forward, ones that match our mission.

With deep apology to our customers,

Jeff Bezos

Founder & CEO

Amazon.com

This short apology—just seventy-five words—begins with the self-referential statement that it is an apology followed by a general description of the offense ("the way we previously handled" illegally sold books). Bezos includes the typical complements—a *for* phrase in the opening sentence ("This is an apology for")—to name the offense and a *to* phrase in the close ("with deep apologies to our customers") to identify his primary addressees. Bezos explains that the action does not represent the true corporate self of Amazon, and he expresses both remorse and embarrassment.

Bezos never literally performs the apology by stating "On behalf of Amazon, I apologize," or even "Amazon apologizes." But we infer an apology because of Grice's maxims of relation and quality, reasoning that Bezos would not say his posting was an apology unless he intended to apologize. We also assume that he believes his statement to be warranted and true. The maxims, in short, tell us how to read between the lines in a cooperative fashion.

Grice's maxims can identify the boundaries of an apology as well. In this case, the maxims of quantity (be just as informative as necessary) and manner (avoid obscurity, ambiguity; be brief and orderly) help us to interpret what Bezos is saying and not saying. The apology is brief, orderly, and unambiguous. The identification of the transgression, however, is obscure. Bezos refers only to "the way we previously handled illegally sold copies" and "our 'solution' to the problem."

The clause "It is wholly self-inflicted" is especially interesting. The word *it* refers to the noun *solution* in the preceding sentence, which Bezos enclosed in scare quotes. The scare quotes indicate that *solution* is not intended literally, and the adjective *self-inflicted* guides us to interpret *solution* as *wound*. That metaphor is reinforced by the references to "scar tissue" and a "painful mistake." Bezos invites customers to see Amazon's actions in a particular way but does not actually say very much about the offense.

Overall, Bezos avoids explicitly naming Amazon's transgression and the harm done to customers, focusing instead on the harm done to Amazon and its relationship with customers. Bezos also does not engage with the social and legal issues that were raised by the deletion, and he omits any discussion of refunds or reimbursements, though later each of the buyers of deleted ebooks received a thirty-dollar credit or check. It was a serviceable apology, and when we examine it closely we see both its intent and limitations.

Unhappy Meals

Now we'll try a slightly longer example. In May of 2001, McDonald's Corporation, which has served over two hundred billion orders of French fries, admitted something surprising. In the United States, potatoes were partly fried using beef fat, then frozen and shipped to the restaurants. There the spuds were refried using just vegetable oil. Eric Schlosser's *Fast Food Nation*, published the same year, had noted this prefrying technique, and vegetarians and Hindus in the United States began asking McDonald's about the practice.

McDonald's acknowledged the use of beef fat in the United States but emphasized that it observed the religious preferences for food preparation in Hindu and Islamic countries. Nevertheless, the revelations led to protests, including the burning of Ronald McDonald dolls, in India and elsewhere. The company explained that the change to vegetable oil had been to reduce cholesterol and that it had never promoted French fries as a vegetarian item, though Seattle attorney H. B. Vatri still filed a class-action lawsuit on behalf of millions of vegetarians and Hindus in the United States. McDonald's settled the suit with a donation of ten million dollars to various vegetarian and religious groups. In its June 2002 written apology, the McDonald's Board of Directors released a statement that began:

> McDonald's sincerely apologizes to Hindus, vegetarians and others for failing to provide the kind of information they needed to make dietary decisions at our U.S. restaurants.

This statement succeeds grammatically, having both direct and indirect objects, as well as the emphatic adverb *sincerely*. The compound indirect object is both specific and general (identifying Hindus and vegetarians but also others). The gerund *failing to provide* designates the transgression, but only as a harm of omission. If we just looked at this opening, Grice's maxims would lead us to wonder whether McDonald's was providing enough information, that is, whether they were following the maxim of quantity. However, the next two paragraphs of the apology acknowledge the error (albeit with the passive-voiced *mistakes were made*), express regret, apologize, and commit to doing better in the future.

> We acknowledge that, upon our switch to vegetable oil in the early 1990's for the purpose of reducing cholesterol, mistakes were made in communicating to the public and customers about the ingredients in our French fries and hash browns. Those mistakes included instances in which French fries and hash browns sold at U.S. restaurants were improperly identified as "vegetarian."
>
> We regret we did not provide these customers with complete information, and we sincerely apologize for any hardship that these miscommunications have caused among Hindus, vegetarians and others. We should have done a better job in these areas, and we're committed to doing a better job in the future.

We might ask for still more information (who made these mistakes?), but the maxim of quality is met by McDonald's saying "We did not provide customers with complete information" and by generally identifying the kind of missing information (information relevant to "dietary decisions"). The final two paragraphs of the apology talk about what will be different in the future: enhanced disclosures and an advisory panel. The final sentence notes the ten-million-dollar donation to charity and education being made "as part of this settlement," though the settlement is not mentioned previously.

> As a direct result of these events, McDonald's has enhanced its disclosures concerning the source of ingredients in its food products. This information is available at McDonald's website, www.mcdonalds.com, and will be available at each store.
>
> McDonald's has created a Dietary Practice/Vegetarian Advisory Panel consisting of experts in consumer dietary practices that will advise McDonald's on relevant dietary restrictions and guidelines, which McDonald's and others can use for marketing to persons who follow those restrictions. As part of this settlement, McDonald's is donating $10 million to Hindu, vegetarian and other groups whose charitable and educational activities are closely linked to the concerns of these consumers.

This example shows the importance of looking at the apology statement in the full linguistic context. By itself, the statement "McDonald's sincerely apologizes…for failing to provide the kind of information needed" seems less informative than would be hoped. As the opening to a larger text, however, it prefaces a coherent set of themes. The general transgression "failing to provide" segues to the explanation and acknowledgement of the mistakes and the expression of regret in the second and third paragraphs. The first half ends with a restatement of the apology, which identifies a general harm ("any hardship").

The remaining two paragraphs look to the future and what McDonald's is doing, creating, and donating. The apology also refers to two points that are strategically not developed further: the agency of the mistakes is left unspecified and the relation of the apology to the legal settlement is merely an allusion. Stripped to its essentials, the McDonald's apology works like this:

MCDONALD'S APOLOGY STEP BY STEP

McDonald's sincerely apologizes

We acknowledge…mistakes were made

We regret we did not

… [again] we sincerely apologize for any hardship

… and we're committed to doing a better job in the future

As a direct result of these events, McDonald's has enhanced...

McDonald's has created...

As part of this settlement, McDonald's is donating…

The 240-word statement has a consistent string of subjects throughout. Almost every sentence begins with "McDonald's" or "we." What's more, the full statement uses the shift between "McDonald's" and "we" to signal its acknowledgement and regret of past failings (We acknowledge, We regret, We should have). The present and future actions use the brand name, while the specifics of the transgression are in the vague and agentless passive voice. It is perhaps reading too much into the alternation of pronouns to impose a Goffman-like interpretation of "we" as a former self and "McDonald's" as a new self, but the systematic use of sentence subjects is evident: there is a point in the text where "we" becomes "McDonald's." As the apology shifts from past actions to future ones, the self-reference shifts from the pronoun to the corporate name.

Beyond the linguistic details, the McDonald's apology also highlights the tension between the instrumental step of simply acknowledging error and the moral exploration of the transgression. As a corporation, McDonald's had obligations to its stockholders to minimize the damage to its reputation by resolving the issue speedily. It also had an obligation to its employees not to scapegoat those who misunderstood the French-fry cooking process and might have provided wrong information. In developing its apology, McDonald's tried to balance full exploration of the harm with preservation of the company's corporate face and internal morale.

What the Word *Apology* Does

The three progressively longer examples in this chapter have shown how we use the word *apologize*. The verb expresses a formal, literal apology that, when combined with direct and indirect objects, identifies both the transgression and the recipient of the apology. *Apologize* is a word that performs an action. But all uses of *apologize* are not equal. For those who want to back away from their words, grammar has mechanisms for indirection and misdirection. Speakers can use conditional clauses and indefinite objects, which permit the appearance of an apology without its core features of naming and regretting. Grammar permits vagueness as well, through the use of general nouns like *my behavior, my mistake, the insult, the inconvenience*, or by simply omitting the object altogether. And noun clauses with *that* can create ways to apologize for situations rather than one's own actions, as when a professor apologizes that the exams are not graded.

Other grammatical mechanisms allow the shaping of an apology socially and stylistically without necessarily weakening its meaning. Modal expressions (such as "I would like to apologize") soften a performative with deference, but we interpret this as a normal colloquial rephrasing not a serious evasion. The use of the noun *apology*, which historically predates the verb use, falls somewhere in the middle. To offer or extend an apology treats the apology as a metaphorical commodity. An offer is more deferential than a direct speech act, and it emphasizes the hearer's opportunity, even obligation, to respond. And grammatical options can be combined and used in novel ways. Jeff Bezos's "This is an apology" uses the noun form to depersonalize the apology. George Allen's "I do apologize if..." employs an emphatic *do* to suggest that no broader apology is really needed. And recall Mel Gibson's phrasing, "I want to apologize specifically to everyone in the Jewish community," in which Gibson softens his tone with *want to* and uses the adverb *specifically* to figuratively look his audience in the eye. Compare that to Gibson's earlier phrasing, "Also I take this opportunity to apologize to the deputies involved," which situates the apology almost as an afterthought. As consumers (and producers) of apologies, we must reflect on each grammatical choice and ask how the grammatical devices at play shape the nuances of the apology.

In the next chapter, we take up the words *sorry, regret, wrong,* and *forgive,* and the expression *my bad.* First, however, we offer some additional examples of the word *apologize*: Charles Coughlin's apology to Franklin Roosevelt, Captain Joseph Hazelwood's apology for the Valdez oil spill, former president Jimmy Carter's apology for a book about Israel, and National Rifle Association (NRA) spokesman Wayne LaPierre's apology to law enforcement officials.

The Radio Priest

"I now offer to the president of the United States my sincere apology."
—FATHER CHARLES COUGHLIN, *1936*

In 1926, Father Charles Coughlin, a Roman Catholic priest serving in Detroit, began delivering sermons using the then-new technology of radio. Coughlin's earliest radio sermons were on theology, but as the country sank into the Great Depression, Coughlin increasingly called for populist economic reform. In the 1932 election, he was a strong supporter of Franklin Roosevelt, seeing the choice as between "Roosevelt or Ruin" and claiming "The New Deal is Christ's Deal."

Roosevelt turned out to be less radical than Coughlin had hoped. By the mid-1930s, Coughlin viewed the president as a tool of Wall Street and was criticizing Roosevelt's policies to his millions of listeners. In a radio address (they were no longer called sermons), Coughlin explained that "Roosevelt or Ruin" had become "Roosevelt and Ruin." And in his 1936 speech to Francis Townshend's convention advocating old-age pensions, Coughlin flat out called the president a liar:

> The great betrayer and liar, Franklin D. Roosevelt, who promised to drive the money changers from the temple, had succeeded in driving the farmers from their homesteads and the citizens from their homes in the cities.... I ask you to purge the man who claims to be a Democrat, from the Democratic Party, and I mean Franklin Double-Crossing Roosevelt.

Under pressure from both church and political leaders, Coughlin published an open letter of apology to Roosevelt in his magazine *Social Justice*:

> Excellency
>
> In the heat of civic interest in the affairs of my country and in righteous anger at the developments that, it is my conviction, have contributed largely to want in the midst of plenty, I addressed to the President of the United States, in a speech at Cleveland, Ohio, July 16, the word "liar."
>
> For that action I now offer to the president of the United States my sincere apology.

The present tense performative *I now offer* is followed by the indirect and direct objects. The introductory phrase *for that action* refers back to the characterization of the offense that appears in the opening paragraph of the letter: referring to the president as a liar. The language of Coughlin's open letter is formal and clerical, from the salutation "Excellency" to the phrasing of the apology as an offer and of the apology as "sincere." The formality acknowledges the power relationship between a head of state and a citizen of that state and reinforces, perhaps ironically, Coughlin's status as a humble petitioner seeking forgiveness.

The language also distances Coughlin from the apology and the offense. The formality allows Coughlin to extend a polite offer but to defend his intent, which he characterizes as "civic" and "righteous." Imagine if the letter had instead begun, "Dear President Roosevelt: I apologize for calling you a liar in my speech of July 16. I was wrong to be disrespectful." That would have been a rather more direct apology.

In the 1936 presidential election, Coughlin supported William Lemke, the third-party agrarian radical running on the Union Party ticket. After the election he muted his criticism of Roosevelt for a time, as some radio stations began refusing to carry his speeches, and church leaders and influential Catholics such as Joseph Kennedy made their disapproval clear. Coughlin's strident tone reappeared in 1937, however, when he referred to the president's "personal stupidity" in nominating Hugo Black to the Supreme Court. Coughlin was rebuked by Edward Mooney, the Archbishop of Detroit, and Coughlin canceled his radio program. In *Social Justice*, however, he became increasingly isolationist, anti-Semitic, and pro-Nazi. Finally, in May of 1942, when the magazine accused Jews of starting World War II, Mooney ordered Coughlin to stop his political activities or be defrocked. Coughlin ended his public career but remained the pastor of the Shrine of the Little Flower in Royal Oaks, Michigan, until his retirement in 1966. He died in 1979.

Captain Joe

"I would like to offer an apology, a very heartfelt apology, to the people of Alaska for the damage caused by the grounding of a ship that I was in command of."
—CAPTAIN JOSEPH HAZELWOOD, *2009*

Just after midnight on March 24, 1989, the Exxon *Valdez*, a single-hulled 987-foot-long oil tanker, ran aground on the Bligh Island Reef, dumping over ten million gallons of crude oil into Alaska's Prince William Sound. The captain was not on the bridge. Captain Joseph Hazelwood was in his quarters, and the ship's third mate was in command. Operating without radar—which had been broken for more than a year—the mate and the seaman at the helm struck the reef just after midnight.

Hazelwood had joined Exxon (then the Humble Oil Company) as a third mate in 1968, and he eventually became Exxon's youngest captain. He was also a drinker. His driver's license had been suspended in September 1988 for driving under the influence—his third such offense—and he had been in a rehab program in 1985 at a hospital in Amityville, New York. Hazelwood's background, his refusal to speak with National Transportation Safety Board investigators after the crash, and the sad irony of a ship's captain with a revoked driver's license led the public and Exxon to blame Hazelwood for the spill. He was fired and indicted on three felony counts of second-degree criminal mischief.

Hazelwood was acquitted of the felony charges but convicted of a misdemeanor charge of negligent discharge of oil, fined fifty thousand dollars, and sentenced to one thousand hours of community service in Alaska. His shipmaster's license was suspended for just nine months, but he left the merchant marine to work as a legal investigator. He became a private person.

Twenty years later, Hazelwood had an opportunity to reflect and apologize. When an oil industry watchdog group commissioned a book of oral histories on the spill, writer Sharon Bushell interviewed Hazelwood. In *The Spill: Personal Stories from the Exxon Valdez Disaster*, Hazelwood argued that he was wrongly blamed. But he also apologized:

I was the captain of a ship that ran aground and caused a horrendous amount of damage. I've got to be responsible for that. I would like to offer an apology, a very heartfelt apology, to the people of Alaska for the damage caused by the grounding of a ship that I was in command of.

Hazelwood's dilemma is clear. He does not feel that he was to blame—elsewhere in the interview he says, "The true story is out there for anybody who wants to look at the facts, but that's not the sexy story and that's not the easy story." But he accepts responsibility and offers an apology that was impossible to make earlier. His apology reflects his wish to take responsibility but not blame. It is existential rather than personal, even down to the use of the indefinite article: he "was the captain of a ship"; he has "got to be responsible." It is an apology, but it is a morally fragmented apology for the damages not for Hazelwood's actions.

Hazelwood's apology also raises another question. In light of our understanding of apology as a call to apologize, a naming and regretting, and a response, who would respond to Hazelwood when he speaks to the "people of Alaska"? Some apologies are offered without the expectation of a response.

Improper and Stupid Wording

"I apologize to you personally, to everyone here."
—JIMMY CARTER, *January 2007*

Jimmy Carter has had an active and productive ex-presidency. He established the Carter Center, a nongovernmental organization that supports human rights and promotes health. He served as an unofficial envoy to trouble spots in Asia and Africa, monitored elections in Venezuela and Haiti, built homes for Habitat for Humanity, and offered insights—sometimes unwelcome—on the policies of his successors. He has published over twenty books and won a Nobel Peace Prize for his humanitarian work.

Carter has also remained involved in Middle East affairs. As president, he facilitated the Camp David Accords, which led to the Egypt-Israel Peace Treaty, though progress on the issue of Palestine proved more elusive. In 2002, Carter and others from his Center worked with Israelis and Palestinians on the Geneva Accord model for peace.

In late 2006, however, Carter's efforts took a step backward when he published a book arguing that Israeli policies deprived Palestinians of basic human rights and comparing the situation there to the racial divide in South Africa from 1948 to 1994. *Palestine: Peace Not Apartheid* was criticized as biased and inaccurate. A class-action lawsuit (later dropped) was filed over supposed mistakes in the book, fifteen members of the Carter Center board resigned in protest, and Democratic politicians distanced themselves from Carter's views. The book did receive one unlikely endorsement—from Osama bin Laden.

Carter defended the book and himself, offering accounts of his motives, expertise, research process, and character. But in January 2007, he apologized for one particular sentence. At a question-and-answer session at Brandeis University, Carter was asked about a statement in the book that seemed to endorse terrorism. Carter had written a passage suggesting that suicide bombings and other acts were legitimate tactics:

> It is imperative that the general Arab community and all significant Palestinian groups make it clear that they will end the suicide bombings and other acts of terrorism when international laws and the ultimate goals of the Roadmap for Peace are accepted by Israel.

Challenged by students, he apologized, "The sentence was worded in a completely improper and stupid way," adding, "I have written my publisher to change that sentence immediately. I apologize to you personally, to everyone here… It was a mistake on my part."

Carter's apology names just one offense—one sentence—and was unsuccessful in quelling the broader objections to his book and his proposals for peace. Carter continued to defend his views and to arrange peace talks with leaders of Hamas, the terrorist organization.

In 2009, Carter apologized again, in an open holiday letter to the Jewish community. Noting that holidays were a time of reflection, Carter expressed his hope that Israel would "flourish as a Jewish state within secure and recognized borders in peaceful co-existence with its neighbors" and he ended by offering an *al het*.

> We must recognize Israel's achievements under difficult circumstances, even as we strive in a positive way to help Israel continue to improve its relations with its Arab populations, but we must not permit criticisms for improvement to stigmatize Israel. As I would have noted at Rosh Hashanah and Yom Kippur, but which is appropriate at any time of the year, I offer an Al Het for any words or deeds of mine that may have done so.

Literally meaning "for the sin," an *al het* is a Yom Kippur prayer listing sins and asking forgiveness. Some Jewish leaders, such as the ADL's Abraham Foxman, welcomed Carter's *al het*, while others questioned its sincerity, citing the ex-president's continued provocative writings and actions on Palestinian-Israeli relations. There was even speculation that the apology was tied to the political aspirations of Carter's grandson.

Carter's two apologies take different approaches. His 2007 apology is extremely limited, focusing on one sentence while defending the rest of his book. And his 2009 *al het* is very general, asking forgiveness for "any words or deeds" that may have stigmatized Israel but without naming his actions, revisiting his positions, or offering a new direction. He even avoids the words *apology* or *sorry* in favor of a Hebrew term that defamiliarizes his apology. Carter's apologies show him wanting to have it both ways: he wanted to be forgiven but also remain as consistent with his earlier views as possible.

Jackbooted Government Thugs

"If anyone thought the intention was to paint all federal law-enforcement officials with the same broad brush, I'm sorry, and I apologize."
—WAYNE LAPIERRE, *NRA executive vice president, May 17, 1995.*

The NRA has long used derisive, even aggressive language in its portrayal of the Bureau of Alcohol, Tobacco, and Firearms (ATF). As the NRA evolved from promoting marksmanship and gun safety to lobbying activities, its direct mail message paralleled the rhetoric of antigovernment militia groups. Federal agents were called "government thugs," "armed terrorists," "gestapo," "SS," and "intruders," and a 1994 special report in the organization's magazine even referred to disputes over gun control during the Clinton administration as "the final war."

On April 13 1995, the NRA sent a fundraising letter referring to the ban on assault weapons as giving "jackbooted Government thugs more power to take away our constitutional rights, break in our doors, seize our guns, destroy our property and even injure and kill us." The letter claimed, "In Clinton's Administration, if you have a badge, you have the Government's go-ahead to harass, intimidate, even murder law-abiding citizens." And it referred to confrontations at Ruby Ridge, Idaho, in 1992 and Waco, Texas, in 1993 as examples of federal excess. "Not too long ago it was unthinkable for Federal agents wearing Nazi bucket helmets and black storm trooper uniforms to attack law-abiding citizens. Not today. Not with Clinton," the NRA letter said. The letter was dated just six days before the April 19, 1995, Oklahoma City bombing in which terrorist Timothy McVeigh bombed the Alfred P. Murrah Federal Building, killing over six hundred people. Congressional leaders and others challenged the letter as inappropriate.

The six-page NRA letter provoked an especially strong reaction from George H. W. Bush, who had been president during the Ruby Ridge incident. Bush wrote to the NRA on May 3, resigning from the organization. Soon the NRA was apologizing. In a May 17 telephone interview with a *Seattle Times* reporter, NRA executive vice-president Wayne LaPierre said, "I really feel bad about the fact that the words in that letter have been interpreted to apply to all federal law-enforcement officers. If anyone thought the intention was to paint all federal law-enforcement officials with the same broad brush, I'm sorry, and I apologize." LaPierre insisted that the fundraising letter was intended to criticize isolated actions, primarily involving the ATF. His ambiguous, conditional apology left unclear what it was he felt bad about—that people misinterpreted his intention or the letter itself. And his statement actually reiterated the insult to the ATF: if the intention was not to paint *all* federal law enforcement officials as jackbooted thugs, then the intention was to portray *some* of them that way.

LaPierre's statement was criticized as a "narrow apology" and a "faux mea culpa." The national president of the Fraternal Order of Police said, "That was no apology. LaPierre can't get off the hook by saying, 'Oops, I was really only talking about ATF.' Law enforcement is a family, and when you attack one member, you attack us all." LaPierre's language, with its reiteration of the original harm, failed to address the moral issue or to resolve the controversy.

4

Sorry, Regrets, and More

"I'm Very Sorry for That"

When he became president in 1993, Bill Clinton quickly set up the Task Force on National Health Care Reform. Headed by first lady Hillary Clinton, the task force was intended to make good on Clinton's campaign promise to enact universal health care. The effort failed, as had previous efforts beginning with Theodore Roosevelt, and health-care reform became a major factor in Democratic losses in the 1994 midterm elections. Opponents personalized the failure by portraying the task force as an intrusive bureaucracy being imposed by the first lady. They called it HillaryCare.

After the 1994 midterm losses, Bill Clinton began to adjust his priorities and adapt his approach. Hillary Clinton also began to think about her role, at one point organizing an off-the-record lunch with a group of columnists and journalists that included syndicated columnist Ann Landers, Cindy Adams and Louis Romano of the *New York Post*, Marian Burros of the *New York Times*, and others. At the lunch, Clinton described how she believed her health-care efforts had been twisted by opponents and how she herself had been portrayed. She told the journalists, "I regret very much that the efforts on health care were badly misunderstood, taken out of context and used politically against the Administration. I take responsibility for that, and I'm very sorry for that." What Clinton was saying was that the fault lay with others who were distorting her efforts on health care and that she should have better understood the political machinations.

Was Clinton apologizing? She regrets three grammatically passive actions—efforts on health care being misunderstood by the public, efforts being taken out of context, and efforts being used by political opponents— and she says she is sorry. However, her sorry refers to the actions of others who misunderstood or misrepresented health-care reform. Sorry indicates regret for a situation, not regret for an offense. Taken alone, her sorry is more like the usage in "I'm sorry that I missed your call" than "I'm sorry that I lost your book."

Clinton confused matters somewhat by also saying "I take responsibility for that." With that phrasing she also asserted responsibility for the public's misunderstandings and her opponents' misrepresentations. She treated what happened as something she might have prevented with different actions—in other words she treated it as a transgression. Her "I'm very sorry for that" was thus ambiguous, carrying both the sense of reporting on a regrettable situation and that of taking the blame for that situation. The conversational logic of her statement was unresolved.

When Clinton's comments came out, she was criticized for apologizing. The *Chicago Sun Times* headline was "Hillary 'Sorry' About Health Care," and the article led with the statement that "over a plate of heart-healthy American cuisine, Hillary Rodham Clinton took full responsibility for the failure of the health-care program she helped design...and said she was 'sorry.'" The *Arkansas Democrat-Gazette* wrote "First Lady Says She's Sorry, But Insists She Won't Hide For Next 2 Years" and the *New York Times*— which broke the story—wrote that "Mrs. Clinton put most of the fault on herself."

As the story developed, others commented on the first lady's words and whether or not saying sorry was a stereotypical feature of women's speech. One state legislator said, "When [Clinton] says she is responsible for the failure of health care, that is the woman trying to take all the burdens on herself. She could have been Mother Teresa and that health care bill still would have failed." Linguist Deborah Tannen even discussed the incident and its relationship to gender in a *New York Times Magazine* article, quoting an unnamed political scientist saying, "To apologize for substantive things you've done raises the white flag. There's a school of thought in politics that you never say you're sorry."

Ironically, Clinton had noted, "I can only guess that people are getting perceptions about me from things I am saying or doing in ways that don't correspond with things I am trying to get across." Were her words treated as an apology because she was woman? We'll come back to the question of perceived apology and gender in Chapter 10. For the moment, however, let's start by taking a closer look at the grammar of *sorry* and how it differs from *apologize*.

The Grammar of *Sorry*

Saying "I'm sorry" is different from saying "I apologize." The former reports on an internal state of the speaker but does not literally perform an apology. Instead, speakers and hearers use the conversational maxims of quality, quantity, relation, and manner to imply or infer an apology. By itself, the minimal report "I'm sorry" (or, the simple "Sorry" used for minor transgressions) doesn't tell us much. Much of the meaning-making comes from the complements that follow *sorry*.

Like *apologize, sorry* can occur with a gerund complement or a conditional (*if*) complement—I can be sorry for speaking out of turn or I can be sorry if I have offended you. Unlike *apologize, sorry* can occur with an infinitive complement. If the following infinitive is *to be, sorry* is understood as an apology ("I'm sorry to be such a bother"), while if the verb is one of perception it is often understood as report of empathy ("I'm sorry to hear about your loss").

Sorry differs from *apologize* in that it frequently occurs with a noun clause. Noun clauses, you'll recall, are tricky because the choice of the subject of the clause can affect the meaning: I can be sorry that I was so inconsiderate or I can be sorry that you were offended. When the subjects of the both clauses are the first person *I* (or *we*), the speaker is sorry for something he or she has done. But when the subordinate clause subject does not match the first-person subject of the main clause, then the speaker is sorry for something that happened. So "I'm sorry that it's raining" expresses disappointment but not apology. *Sorry* also differs from *apologize* in not allowing an expressed indirect object. That means that the grammar of *sorry* does not indicate to whom the apology is addressed. An apology using *sorry* must either rely on context (by uttering the expression face to face or in a person-to-person communication like a letter or email) or on making the recipient of the apology clear by mentioning it elsewhere.

Sorry provides somewhat more grammatical flexibility than *apologize* and somewhat more semantic flexibility. When a speaker says "I'm sorry," he or she may be implying an apology or making a report. Thus, when businesswoman Martha Stewart was convicted of several charges related to insider stock trading in March 2004, she said she was sorry. In court she told the judge:

> Today is a shameful day. It is shameful for me, for my family, and for my beloved company and all of its employees and partners. What was a small personal matter became over the last two and a half years an almost fatal circus event of unprecedented proportions spreading like

oil over a vast landscape, even around the world. I have been choked and almost suffocated to death.

She ended by saying "I'm very sorry it has come to this." Was Stewart apologizing? Perhaps she intended it to be taken that way. But her ambiguous language can also be understood as meaning that she regrets the unfortunate situation she is in. And both the abstractness of the shame ("Today is a shameful day") and the vague passiveness of the language ("a small personal matter...has become," "I have been choked..." "...it has come to this") suggest that she is not performing an apology but merely reporting her feelings.

The distinction between performing an apology by saying "I apologize" and reporting a mental state by saying "I'm sorry" provides insight into another aspect of apologetic discourse—apologies sometimes combine the two expressions. Thus when England's Prince Harry apologized for dressing in a Nazi uniform for a 2005 costume party, he said this: "I am very sorry if I caused any offense or embarrassment to anyone. It was a poor choice of costume and I apologize." The use of "I apologize" extends and supplements the conditional "I am very sorry if" in the first sentence. There is also a bit of a verbal trick in the positioning of the word *apologize*. The prince is apologizing for an abstraction—a poor choice of costume—not for offensive behavior or the values implied in dressing as a Nazi. Putting the apology last allows the speaker to shape the transgression in a more innocuous way. A similar verbal trick arises with the positioning of *sorry* in our next example, from the 2004 presidential election.

Rather Sorry

Shortly before the 2004 presidential election, CBS broadcast a *Sixty Minutes* segment calling into doubt President George W. Bush's National Guard record. The September 8 report by Dan Rather aired on *Sixty Minutes Wednesday* and showed four documents that appeared to have been written by Bush's commanding officer. The documents created the impression that Bush had disobeyed orders to report for a physical, had been grounded from flying, and had used political influence to receive more positive evaluations than he deserved. The presumed author of the memos, Lieutenant Colonel Jerry Killian, had died in 1984, and the memos were provided to a CBS producer by another retired National Guard lieutenant colonel, Bill Burkett, who claimed to have burned the originals after faxing them to CBS. Prior to airing the segment, CBS producers consulted with several document experts and interpreted the results in the most positive light for the potential news story, but failed to contact a crucial typography expert.

Immediately after the story aired, bloggers and then the print news media began to question the authenticity of the documents. For a time, CBS and Rather defended the segment, but soon they had to disavow it. On the September 20 *CBS Evening News*, Rather explained that in light of additional research on the authenticity and source of the documents:

> I no longer have the confidence in these documents that would allow us to continue vouching for them journalistically. I find we have been misled on the key question of how our source for the documents came into possession of these papers. That, combined with some of the questions that have been raised in public and in the press, leads me to a point where—if I knew then what I know now—I would not have gone ahead with the story as it was aired, and I certainly would not have used the documents in question.
>
> But we did use the documents. We made a mistake in judgment, and for that I am sorry.

Dan Rather first explains the situation and concludes that he would have acted differently if he had more information. At the end, he names the offense—a mistake in judgment—and he explains that he is sorry, inviting viewers to infer an apology. Because an apology was in order, *sorry* was indeed understood as implying an apology instead of simply regrets that something happened. Conversational logic suggests that Rather would not be saying CBS made a mistake and that he was sorry if he did not intend an apology.

I hope you noticed how Rather used the plural *we* in the last two sentences cited above, switching from an earlier *I*. He switches from "I no longer have confidence," "I find we have been misled," and "I would not have gone ahead," to "we did use" and "we made a mistake." He depersonalizes the naming of the offense then switches back to *I* at the end to personalize his regret. Rather uses pronouns to ever so slightly separate himself from the offense.

Following the incident, CBS commissioned an independent review panel whose report led to several executive- and producer-level firings. The panel's report noted that Rather still felt the documents were accurate and that he had merely "delivered the apology" in support of the corporate decision to back off the story. Two months after the panel report was issued, Rather left the CBS anchor position, a year ahead of his planned retirement, and sued the network. In the lawsuit, Rather argued that he was forced to apologize by CBS, that he was not responsible for the errors in the reporting, and that he was being made a scapegoat. The seventy-million-dollar suit was unsuccessful.

Soon after the original story aired, CBS also issued a separate statement saying, "Based on what we now know, CBS News cannot prove that the documents are authentic, which is the only acceptable journalistic standard to justify using them in the report. We should not have used them. That was a mistake, which we deeply regret." Here CBS makes its apology with *regret* rather than *sorry*. But how does *regret* differ from *sorry*?

Regrets

The sorries expressed by Hillary Clinton and Dan Rather illustrate self-reports of speakers' attitudes about their actions or inactions. Just as common is the verb *regret*, which also reports on a speaker's internal state. The grammar of *regret* largely parallels that of *sorry*. *Regret* does not allow indirect objects, but it does take direct object nouns and pronouns, conditionals, noun clauses, gerunds, and infinitives as complements. I can regret my actions, regret it if anyone was offended, regret that I behaved so poorly, regret calling him mean, or regret to have to tell you bad news. Again, a gerund can provide an especially strong grammatical foundation for an implied apology: "I regret calling him mean" aligns the subject of the main clause with the understood subject of the gerund. A noun clause can similarly invite interpretation as an apology when the subjects match, as in "I regret that I behaved so poorly." Both gerunds and noun clauses, however, can complement *regret* in ways that merely report on situations without assuming agency for them: "I regret your being inconvenienced" and "We regret that they feel that way." Here, the speaker regrets a situation but does not assume responsibility for it.

Regret also occurs with noun phrases, as we have seen: "I sincerely regret the unfortunate choice of language" (Harry Truman), "I...profoundly regret my horrific relapse" (Mel Gibson), and "I deeply regret any offense my remark in the *New York Observer* might have caused anyone" (Joe Biden). And *regret* of course may be a noun, which provides a further option for apologies: "I always put the victim first but here I didn't follow my principle and that is my greatest regret" (said by Scotland Yard assistant commissioner John Yates on his decision not to reopen an investigation into *News International* in 2009) or "I'm very disappointed and want to express my regret to The Open fans" (Tiger Woods commenting on his performance at the 2011 British Open). Having or expressing regrets makes the attitude more abstract—it is more a thing than a mental action—and distances the regretter from the regret.

Like *sorry*, *regret* is ambiguous. Literally, *regret* refers to one's attitudes toward an event or action. It can be used to indicate an apologetic stance toward one's own actions but can also merely comment on a disagreeable state of affairs. Often the difference is clear. When a Soviet court sentenced captured pilot Francis Gary Powers to a ten-year sentence in 1960, President Dwight Eisenhower's press secretary released a statement that Eisenhower "deplored the Soviet propaganda activity associated with the episode beginning last May and regrets the severity of the sentence." Eisenhower was not apologizing. He was expressing disapproval. When President John F. Kennedy sent troops to oversee the integration of the University of Mississippi, he noted that it was his responsibility to enforce the court decision even though the government had not been a part of the court case. Kennedy said: "I deeply regret the fact that any action by the executive branch was necessary in this case, but all other avenues and alternatives, including persuasion and conciliation, had been tried and exhausted." Kennedy was explaining and regretting that circumstances made federal action necessary. But he was not apologizing.

Sometimes in partisan politics there is public debate about whether an expression of regret implies apology. This was the case when secretary of state William Jennings Bryan presented a treaty to the Senate expressing "sincere regret" to the nation of Colombia. Was this an apology? We will get to this controversy in just a moment. First, one last question.

Does "I regret" mean the same thing as "I'm sorry"? There is overlap of course, but as we have seen, *sorry* reports on internal emotional states and de-emphasizes the calculus of acts and consequences. *Regret*, on the other hand, places more weight on situations and on the analysis of acts and consequences. Thus, *sorry* is typically used for mild transgressions (jostles and spills) and *regret* for more formal, serious, and detached situations. Of course, as speakers of English, we use and understand the nuances intuitively. The overlap and distinction between regretting and being sorry are evident in fixed expressions like "I regret to inform you that we selected another applicant" as opposed to "I'm sorry for your loss." *Sorry* is too personal for some professional and business exchanges, while *regret* is usually too impersonal and detached for condolences.

Did the Wilson Administration Apologize to Colombia?

In the early part of the twentieth century, US relations with Colombia deteriorated because of the Panama Canal conflict. The geographically strategic state of Panama had been a part of Colombia since 1821. Panamanian secession efforts had repeatedly failed, most notably during the Thousand Days War of 1899 to 1902. At the same time, the United States was negotiating with the Colombian government to gain rights to a five-hundred-square-mile area for a canal.

Events turned when the Colombian Senate rejected the Hay-Herrán Treaty, which would have given the United States rights to the canal zone in perpetuity in return for a $10 million initial payment and annual payments of $250,000. Determined to have the canal, the Roosevelt administration threw its support behind the Panamanian independence movement. American ships, ordered to the area by President Roosevelt, blockaded Colombian forces. In November 1903, Panama proclaimed its independence and was immediately recognized by the United States. American troops landed with the stated role of keeping order and protecting American lives and property, but also to interfere with and intimidate Colombian forces. Five days after independence was declared, the treaty the United States had sought was signed, and in 1904, work began on the five-hundred-mile-long canal.

The Colombians, and many Americans as well, insisted that the separation of Panama was an immoral and illegal action instigated by American commercial interests and abetted by Roosevelt. Later in the Roosevelt administration and through the Taft years, efforts were made to repair the rift. Diplomatic contacts continued, and when Woodrow Wilson became president, one of his priorities was to improve relations with the strategic region of Central and Latin America. By 1914, a treaty had been negotiated to ensure full recognition of Panama. The Thomson-Urrutia Treaty proposed to pay Colombia twenty-five million dollars and to grant special canal privileges in return for Colombia's recognition of Panama's independence and sovereignty. The treaty also included this sentence:

> The government of the United States of America, wishing to put at rest all controversies and differences with the Republic of Colombia arising out of which the present situation on the Isthmus of Panama have resulted, on its own part and in the name of the people of the United

States expresses sincere regret that anything should have occurred to interrupt or to mar the relations of cordial friendship that had so long subsisted between the two nations.

When the treaty was presented in April of 1914, it met with strong opposition from Roosevelt's supporters in the Senate. Roosevelt himself lobbied against it, calling the payment "blackmail." And some senators objected to the words *sincere regret* as an apology to Colombia. California senator George Perkins, for example, said, "I do not believe that the United States Senate will ever ratify this treaty, which implies an apology to Colombia and payment of $25,000,000 in reparations. Colombia should apologize to the United States." The *New York Times* added its opinion that "a formal apology is uncalled for," since the Colombians were trying to prevent construction of the canal.

James Du Bois, the minister to Colombia under William Howard Taft, argued that the treaty was not an apology at all but rather a "simple expression of regret." Du Bois reported telling the Colombian negotiators that the United States "would never apologize for a political act" and noted that neither he nor the Colombian negotiators viewed the statement as an apology. The apology claim was, he said, "only the cry of the Roosevelt people to defeat the treaty." Woodrow Wilson too denied that the treaty had an apology, describing that view as "pure guff." Nebraska senator Gilbert Hitchcock elaborated: "The language of the treaty falls very far short of an apology, and an apology in this case is not called for."

The wording of the treaty supports the view that there was no apology. Look back at the phrase "expresses sincere regret that anything should have occurred to interrupt or to mar the relations of cordial friendship." The noun clause following *regret* is nonspecific. Expressing regret for "anything that might have occurred" does not name any particular transgression. An apology might be inferred, but the implication is weak given the vagueness in the sentence and in the context. Nevertheless, those who argued against the treaty carried the day through the Wilson administration. The treaty would not have included the word *regret*, they argued, unless apology was implied. By 1915, it was clear that the treaty would not be ratified with the expression of regret included. Wilson was soon occupied by other issues and never returned to the treaty. But in 1921, two years after Theodore Roosevelt had died, the new Harding administration succeeded in passing the treaty, with the expression of regret omitted.

Shortcuts

The expressions "I was wrong" and "Forgive me" are also sometimes taken to imply apologies. "I was wrong" concedes error. "Forgive me" asks for reconciliation. To conversationally cooperative listeners, either can imply the full apology process. Recall our earlier modeling of the apology process as made up of a call to apologize, a two-part expressed apology (a naming and a regretting), and a response. When we shortcut a full apology by merely saying "I was wrong," we are relying on the naming of the offense to perform the work of the apology without the sorry-saying. And when we shortcut a full apology with "Forgive me," we are jumping directly to the response step of the process.

Sometimes such shortcuts are sufficient, especially if the person apologizing is sufficiently contrite or if the audience is particularly receptive. Consider this terse public admission by Senator John McCain: "It was the wrong thing to do, and I have no excuse for it." McCain was referring to a joke he had made about Chelsea Clinton's appearance and parentage, which he characterized as a "very unfortunate and insensitive remark." Saying he was wrong suggests regret, and saying he had no excuse condemns the behavior. The statement thus contains two key elements of an apology: regret and condemnation of one's behavior. McCain was not literally apologizing here, but his statement uses conversational logic to invite the inference.

Shortcutting the apology process is understandable. John McCain had apologized privately to the Clinton family, so he perhaps felt no need to apologize expansively in public. But for a serious offense, a shortcut apology often seems like a verbal trick to gain the social benefits of apologizing without having to say you are sorry. Thus, McCain seems to be not quite apologizing. And the converse is true as well. As we will see a bit later (in Chapter 6, when we look at the Iran-Contra scandal), admitting a mistake can be treated as an apology, even when no apology is intended.

For very minor offenses, of course, a shortcut is often exactly what is called for. For the stepped-on foot or jostled elbow, a linguistically elaborate process is overkill. For small social offenses, we may skip the call to apologize and the naming of the offense. Both are apparent from the immediate situation, so we move right to a quickly spoken "Sorry," "'Scuse me," "Pardon," or "My fault," which may or may not be followed by a response from the person harmed. The French-derived counterparts of "Forgive me," "Excuse me," and "Pardon me" are especially common for very minor transgressions. And they are conventionally used to pre-apologize for an imposition. We say "Pardon me, do you have the time?," or "Excuse me, can I ask you a question?"

Just as we take a shortcut by saying "I was wrong," we can also imply an apology with the simple possessive phrase *my fault*. Even shorter is the phrase *my bad*, used as a tic of adolescent speech in the 1995 movie *Clueless*. Lexicographers have traced the origin of the phrase to basketball. Ben Zimmer, who for a time wrote the On Language column at the *New York Times*, favors the view that *my bad* originated on playgrounds in the 1970s and 1980s. He cites *Oxford English Dictionary* examples from the 1980s as proof, including a 1986 guide which gives this definition: "My bad, an expression of contrition uttered after making a bad pass or missing an opponent." Today, *my bad* lends itself to any quick expressions of apology where the call to apologize is apparent and no response is expected.

More Regrets

English provides us with a wide range of lexical choices for apologies. At one end, we have the literal performative *I apologize*, which anchors a full elaboration of a harm and regrets. At the other, we have the fast-moving *my bad*. In between are reports, like *I'm sorry* and *I regret*; the concession *I was wrong*; and the requests to *forgive, pardon*, and *excuse*—all of which can also be taken as implied apologies under certain conversational assumptions. We've also seen how apologies are shaped by the choice of verb and adjective complements and other grammatical choices. We'll end with four additional examples in which the meaning of *sorry* or *regret* was contested: Ohio governor Richard Celeste's apology for the Kent State University shootings, Jane Fonda's apologies for some of her antiwar efforts, Franklin Roosevelt's regrets to African-American leaders, and the University of Iowa apology for experiments on orphans.

Ohio, 1970

"To all those who were wounded and all who have suffered, I am sorry."
—OHIO GOVERNOR RICHARD CELESTE, *May 4, 1990*

In 1970, the nation was divided by the Vietnam War. When President Richard Nixon announced the invasion of Cambodia on April 30, protests erupted on many college campuses, the most tragic of which occurred at Kent State University in Ohio. On May 2, members of the Ohio National Guard were sent to Kent State after the University's ROTC building was burned down. On May 3, Governor James Rhodes went to the campus and vowed to use "every force possible" to maintain order. And at about noon on the following day, guardsmen fired sixty-seven rounds at unarmed college students. Four students were killed and nine others wounded.

President Nixon established the President's Commission on Campus Unrest, which found the shootings "unnecessary, unwarranted, and inexcusable." Nevertheless, a state grand jury exonerated the guardsmen. Federal officials reviewed the case and allegations of a conspiracy among the guardsmen, but declined to prosecute. In 1972 and 1973, parents and students filed lawsuits to challenge those decisions, and in the summer of 1973 a new attorney general, Elliot Richardson, ordered the case reopened. Eventually, eight guardsmen were indicted, though a federal judge dismissed the charges.

Two civil suits were filed (one overturned due to jury tampering), and Ohio eventually reached an out-of-court settlement with victims and parents in 1978, awarding them $675,000 in compensation. Governor Rhodes and twenty-seven Ohio National Guardsmen also expressed official "regret" about the shootings and the killings. Was their regret an apology? *Time* magazine reported the adjutant general of the Guard, Sylvester Del Corso, as explaining that the statements of regret were not apologies: "There is no apology," Del Corso said. "We expressed sorrow and regret just as you would express condolences to the family of someone who died."

An apology did finally come in 1990, with *regret* yielding to *sorry*. On May 4, the twentieth anniversary of the shootings, Kent State dedicated a memorial. Governor Richard Celeste, who took office in 1985, apologized to the families of the dead students and to the nine who were wounded, speaking the name of each victim:

Speaking your mind, casting a stone or hurling an obscene comment—none of these deserve death. To all those who were wounded and all who have suffered, I am sorry.

To Allison Krause, your family and your friends, I am sorry. To Jeff Miller, your family and your friends, I am sorry. To Sandy Scheuer, your family and your friends, I am sorry. To Bill Schroeder, your family and your friends, I am sorry.

Hanoi Jane's Regrets

"I will go to my grave regretting the photograph of me in an anti-aircraft gun . . . "
—JANE FONDA, *1988*

By 1970, actress Jane Fonda had become an opponent of the Vietnam War. She visited military towns in the United States to talk to soldiers, spoke at rallies and college campuses, helped to raise funds for antiwar organizations, and donated her own money to antiwar efforts. In 1972, Fonda took a direction that many thought overstepped the bounds of political protest. That July, she visited Hanoi, the capital of North Vietnam. While there, she participated in anti-American propaganda, giving statements about bombings, making radio broadcasts denouncing American leaders and—at the end of her trip—allowed herself to be photographed seated on a North Vietnamese antiaircraft gun battery.

By the late 1980s, a fiftyish Fonda regretted some of what she had done. In a 1988 interview with Barbara Walters, Fonda used all of the words associated with apology. She explained that she had at times been "thoughtless and careless," was "very sorry," and wanted to "apologize to [members of the military] and their families" for the harm her words had done. She added:

> I will go to my grave regretting the photograph of me in an anti-aircraft gun, which looks like I was trying to shoot at American planes. It hurt so many soldiers. It galvanized such hostility. It was the most horrible thing I could possibly have done. It was just thoughtless.

In 2005, Fonda published an autobiography in which she again expressed regret for the antiaircraft gun photo and for her later comments that attacked POWs. But she also defended the other aspects of her antiwar activism. In the chapter titled "Framed," Fonda wrote,

> I *do* regret that I allowed myself to get into a situation where I was photographed on an anti-aircraft gun. I have explained how that happened and how it sent a message that was the opposite of what I was feeling and doing. I regret the angry remark I made when the POWs returned home that enabled apologists for the war to orchestrate the myth of Hanoi Jane. I was framed and turned into a lightning rod for people's anger, frustration, misinformation, and confusion about the war.

Fonda's autobiography also generated some discussion of what constitutes an apology. Critics faulted her apologies as self-serving, focusing on her use of the word *regret* and arguing that an expression of regret is not an apology. Dexter Lehtinen, writing in the *National Review*, complained (inaccurately) that Fonda "never use[d] the word 'apology.'...only regrets." He argued that "an unqualified apology offered with sincere regret" would be helpful but Fonda's "pseudo-apology...only serves to aggravate the injury." And Oliver North, appearing on Fox News, critiqued Fonda's apology as well, saying, "She has not apologized. I mean again, I'm not trying to be pedantic about it, but an apology is, 'I'm sorry for what I said. I'm sorry I hurt you, Alan, and I hope you can forgive me.' That's an apology." Unlike Hillary Clinton, who found her regrets and sorries about health care inaccurately framed as an apology, Fonda found her attempts to apologize viewed as mere self-serving regrets. Once again, the response to an apology and the framing of its logic is an aspect of its success or failure.

Stabbed in the Back

"I regret that there has been so much misinterpretation of the statement of War Department policy issued from The White House on October 9."
—FRANKLIN ROOSEVELT

World War II broke out in September 1939, but the American people remained isolationist for two more years. As Britain faltered in the summer of 1940, Franklin Roosevelt convinced a wary nation to expand its defense industry to help supply the British. The expansion of the armaments industry took place at a time when African-American unions were just beginning to break barriers. In 1936, the Brotherhood of Sleeping Car Porters had been accepted as a full member of the American Federation of Labor. Its charismatic leader Asa Philip Randolph had organized Pullman porters against propaganda and intimidation, and by 1940, he was ready for a new struggle—bringing African-Americans into the defense industry. A quarter-million jobs were being created, but both the defense and construction industries largely ignored African-American workers. Randolph also wanted to end segregation of units in the armed forces. In a US army of a half-million, less than five thousand were African-Americans, none serving in elite units.

Randolph had described these problems in an address to the 1940 porters' union convention. Also speaking to the porters' union was Eleanor Roosevelt, who became an advocate for a presidential meeting. On September 27, 1940, shortly before the election that would give him a historic third term, Roosevelt met with Randolph; Walter White, the head of the National Association for the Advancement of Colored People (NAACP); and T. Arnold Hill, from the Urban League. The three left the meeting with the impression that they had succeeded in making their case for integration. Roosevelt's cabinet, however, was wary of making such a major change in the military. On October 9, the administration issued a revised War Department Statement of Policy on Negroes, reiterating segregation:

The policy of the War Department is not to intermingle colored and white enlisted personnel in the same regimental organizations. This policy has been proved satisfactory over a long period of years, and to make changes now would produce situations destructive to morale and detrimental to the preparation for national defense.

Press secretary Stephen Early implied that Randolph, White, and Hill had concurred in the policy, an implication that was carried in press reports. The next day, Randolph, White, and Hill released the memo they had brought to the White House meeting in which they argued for ending segregation. They also sent a telegram to Roosevelt which said in part:

> We are inexpressibly shocked that a President of the United States at a time of national peril should surrender so completely to the enemies of Democracy who would destroy national unity by advocating segregation. Official approval by the Commander-in-Chief of the Army and Navy of such discrimination and segregation is a stab in the back of Democracy.

Roosevelt replied in a letter of October 25, writing,

> I regret that there has been so much misinterpretation of the statement of War Department policy issued from The White House on October 9. I regret that your own position, as well as the attitude of both The White House and the War Department, has been misunderstood.

Roosevelt's use of *regret* here, with a noun clause containing passive verbs, is no apology. He is not regretting any action of his or his administration. Instead he is lamenting something that he says occurred: misinterpretations and misunderstandings. The implication is that Randolph, White, and Hill were among those misinterpreting. Roosevelt's response was reported in the African-American magazine *The Crisis* with the headline "Roosevelt Regrets that Army Policy was 'Misinterpreted'," the quotes around *misinterpreted* emphasizing that Roosevelt's *regrets* were not an apology. They were the president's condescending way of restating his position and his claim that other understandings and interpretations were erroneous.

There were no further clarifications of the policy, and Randolph, White, and Hill were unsuccessful at first in getting another White House meeting. Later that year, Randolph proposed the idea of a ten-thousand-man march on Washington. His slogan was "We loyal Negro Americans demand the right to work and fight for our country." In January 1941, Randolph issued his call for a July 1 march. As the estimated number of marchers moved upward from ten thousand to one hundred thousand, Roosevelt asked the first lady to appeal to Randolph to cancel it. She was unsuccessful and suggested a meeting with the president, which occurred June 18, 1941. At that meeting, Randolph was still unable to persuade Roosevelt to end segregation in the military, but Roosevelt did agree to issue an executive order prohibiting discrimination in the defense industries and establishing a Fair Employment Practices Committee. Roosevelt signed Executive Order 8802 on June 25, 1941. It said, "There shall be no discrimination in the employment of workers in defense industries or government because of race, creed, color, or national origin." Randolph canceled the march.

The Monster Study

"The University of Iowa is deeply sorry for the regrettable stuttering experiments on children at the Iowa Soldiers Orphans' Home 60 years ago that have been called to our attention in recent days."
—DAVID SKORTON, *for the University of Iowa, 2001*

In the 1920s, the University of Iowa was known for its pioneering research into the causes and treatments of stuttering. Among other things, the speech pathology faculty tested stutterers surprised by loud noises, sitting in ice water, hypnotized, under the influence of alcohol, and with their dominant arms immobilized in casts. Eventually one Iowa professor, Wendell Johnson— himself a stutterer since the age of five—concluded that stuttering was learned behavior. He would later call this view the diagnosogenic theory, and it became the basis for childhood treatment until the 1980s.

To test his belief that stuttering was learned—and could thus be unlearned—Johnson devised many research studies over the years. One of his earliest, however, was an experiment to determine whether a stutter could be induced in non-stuttering children. In 1939, Johnson and a master's student named Mary Tudor began an experiment using twenty-two children from the Soldiers and Sailors Orphans' Home in Davenport, Iowa.

Ten of the children originally stuttered and twelve did not. All were told that they were going to receive speech therapy. Half of the stutterers were told that their speech was fine; half were told that they did indeed have a speech defect. The twelve fluent children underwent the same regime: six were told that they spoke fine and six others were told that they were beginning to stutter. Part of Mary Tudor's script for the five-month experiment was to tell these fluent subjects:

> The staff has come to the conclusion that you have a great deal of trouble with your speech.... You have many of the symptoms of a child who is beginning to stutter. You must try to stop yourself immediately. Use your will power.... Do anything to keep from stuttering.... Don't ever speak unless you can do it right.

The six students became afraid to speak, their academic work suffered, and some grew self-conscious and withdrawn. They did not become stutterers, but as Tudor concluded in her master's thesis, they did adopt the tics and traits of stutterers. And the children were never apprised of true purpose of the study and—aside from a return visit by Tudor—never received follow-up therapy.

For many years, the orphans' study was little known. Wendell Johnson never referred to it and later Iowa graduate students who learned of it sometimes called it "The Monster Study." In 2001, a reporter for the *San Jose Mercury News* exposed the research, suggesting that Johnson and others had intentionally suppressed it. Mary Tudor, then in her eighties, was quoted in the news articles. She reflected: "I didn't like what I was doing to those children. It was a hard, terrible thing." She added: "It was a different world then. You did what you were told. If I got the same assignment today, I wouldn't do it, now that I'm a mother and grandmother."

While Tudor implies an apology, the university states one more explicitly. In June of that year, David Skorton, the university vice president for research, issued a statement apologizing:

> The University of Iowa is deeply sorry for the regrettable stuttering experiments on children at the Iowa Soldiers Orphans' Home 60 years ago that have been called to our attention in recent days by the *San Jose Mercury News*. While there were no effective safeguards in place in 1939 to prevent such experiments from occurring at universities, the University of Iowa today has in place a strict policy and procedures to insure the safety of all humans in research and has had these controls in place for some years. We are confident that experiments of this nature cannot happen again.

The university also sent letters of apology to the subjects or their survivors. In 2003, the subjects and families sued the state of Iowa for damages, and when the case was settled in 2007, they were awarded $975,000.

Both Tudor's comments and the University's blend excuses with their regrets, while asserting that they would not behave that way today. Mary Tudor suggests that she is a different person with a different moral sense. She struggles to name the offense—calling it an "assignment" and blaming the "different world"— even as she expresses regret. But she does not use the words *sorry, regret,* or *apologize.* And the university, while "deeply sorry" for the "regrettable experiments," frames them as due to the lack of modern safeguards.

5

True Confessions

"I Have Sinned"

In a serious apology, the naming of the offense may be viewed as a public confession. In this chapter, we turn to ways to confess, looking at two very different types of confession. We start with a television preacher.

Jimmy Lee Swaggart began his career in his hometown of Ferriday, Louisiana. He married young, preached his way around the state, and sang Gospel music at Baptist and Pentecostal churches. Swaggart had a good voice—his cousin was Jerry Lee Lewis—and he recorded Gospel music played on Christian radio stations. In 1961, the young Swaggart began his own radio ministry, which led to a church in Baton Rouge and a weekly half-hour television show. By the mid-1970s, Swaggart was broadcasting daily throughout the Bible Belt. In the 1980s, with a longer program and more stations, he was among the most popular television preachers in the United States.

Along the way, Swaggart made some enemies. One was a fellow minister named Marvin Gorman, who had been defrocked in 1986 after allegations of affairs. Swaggart was among those who helped oust Gorman. A year later, Gorman's son and another man staked out a New Orleans airport motel and photographed Swaggart with a prostitute named Debra Murphree. Marvin Gorman had hoped to pressure Swaggart into getting him reinstated. When that didn't happen, Gorman turned his photos over to the leaders of Swaggart's church, the Executive Presbytery of the Assemblies of God. Swaggart met with the Executive Presbytery in a ten-hour closed session on February 18, 1988, and on February 21, he made a televised address to his congregation. Swaggart confessed and apologized in a tearful speech delivered to an audience of eight thousand in his Baton Rouge Family Worship Center.

When someone names their offense, we expect them to articulate what is hidden. A criminal confesses by acknowledging facts. A penitent confesses by recounting sins and asking forgiveness. Someone with a guilty conscience confesses by revealing what bothers them about their own actions. Confessions will have different forms, but acknowledging one's actions is a core component.

What is fascinating about Swaggart's nearly two-thousand-word speech is how little it says. Swaggart's central message was that he had sinned and was asking for God's forgiveness. His confession was short on specifics of the sin and long on expressions of sincerity, compliments to his listeners, and requests. Swaggart began by acknowledging, "Everything that I will attempt to say to you this morning will be from my heart," but he would "not be able to articulate as I would desire." Swaggart was not just lowering expectations, he was linking inarticulateness and sincerity, implying that heartfelt expressions are by their nature beyond words.

Swaggart asserted his forthrightness by saying that he was not planning "to whitewash" his sin. At the end of the second paragraph he summed up his contrition by saying "I take the responsibility. I take the blame. I take the fault." The repetition obscured the fact that he did not say what he was taking the responsibility, blame, or fault for. Swaggart next offered thanks and praise and asked forgiveness. He thanked the media for its fairness, and in successive paragraphs asked for forgiveness from his wife, his family, church leaders, his church and Bible college, his fellow television ministers and evangelists, and his television audience, repeating variants of the confession-apology: "I have sinned against you. And I beg your forgiveness." The formula of each paragraph consisted of praise for those singled out, a broad confession of sin, and a request for forgiveness.

After apologizing to mortal audiences, Swaggart asked God to forgive him. Here Swaggart emphasized forgetting and asked that his actions be cleansed "in the seas of God's forgetfulness, never to be remembered against me anymore." Swaggart also framed his transgression as "a past sin," born of his conviction that he only needed the help of God to overcome his weaknesses, not the help of others:

> Maybe Jimmy Swaggart has tried to live his entire life as though he were not human. And I have thought that with the Lord, knowing He is omnipotent and omniscient, that there was nothing I could not do—and I emphasize with His help and guidance. And I think this is the reason (in my limited knowledge) that I did not find the victory I sought because I did not seek the help of my brothers and my sisters in the Lord.

Swaggart closed by telling viewers that his ministry would continue, and by quoting Psalm 51, in which King David asks for mercy after committing adultery with Bathsheba. It was a well-received performance, interrupted repeatedly by applause. The Assemblies of God leaders ordered a two-year suspension, but after three months, Swaggart returned to preaching as an independent, nondenominational Pentecostal.

Two Ways to Confess

Swaggart's televised confession was central to his survival as a television preacher. But was it a true confession? Swaggart did not name his offense other than generally, referring to it as a sin.

Rhetorician David Tell sees Swaggart's sermon as falling into one of two competing traditions of confession. The first traces its roots to the *Confessions* of Jean-Jacques Rousseau. The other is an even older tradition found in St. Augustine's *Confessions*. In the Augustinian tradition, the nature of confession lies in public disclosure—in revealing the details of sinfulness. Sin, for St. Augustine, was connected to pride, independence, and self-interest—flaws of individualism. Confession meant submitting oneself to the public judgment of the community. Thus confession was not just between man and God. And because it entailed accountability to one's community, confession valued verbal precision and elaboration. As Augustine biographer James J. O'Donnell emphasizes, confession simultaneously needed to be in "an authentic voice " and needed "to express what is private in a way that can be shared with a wider public." Confession therefore required finding the right words.

Rousseau saw the relation between human nature and language differently. He was skeptical that language could ever express a person's interior depths, explaining that "to say what I have to say would require me to invent a language as new as my project." David Tell writes that for Rousseau self-disclosure was simple and instinctive, without "complex chains of reasoning, logical arguments, and precise calculations." Unreflective speech, in this view, has the purity and sincerity needed for heartfelt expression. By contrast, the measured language of a trained speaker suggests instrumentality and pretense. Confession for Rousseau was a form of inarticulateness, which Tell calls "anti-rhetoric." Tell sees Swaggart's "I have sinned" sermon as an example of such anti-rhetoric. Its effectiveness comes from emotion rather than exposition and detail. Swaggart presents his confession as between him and God and considers a public accounting of the transgressions unnecessary. And to many of Swaggart's followers, that was enough.

Three years later, Swaggart was stopped by the California Highway Patrol for driving on the wrong side of the road. His passenger was a prostitute who told the patrol officer Swaggart had propositioned her. Rather than confess again to his congregation, Swaggart told those at Family Worship Center that "The Lord told me it's flat none of your business." Swaggart's son then announced that his father would be temporarily stepping down as head of Jimmy Swaggart Ministries.

"I Don't Think There Is a Fancy Way to Say That I Have Sinned."

In 1995, President Bill Clinton and twenty-two-year-old intern Monica Lewinsky began a relationship that involved fellatio and other sex play in the Oval Office of the White House. The relationship continued through 1997, ending with a lurid investigation by special counsel Kenneth Starr, a semen-stained blue dress, and an impeachment trial.

The Clinton-Lewinsky relationship came to light in the course of another, different lawsuit. In January 1998, Clinton was deposed as part of a sexual harassment lawsuit filed by former Arkansas state employee Paula Jones. As Jones's lawyer explored rumors of relationships with other women, Clinton testified that he had not had "a sexual affair," "sexual relations," or "a sexual relationship" with Lewinsky. Lewinsky had also filed an affidavit in the case denying a sexual relationship with Clinton.

When Lewinsky confidante Linda Tripp passed along tapes suggesting Lewinsky had perjured herself, Kenneth Starr expanded his investigation of the Arkansas Whitewater land deal to include the President's sexual relationships, and he called Lewinsky to testify. On January 21, 1998, the media reported on Starr's Lewinsky investigation, and on January 26, Clinton made his famous television denial: "I did not have sexual relations with that woman, Miss Lewinsky. I never told anybody to lie, not a single time. Never. These allegations are false."

In late July, Lewinsky reached an immunity agreement with Starr's office about her earlier testimony. In over a week's worth of new testimony, she recanted her earlier denial of a sexual relationship. Clinton, in turn, was subpoenaed and testified by videotape before a grand jury on August 17. In his testimony, Clinton confessed to inappropriate sexual conduct and expressed regret, saying:

I engaged in conduct that was wrong. These encounters did not con-
sist of sexual intercourse. They did not constitute sexual relations as
I understood that term to be defined at my January 17th, 1998, deposition. But they did involve inappropriate intimate contact.

These inappropriate encounters ended, at my insistence, in early
1997. I also had occasional telephone conversations with Ms. Lewinsky
that included inappropriate sexual banter.

I regret that what began as a friendship came to include this conduct,
and I take full responsibility for my actions.

Notice how Clinton's regret is followed by a noun clause that removes him
from the action: "what began as a friendship came to include this conduct."
He doesn't regret doing something. He regrets something happening. Clinton also cited "privacy considerations" to limit the amount of detail he would
provide. But a key part of the rest of Clinton's testimony involved how he
understood the term "sexual relations" in the earlier deposition and whether
Lewinsky's testimony was accurate when she responded that "there is no
sexual relationship." Clinton testified that he understood sexual relations as
necessarily including intercourse, and that therefore his claim not to have had
sexual relations with Lewinsky was technically true.

Later that day, Clinton appeared on television and read a 546-word statement to the public. He explained that in the grand jury testimony he had
answered questions about his private life "that no American citizen would ever
want to answer." Clinton went on to state, twice, that he was completely responsible for his actions and to again enumerate the things he did not do. He ended
by explaining the motivation for his misdirection: fear of embarrassment, desire
to protect his family, and suspicion that the investigation was politically motivated. He framed his conduct as a private family and religious matter.

In his television statement, the go-to verb was again *regret*. Clinton said,
"I misled people, including even my wife. I deeply regret that." He presented
himself passively, especially by emphasizing the things that he did not do. He
spoke of taking responsibility (three times) but cast his actions in terms of
things that happened to him ("I was asked questions," "I was motivated by
many factors," "I was also very concerned") and negative actions ("I did not
volunteer information," "a critical lapse in judgment," and "a personal failure,"
"silence [that]...gave a false impression").

Response to Clinton's statement was negative. Editorials were critical,
Congressional Democrats were disappointed, and polling found that a majority did not think Clinton had offered an outright apology. Analysts compared

it to Richard Nixon's "Checkers" speech, in which Nixon denied illegal slush funds, represented himself as a family man, and blamed his troubles on political enemies. Clinton's personal approval rating dropped, and the *New York Times* called the speech "cavalier" and "cursory." The paper's April 19 editorial went on to say that

> apology, the essential word for such remarks, was missing entirely, as well as any hint of awareness of the inexcusable carelessness with which Mr. Clinton has treated people.... Expressing regret for creating a "false impression" is not an adequate response when he lied to the American people for seven months.

Clinton is a lawyer by training: his defense relied on language—from careful parsing of the phrase "sexual relations" (and the word *is*) to generalities like "responsibility for all my actions." But a successful Augustinian confession required a more contrite and detailed public accounting. Clinton offered rhetorical artifice without offering shame, so his statement failed as a confession. And without a confession, there was no basis for an apology.

Over the next couple of weeks, Clinton continued to treat his behavior and his deceptions as mistakes he had acknowledged and wished to put behind him. Beginning in the second week of September, he presented his behavior in a new way, using religious terms. At the annual White House prayer breakfast on September 11, 1998, the day the Starr Report was issued, Clinton spoke to an audience of more than one hundred religious leaders in the East Room of the White House. Clinton acknowledged that he had not been "contrite enough" and said, "I don't think there is a fancy way to say that I have sinned." He went on to say:

> But I believe that to be forgiven, more than sorrow is required—at least two more things. First, genuine repentance—a determination to change and to repair breaches of my own making. Second, what my Bible calls a "broken spirit"; an understanding that I must have God's help to be the person that I want to be; a willingness to give the very forgiveness I seek; a renunciation of the pride and the anger which cloud judgment, lead people to excuse and compare and to blame and complain.

While he would defend himself legally, Clinton explained that "legal language must not obscure the fact that I have done wrong." He ended by quoting from the Yom Kippur liturgy and asked that God give him "a clean heart."

The language and even the structure of Clinton's September 11 statement paralleled Swaggart's. Clinton's apology had evolved from an earlier reliance on words to a confession of sin and shame. On September 12, the *New York Times* applauded the speech for "its unmitigated confession."

Clinton continued to apologize at crucial junctures. On December 11, when the House Judiciary Committee approved articles of impeachment, he said:

> What I want the American people to know, what I want the Congress to know is that I am profoundly sorry for all I have done wrong in words and deeds. I never should have misled the country, the Congress, my friends, or my family. Quite simply, I gave into my shame.

And after his Senate acquittal on February 12, 1999:

> Now that the Senate has fulfilled its constitutional responsibility, bringing this process to a conclusion, I want to say again to the American people how profoundly sorry I am for what I said and did to trigger these events and the great burden they have imposed on the Congress and on the American people.

These later apologies reiterated the themes of sorrow and shame. But it was Clinton's September apology that marked the shift from victim of politically inspired lawsuits to a sinner. As he turned to religious language, Clinton went from framing himself as legally not guilty to sinful and ashamed, asking for help in returning to the moral community he had fallen away from. It was his turn from legal language to religious language—to the language of Rousseau—that made Clinton's later apologies effective. He moved from regret to being sorry.

Naming the Offense or Naming the Offended?

Swaggart and Clinton both confessed without much detail about their misdeeds. In our earlier discussion of apologies (in Chapter 2, especially), we identified naming the offense as an important aspect of a genuine apology. Ideally, apologizers should acknowledge what they have done wrong and the way in which their actions have caused harm. Yet both Swaggart and Clinton apologized without specifically naming their offenses. They apologized for sinfulness, without naming the sin. Both apologies largely succeeded without the specificity we would expect. Why is that?

In part, the avoidance of detailed naming relates to the nature of the transgressions. The details of sexual indiscretions are not something the public wants to hear in sermons or presidential speeches. And naming was unnecessary because the public already knew the details of the transgressions from other sources. Swaggart had confessed his lifelong addiction to pornography in the earlier closed meeting with the Assembly of God leadership—a confession quickly leaked to the press. And the details of the Clinton-Lewinsky relationship had been graphically detailed in the Starr Report.

These apologies succeeded because Swaggart's sermon and Clinton's speech focused on forgiveness. The specificity of naming the offense was transferred to a specificity of naming those harmed. Clinton identified his family, friends, staff, cabinet, Monica Lewinsky and her family, and the American people. Swaggart asked for forgiveness from his wife and family, church leaders, his church and Bible college, his fellow televangelists, and his audience. Confessing was acknowledging what the public already knew and naming those who had been most harmed.

Clinton's belated sincerity helped him to repair relationships, and Swaggart's tearful sermon preserved enough of his flock that he was able to continue his television ministry until his next offense. Sometimes—perhaps more often than we realize—confession and apology follow Rousseau more so than Augustine. Anti-rhetoric asserts the inner goodness and repentance of the sinner, not the details of the transgressions. But sometimes it fails quite badly.

The Appalachian Trail

For six days in June of 2009, the governor of South Carolina went missing. Mark Sanford, elected in 2002 and re-elected in 2006, was the head of the Republican Governor's Association and considered by some to be a strong candidate for the Republican presidential nomination in 2012. On June 18, just before Father's Day, Sanford vanished. He had told his staff that he would be hiking the Appalachian Trail for a few days, but state police could not locate him, and neither his staff nor his wife could reach him by phone.

It turned out that Sanford was in Argentina. He had gone there to be with his lover, María Belén Chapur, with whom he had begun an affair the previous year. South Carolina reporter Gina Smith confronted Sanford as he was flying into the Atlanta airport from Argentina. His deception and midlife crisis (as his wife later called it) became national news. Sanford initially claimed he had wanted to do something more exotic than Appalachian hiking and had been driving alone along the Argentine coast, but the real story of an affair quickly emerged.

At a June 24 news conference in Columbia, South Carolina, Sanford apologized. He opened his remarks by recounting his discussion of the Appalachian Trail that morning with reporter Gina Smith. Then he explained that he would tell that larger story. "I'm a bottom line kind of guy," he said, "I'll lay it out. It's gonna hurt, and we'll let the chips fall where they may." Sanford apologized to his wife and their four sons for "letting them down," and he apologized to his staff and constituents because he "let them down by creating a fiction with regard to where I was going." He continued to apologize to friends and to his in-laws for letting them down. About midway through he summed up by saying:

> I've let down a lot of people. That's the bottom line. And I let them down and in every instance I would ask their forgiveness. Forgiveness is not an immediate process, it is in fact a process that takes time and I'll be in that process for quite some weeks and months and I suspect years ahead. But I'm here because if you were to look at God's laws, in every instance it is designed to protect people from themselves. I think that that is the bottom line of God's law. It is not a moral, rigid list of do's and don'ts just for the heck of do's and don'ts, it is indeed to protect us from ourselves. And the biggest self of self is indeed self. If sin is in fact grounded in this notion of what is it that I want, as opposed to somebody else. And in this regard let me throw one more apology out there and that is to people of faith across South Carolina or for that matter across the nation.

Having apologized, Sanford confessed, "And so the bottom line is this. I've been unfaithful to my wife." He summed it all up by saying, "I hurt a lot of different folks. And all I can say is that I apologize."

Sanford's bizarre and erratic apology failed. The details of the situation were not yet fully known, so more explanation was needed, not less. The off-the-cuff language of Sanford's statement—referring to "the bottom line," "throwing out" one more apology, letting the chips fall where they may, as well as the opening digression concerning the Appalachian Trail—established a far too casual tone. His invocation of religion was unconvincing and at times incoherent (for example when he says "the biggest self of self is indeed self"). And his lack of empathy for his wife and lack of contrition over the affair added to the sense that the apology and confession were expedient rather than sincere. Sanford confessed and apologized, and—as Rousseau would recommend—he showed his heart. But his heart seemed unapologetic.

The stories of Swaggart, Clinton, and Sanford show confession as an important step in apology and forgiveness. But confession can follow different paths, from the lawyerly parsing of transgressions to the sinner's appeal for forgiveness to thoughtless incoherence. We follow with four historical case studies: Alexander Hamilton's confession for his affair in 1791, the confessions of Augustine and Rousseau themselves, and Robert McNamara's confessional memoir about the Vietnam War.

America's First Sex Scandal

"This confession is not made without a blush."
—ALEXANDER HAMILTON, *1797*

Alexander Hamilton's picture appears on the ten-dollar bill. He was the author of many of the Federalist Papers, a confidante of George Washington, and the first secretary of the treasury. And before he was shot and killed in a duel with Aaron Burr in 1804, he was also involved in one of the country's first sex scandals.

Hamilton was appointed secretary of the treasury by Washington in 1789. In 1791, he began an affair with a twenty-three-year-old woman named Maria Reynolds, who claimed that her husband had abandoned her. The husband, James Reynolds, knew about the affair and began to blackmail Hamilton into paying over one thousand dollars to continue his trysts. The following year James Reynolds became embroiled in a financial scandal and implicated Hamilton, accusing the secretary of giving him money from the US treasury to use for speculation. Senator James Monroe, and Congressmen Frederick Muhlenberg, and Abraham Venable investigated. Hamilton privately confessed to the affair and even shared his love letters with the investigators. They were satisfied and Hamilton continued as treasury secretary until 1795.

Then, as now, nothing stayed secret for long. Rumors about Hamilton's affairs began, and in 1797, a muckraking pamphleteer named James Callender reprinted the secret letters and implied that Hamilton had used government funds to pay the blackmail. Hamilton was no longer able to keep his indiscretion private and responded with a publication of his own called *Observations on Certain Documents*. In the pamphlet, he apologized for his affair but defended himself against charges of corruption:

> The charge against me is a connection with one James Reynolds for purposes of improper pecuniary speculation. My real crime is an amorous connection with his wife; for a considerable time with his privity and connivance, if not originally brought on by a combination between the husband and wife with the design to extort money from me.
>
> This confession is not made without a blush. I cannot be the apologist of any vice because the ardour of passion may have made it mine. I can never cease to condemn myself for the pang, which it may inflict in a bosom eminently entitled to all my gratitude, fidelity, and love. But that bosom will approve, that even at so great an expence, I should

effectually wipe away a more serious stain from a name, which it cherishes with no less elevation than tenderness. The public too will I trust excuse the confession. The necessity of it to my defence against a more heinous charge could alone have extorted from me so painful an indecorum.

Hamilton went on at some length about how the affair with Maria Reynolds began, about his "frequent meetings" with her when Mrs. Hamilton was absent, and about his meetings and correspondence with both the husband and wife. He explained that

> Thus has my desire to destroy this slander, completely, led me to a more copious and particular examination of it, than I am sure was necessary. The bare perusal of the letters from Reynolds and his wife is sufficient to convince my greatest enemy that there is nothing worse in the affair than an irregular and indelicate amour. For this, I bow to the just censure which it merits. I have paid pretty severely for the folly and can never recollect it without disgust and self-condemnation—It might seem affectation to say more.

Hamilton's 28,000-word apology is Augustinian. He offers a "copious and particular" detailing of his relationship with James and Maria Reynolds, defending himself against one charge by confessing in detail to another transgression.

Some of Hamilton's political opponents thought that the story of the affair was concocted to cover up more serious political corruption. Others would later reprint the confession to embarrass him. But George Washington continued his patronage and prevailed on his successor to appoint Hamilton as his second-in-command when Washington was again called upon to head the army. Hamilton also played a role in the 1800 presidential election, which was decided in the House of Representatives, when he threw his support to Thomas Jefferson over Aaron Burr. Four years later, Burr challenged Hamilton to a duel and fatally shot him.

St. Augustine's Confessions

"I defiled, therefore, the spring of friendship with the filth of concupiscence, and I beclouded its brightness with the hell of lustfulness."
—AUGUSTINE OF HIPPO, C. 397

The man we know as St. Augustine was born in the mid-fourth century—in 354—in what is now Algeria. His father was a pagan and his mother a Christian, so he grew up exposed to both traditions. For a time as a youth he lived as a hedonist in Carthage, and he also began to follow Manichaeism, the dualistic religion of the Persian prophet Mani. As a profession, Augustine taught grammar and rhetoric in Thagaste, Carthage, Rome, and finally in the imperial court at Milan.

Augustine had a lover, a concubine whom he abandoned when his mother arranged a marriage for him. But the arranged marriage never came about, and in 386 Augustine converted to Christianity and gave up teaching rhetoric for the priesthood. His *Confessions* were written between 397 and 398, more than a decade after his conversion. The *Confessions* combine theology and autobiography and include Augustine's reflections on sexual morality and his regrets for his own youthful hedonism. Augustine also explained his intent to his mortal audience so that his readers might better understand their own actions:

> To whom am I narrating all this? Not to thee, O my God, but to my own kind in thy presence—to that small part of the human race who may chance to come upon these writings. And to what end? That I and all who read them may understand what depths there are from which we are to cry unto thee.

His goal is a deep public exposition of self-knowledge. Augustine writes for himself and for "all who read" his *Confessions*. And as he confesses, Augustine reveals the specifics of his motivations—peer pressure and lust—that led him to ignore his mother's advice on chastity.

> [I]... rushed on headlong with such blindness that, among my friends, I was ashamed to be less shameless than they, when I heard them boasting of their disgraceful exploits— yes,
> and glorying all the more the worse their baseness was. What is worse, I took pleasure in such exploits, not for the pleasure's sake only

but mostly for praise. What is worthy of vituperation except vice itself? Yet I made myself out worse than I was, in order that I might not go lacking for praise. And when in anything I had not sinned as the worst ones in the group, I would still say that I had done what I had not done, in order not to appear contemptible because I was more innocent than they; and not to drop in their esteem because I was more chaste.

Augustine is describing—analyzing—a person who no longer exists. His former self took pride and pleasure in vice and saw innocence as contemptible. Augustine now sees love as sexual enjoyment on God's account and lust as mere corporeal desire. In Book Three of the *Confessions* he also talks about lust arising from "a deep-seated want":

There seethed all around me a cauldron of lawless loves.... To love then, and to be beloved, was sweet to me; but more, when I obtained to enjoy the person I loved. I defiled, therefore, the spring of friendship with the filth of concupiscence, and I beclouded its brightness with the hell of lustfulness.

Unlike Swaggart, Clinton, and Sanford, Augustine is not seeking forgiveness but trying to understand his earlier hedonism. By articulating it, he is able to reflect on his actions and motivations.

Cries of Nature

"I know my heart, and have studied mankind."
—JEAN-JACQUES ROUSSEAU, c. 1764

Jean-Jacques Rousseau was born in Geneva in 1712, part of the generation that would include David Hume, Adam Smith, Denis Diderot, and Ben Franklin. Rousseau's mother died a week after he was born, and he was raised by his father, a clockmaker, and by an aunt and uncle. At thirteen, Rousseau apprenticed for a time to an engraver. Beatings were common, from his father, his uncle, and the engraver. In his teens, Rousseau moved on to Annecy where he came under the tutelage of Françoise-Louise de Warens, a woman thirteen years his senior. De Warens convinced Rousseau to give up the strict Calvinism of his youth and convert to Catholicism. The two also eventually became lovers.

Charming and handsome, Rousseau supported himself through patronage and work as a secretary, teacher, and musician. In 1745, he began a common-law relationship with a housemaid named Therese Levasseur, with whom he would eventually have five children, all of whom were left at an orphanage for care. Rousseau also continued to have many affairs and was often in heated philosophical, literary, and political disputes. Nevertheless, Rousseau became a celebrity writer, authoring both novels and the moral and political philosophy that would inspire the French Revolution after his death. He also reconverted to Calvinism in 1754 and in 1764 began to write—and to give controversial public readings from—his autobiography, titled *Confessions* (in a nod to Augustine). After Rousseau's sudden death in 1778, his *Confessions* were published, the first parts appearing in 1782 and the remainder in 1789.

Organized into a dozen books, *Confessions* is a memoir of both his private and public lives. Rousseau aimed to celebrate himself—both the bad and good. His opening paragraph ends with the line, "My purpose is to display to my kind a portrait in every way true to nature, and the man I shall portray will be myself." He explains that on Judgment Day, he will ask God to

> assemble round thy throne an innumerable throng of my fellow-mortals, let them listen to my confessions, let them blush at my depravity, let them tremble at my sufferings; let each in his turn expose with equal sincerity the failings, the wanderings of his heart, and, if he dare, aver, I was better than that man.

Rousseau lays bare his life's experiences and transgressions, challenging others to do the same. He describes his pleasure at being spanked, his thefts, his cruelties, and his affairs. His goal is self-expression and self-understanding of his humanness, with periodic regrets. In one of his most memorable transgressions, young Rousseau had stolen a pink and silver ribbon and, when it was discovered that he had it, claimed that it had been given to him by the housemaid. The young maid was dismissed. Rousseau reflects:

> The cruel remembrance of this transaction, sometimes so troubles and disorders me, that, in my disturbed slumbers, I imagine I see this poor girl enter and reproach me with my crime, as though I had committed it but yesterday.... The weight, therefore, has remained heavy on my conscience to this day; and I can truly own the desire of relieving myself, in some measure, from it, contributed greatly to the resolution of writing my *Confessions*.

Rousseau recounts both the wicked and laudable events of his life not just to condemn his earlier self but to forgive himself as well. It is as if by recounting his depravities he can put them behind him. But Rousseau is not so much interested in exploring the nature of his harms—why he behaved so badly—as in transferring the weight of his "depravity," as he calls it, to his readers and thus relieving himself of some of his burden. He shares and exposes but does not explore.

Apology in Retrospect

"We were terribly wrong."
—FORMER SECRETARY OF DEFENSE ROBERT MCNAMARA, *in a 1997 memoir*

Robert McNamara studied economics, mathematics, and philosophy as a young man at Berkeley. He took an MBA at Harvard, worked briefly as an accountant and professor of accounting, served in World War II, and joined the Ford Motor Company as manager of planning and financial analysis. He was, in the jargon of the time, a whiz kid—and by 1960 he had become president of Ford, the first company president from outside the Ford family.

President Kennedy tapped McNamara to bring his systems-analysis approach to the Department of Defense. And as Vietnam became a national priority in the Johnson administration, McNamara became the chief architect and spokesman for that ill-fated war. McNamara crafted a plan that led to the commitment of over half a million troops to Vietnam. The approach was that of the business strategic planner: determine objectives, develop action steps, assign costs, and monitor progress. And McNamara's military strategy was one of attrition, grounded in the idea that escalated troop levels would eventually wear down resistance. Eventually, though, McNamara began to reassess. He even rejected troop increases at one point only to be overruled by the president. McNamara left the Johnson cabinet in February of 1968 to become the president of the World Bank, a position he held until retiring in 1981.

In 1995, McNamara published a memoir titled *In Retrospect*, in which he acknowledged mistakes and expressed regrets. McNamara said, "We of the Kennedy and Johnson administrations acted according to what we thought were the principles and traditions of our country. But we were wrong. We were terribly wrong." That sentiment runs throughout the book itself. He characterized the war in terms of flawed decision-making, misread and underestimated situations, ill-founded judgments, and failures of analysis. In the book, McNamara recounts that he began to have doubts that the war could be won as early as 1965 but remained silent out of a sense of duty.

McNamara had often been regarded as verbally deft. A *Time* profile in 1971, for example, described him as an "assured technician" with an "unstoppable stream of convincing detail," "a swift answer for every question," and "a sharp rebuttal for every doubt." That impression carried over to McNamara's memoir as well, which was criticized as self-serving, insufficiently contrite, and blame-shifting. The *New York Times* referred to "stale tears, three decades late." Law professor Robert Strassfeld characterized McNamara's failing this way:

> While any memoirist is necessarily selective in his retelling of the past, McNamara sometimes appears bent on minimizing his fault by his choices of what to tell and what to omit. Moreover, he ignores or remains blind to much that he ought to address in a mea culpa.

McNamara's narrative—his confession, as Strassfeld calls it—exemplifies the battle of memory against the messiness of the past. Confronted with a divided self, McNamara reconstructs a simpler, coherent story of flaws, misreadings, and underestimations. In the 2003 documentary, *The Fog of War*, McNamara continued to reflect and rationalize:

> What I'm doing is thinking through with hindsight, but you don't have hindsight available at the time. I'm very proud of my accomplishments, and I'm very sorry that in the process of accomplishing things, I've made errors.

When asked if he felt guilty, he said that he did not want to discuss that because it would just create more controversy and would be too complex to discuss. Filmmaker Errol Morris asked if McNamara had the feeling of being damned if you do and damned if you don't, to which McNamara replied: "[T]hat's right. And I'd rather be damned if I don't." Damned or not, McNamara did not seem to be accustomed to answering the call to apologize. He offered only lessons learned, but few regrets. Lacking that aspect, his memoir, while Augustinian in its detailed analysis, fails as a confession. Confession was, as McNamara conceded, too complex for him.

6

Verbal Self-defense

"I Didn't Get It"

In this chapter, we move from confession to excuse, focusing on the ways in which apology is used in campaigns of self-justification. We begin with what the *New Yorker* would later call "An Ogre's Tale."

In the fall of 1992, the *Washington Post* published a series of articles about long-time Oregon senator Robert Packwood. The series detailed the stories of multiple women who accused the sixty-year-old senator of sexual harassment. Packwood succeeded in delaying the publication of the story until after the 1992 election, suggesting that the allegations were both false and politically motivated. His office also collected and faxed to the *Post* reporters affidavits and other material intended to undermine the credibility of his accusers. The story finally appeared on November 22. It included the first of several Packwood apologies, which he had also faxed to the *Post* reporters. It was a conditional apology. Packwood said, "If any of my comments or actions have indeed been unwelcome, or if I have conducted myself in any way that has caused any individual discomfort or embarrassment, for that I am sincerely sorry." Then, after the story broke, Packwood disappeared.

Packwood had checked in to the Hazelden Institute in Minnesota. His office released a statement in his name on November 27: "I never consciously intended to offend any women. I, therefore, offer my deepest apologies to all those involved and to the people of Oregon. If I take the proper steps I hope my past conduct is not unforgivable." Packwood apologized yet again at a December 10 news conference, after his assessment at Hazelden. He opened with a one-thousand-word statement in which he said "I am here today to take full responsibility for my conduct" and "What I did was not just stupid or boorish, my actions were just plain wrong and there is no other better word for it." He talked about his shy youth and about his support for women's issues, building to his point:

> In light of my commitment to women's issues and my deep belief that the work place must be gender neutral, the current charges about my behavior trouble me in a profound way.
>
> I recognize now that my personal conduct has been at variance with these beliefs, not because my convictions are not genuine, but because my conduct was not faithful to those convictions.
>
> Although most of these incidents are a decade or two decades old and no one's job or pay or status in the office was threatened, my conduct was still wrong. I just didn't get it. I do now.

In this statement Packwood asserted his convictions and framed his conduct as failing to live up to his own standards. He promised to change and asked for a chance to earn back constituents' trust.

In the questioning that followed, reporters pressed Packwood. Yet Packwood was still unwilling to name his offenses. Asked what conduct he was apologizing for, he replied, "I'm apologizing—and I'm not even going to debate the conduct as alleged—that's what I'm apologizing for." When a reporter re-asked the question, Packwood said, "I'm apologizing for the conduct that it was alleged that I did, and I say I am sorry." Packwood left his listeners to fill in whether his conduct was harassment, boorishness, or anything at all. Packwood apologized, but would not name his offense.

Packwood undercut his apology further by refusing to apologize for soliciting damaging affidavits about his accusers. Asked about seventeen affidavits his office had faxed to the *Post*, Packwood stonewalled: "I am not going to discuss the issue at all as to how I might characterize their conduct. I'm not going to get into it and I'm not going to respond at all to the issue that you're raising." Whatever he was apologizing for, it obviously did not extend to the character attacks.

Packwood's press conference and his two previous apology attempts illustrate the main themes of his defense over the next three years. He attempted to minimize the offenses by characterizing them as alleged, as decades old, and as not legally harassment. He offered nonspecific apologies, outright denials, excuses rooted in his personality, and attacks on his accusers. He maintained that his beliefs were beyond reproach. It was merely his behavior that was inconsistent.

Packwood had championed women's issues and had long enjoyed the support of feminist groups. But as the facts emerged and more women came forward—thirty-eight in all—that all changed. In an early 1993 trip back to his home state, Packwood continued to attack his accusers and present himself as a victim. He also moved to the right politically to align himself with his party. And, as his case went to the Senate Select Ethics Committee, Packwood again went silent, saying it would be inappropriate to comment on a case before the committee.

Verbal Self-defense—Deny, Bolster, Differentiate, Transcend

Packwood's response illustrates many of the traditional techniques of verbal self-defense. In studying such techniques, scholars initially focused on particular speeches—such as Richard Nixon's "Checkers" speech, in which Nixon defended himself against charges of maintaining a slush fund, or Edward Kennedy's 1969 Chappaquiddick speech describing his actions after the automobile accident that resulted in the death of Mary Jo Kopechne. Such speeches offer accounts of situations and, as Erving Goffman noted, attempt to use language to reduce "the fault of the actor."

In a much-cited article, rhetoricians B. L. Ware and Wil Linkugel described such verbal accounts—which they refer to by the classical term *apologia*—as responses to "an attack upon a person's character." The word *apology*, in fact, has a history of reflecting both apologies and accounts. The earliest aspect of its meaning refers to the idea of defending oneself from accusations; the later sense of the word is the familiar idea of expressing regret. *The Apology of Socrates* is a well-known example of the former sense. It refers to Plato's rendering of Socrates's speech defending himself against the charges of corrupting the youth of Athens and other crimes. The apology as a defense against an accusation was a feature of the Greek and Roman courts, and the meaning of *apology* as defense later made its way into English. Samuel Johnson includes both in his 1755 *Dictionary of the English Language*, defining the verb as "to plead in favour of any person or thing," and the noun as signifying "an excuse rather than vindication."

Ware and Linkugel observed four strategies of verbal self-defense—denial, bolstering, differentiation, and transcendence. Denial is just that—an account that denies guilt (or guilty intent) for an action. Bolstering is an offender's attempt to identify with a positive value. When Packwood claimed he had "absolutely not" engaged in sexual harassment, he defended with denial;

when he asserted he was a supporter of women's rights he was bolstering. For Ware and Linkugel, denial and bolstering seek to reposition the offender rather than change people's views of an offense.

The other two strategies—differentiation and transcendence—are redefining strategies. When defenders try to separate a situation from its negative context, they are differentiating. Thus when Packwood debated the definition of sexual harassment, he engaged in differentiation, arguing that what he did was not technically sexual harassment. Finally, transcendence shifts attention away from the negative situation to ideals that might be viewed more favorably. In the next section, we will look at an attempt by Packwood to transcend with such an abstraction—he portrays himself as a fallen soldier. Although it probably does not do justice to Ware and Linkugel's theory, I think of the four self-defense strategies as "I didn't do it," "I'm not that kind of person," "It's not what it seems to be," and "I'm called to a higher good."

Ware and Linkugel were writing in the 1970s, and their focus was verbal self-defense in response to attacks on character. Later scholars have broadened the scope of apologia from attacks on character to allegations of wrongdoing by institutions. As communication scholar Keith Hearit describes them, such institutional defenses "present a compelling counter description" of bad actions. Another scholar, William Benoit, has expanded Ware and Linkugel's strategies to five types of rhetorical moves and several substrategies. Benoit's five strategies are denial, evasion, reduction, correction, and mortification. Denial can mean denying that a bad action occurred at all or denying that one performed it. And, according to Benoit, it can also mean shifting blame by offering another culprit. The remaining strategies seek to mitigate the offense in various ways. To evade responsibility, an offender might claim to have been provoked or unaware; he or she might assert good intentions and claim that the harm was an accident. Reducing offensiveness includes strategies we have already discussed—bolstering, minimizing, differentiating, and transcending—but it can also entail attacking the accuser or offering compensation (as when Amazon offered credit to those whose copies of *Nineteen Eighty-four* were deleted). An offender can propose corrective action—to do things better and differently in the future. And an offender can apologize. That's the final strategy on Benoit's list—which he calls *mortification*. An offender "admits responsibility and asks for forgiveness."

Should apology really count as a self-defense strategy? As Benoit notes, some scholars of rhetoric do not see apologies as self-defense strategies, because apologies presume guilt. How can you defend yourself if you confess

---

BENOIT'S TAXONOMY

Denial
> Simple denial
> Shifting the blame

Evading Responsibility
> Provocation
> Lack of information, control, or ability
> Accident
> Good intentions

Reducing Offensiveness
> Bolstering
> Minimization
> Differentiation
> Transcendence
> Attacking the accuser
> Compensation

Corrective Action

Mortification

---

to the wrongdoing? We saw the difficulty that Robert Packwood faced as he tried "apologizing for the conduct that it was alleged that [he] did."

An apology is fundamentally different than an excuse or justification. While other account strategies rename or reframe an offense, an apology must name an offense and express regret for it. As we have seen over and over, an explanation may be part of a successful, sincere apology since it can facilitate a shared understanding of the transgression. Explanations offered during the call to apologize can also evolve into apologies and form the basis for reconciliation. But accounts that excuse can also be ways of avoiding apology, and insincere apologies are often those that cynically feign mortification.

When people try to defend and apologize simultaneously, they place themselves in a double bind. Apology communicates regret. Defense mitigates this regret. And as a defense unfolds over time, defenders may have to expand or revise the original apologies. Such continued revisions render the original apologies insincere or incomplete. On the other hand, refusing to apologize for a legitimate harm and offering only excuses is just as problematic. Failing to apologize signals that someone does not accept his or her role in the harm.

Finding a path through such a bind requires good-faith efforts by the person responsible for the harm. If an apology arises from the sincere exploration of a transgression, then elements of accounts—explanations of the offense, commitments to corrective action, or offers of compensation—may naturally find their way into the apology. But if an apology comes as part of a self-serving defense, it will be ineffective.

This was Packwood's problem. His apologies were just insincere verbal moves. He did not name his offenses in any way that acknowledged their seriousness or the moral worth of those he had harmed. His apologies were mixed with other tactics that undercut them. Packwood denied accusations, dodged responsibility with his suggestion of alcohol abuse, and minimized his offenses as mere boorishness. He tried to bolster his own status by requesting an investigation, by touting his feminist voting record, and by moving closer to his party. He claimed to be committed to corrective action. He attacked his accusers. And for a long time Packwood simply refused to comment on the accusations, saying that it would be inappropriate because the investigation was ongoing.

And in the end, Packwood offered one further account.

Packwood's Exit

The Senate Select Committee on Ethics began its investigation in December of 1992, less than two weeks after the publication of the *Washington Post* article. It was the committee's first case of sexual misconduct. The investigation was both aided and complicated by the fact that Packwood was a diarist. Since entering the Senate, he had made diary entries almost daily, usually dictated into a tape recorder and later transcribed by a secretary. The diaries, which included Packwood's recounting of sexual liaisons with staffers and others, were subpoenaed by the ethics committee. Packwood challenged the release of the full ten thousand pages and a compromise was reached by which a federal judge (ironically, Kenneth Starr) screened the diaries to determine what should be excluded. But as the legal proceedings over the tapes and diaries unfolded, it became clear that there was a new problem. Packwood's secretary Cathy Wagner Cormack testified that he had altered diary entries and re-recorded audiotapes, fabricating new material about his accuser's backgrounds, behavior, and reputations. Packwood attacked his accusers in his diary.

By the late summer of 1995, an increasingly belligerent Packwood had lost both the public and his Senate colleagues, and on September 7, he resigned.

As he announced his resignation, Packwood tried once again to transcend his situation, portraying himself as a fallen soldier. He recounted his Senate "battles" for various causes and his friendship with other senators. He even compared himself to Douglas MacArthur:

> ...some in my age group will remember General MacArthur's final speech at West Point: Duty, honor, country. It is my duty to resign. It is the honorable thing to do for this country, for this Senate. So I now announce that I will resign from the Senate, and I leave this institution not with malice but with love, good luck, Godspeed.

Packwood's long series of rhetorical moves—from his initial denials to his final resignation—show accounts at their most ineffective. A good account mitigates responsibility, but Packwood had no convincing explanation. His fall also demonstrates that an insincere apology cannot resolve a transgression and may serve only to reveal the weaknesses of an account. The three-year Packwood spectacle is useful too because it illustrates the full range of strategies available for accounts. Let's now take a look at how verbal defense strategies were used in another type of defense—against accusations of plagiarism.

"If They Decide I'm a Fraud, I'm a Fraud."

Stephen Ambrose broke out of the academic history niche in 1994 with the publication of *D-Day*, a story of ordinary soldiers. From 1996 to 2002, he published eleven popular books, including *Undaunted Courage*, about Meriwether Lewis and Thomas Jefferson. In January 2002, journalist Fred Barnes suggested that Ambrose had plagiarized parts of his 2001 book *The Wild Blue*, the story of young George McGovern's B-24 crew during World War II. Writing in the *Weekly Standard*, Barnes showed that Ambrose had taken several passages from Thomas Childers's *Wings of Morning*. Ambrose footnoted Childers's book as a source but did not enclose the material in quotations, as is scholarly practice.

Ambrose's publisher, Simon and Schuster, initially defended the book, saying, "All research garnered from previously published material is appropriately footnoted." However, Ambrose himself responded, "I made a mistake for which I am sorry. It will be corrected in future editions of the book." Here we see the beginnings of an account with the publisher's denial followed by Ambrose's minimization of the problem as "a mistake" with the promise of corrective action. In a follow up in the *Weekly Standard*, Barnes took Ambrose's statement as an apology, and Thomas Childers also accepted it as appropriately apologetic. Case closed? Not quite.

Other plagiarism evidence quickly emerged, some dating all the way back to Ambrose's Ph.D. dissertation on General George Armstrong Custer. As the accusations mounted, Ambrose defended by differentiating his writing practices from plagiarism. He told the *New York Times*, "I am not out there stealing other people's writings. If I am writing up a passage and it is a story I want to tell and this story fits and a part of it is from other people's writing, I just type it up that way and put it in a footnote. I just want to know where the hell it came from." Here Ambrose suggests that his practice of verbatim paraphrasing is just a feature of uncluttered storytelling. Footnoting differentiates it from theft.

Ambrose had his defenders, who attempted to bolster his reputation. One was 1972 presidential candidate George McGovern, a one-time history professor, who supported Ambrose in a January 28, 2002, letter to the *New York Times*. McGovern wrote that Ambrose "is not only a superb historian, but also a gifted writer whose books are devoured by the public, and a patriot who has donated millions of dollars to environmental and educational causes." McGovern's defense is deductive: Ambrose's positive qualities should immunize him from his offenses. Ambrose also attacked his accusers, specifically journalist Mark Lewis, who had published several articles about Ambrose's writing. Ambrose responded angrily to one of these in a February 6 letter to the *Wall Street Journal*. He wrote that Lewis would have never found the "examples of plagiarism" without Ambrose's footnotes, implying that since the passages were footnoted, they could not be plagiarism.

Ambrose, a long-time smoker, died of lung cancer not long after the plagiarism was revealed. In a May 11, 2002, interview with the *Los Angeles Times*, he revealed his cancer prognosis. Ambrose also summed up his feelings about the plagiarism accusations. "Screw it," he said, "If they decide I'm a fraud, I'm a fraud. I don't know that I'm all that good at academics. I'm a writer." Ironically, his death in October 2002 insulated his reputation to some extent. But Ambrose's account cannot be said to have been successful. His early apologies did not name his offenses so much as they renamed them—as mistakes or omissions rather than copying or plagiarism, blending apologies with the assertion that he had really done nothing wrong. He minimized the extent of the offense, differentiated plagiarism from error, and blamed the pace with which he wrote. And he generally ignored other criticisms of his scholarship that arose along with the plagiarism concerns.

The overall effect, as his "Screw it" comment suggests, was of someone who did not regret what he had done.

"I Am a Historian…It Is Who I Am."

Shortly after it revealed Stephen Ambrose's plagiarism, the *Weekly Standard* also published another expose. It reported that Pulitzer Prize-winning Doris Kearns Goodwin had plagiarized parts of her 1987 book, *The Fitzgeralds and the Kennedys*, from Lynne McTaggart's *Kathleen Kennedy: Her Life and Times* and two other works. Goodwin and her publisher, again Simon and Schuster, were quoted in the article, the publisher conceding that "in the original book there were some mistakes made." Goodwin admitted that she had previously reached a large private settlement with McTaggart over the copied passages, and the *Weekly Standard* noted that the 2001 edition contained additional footnotes and an acknowledgment of McTaggart's work in preface.

After the *Weekly Standard* piece appeared, Goodwin responded almost immediately in an eight-hundred-word *Time* magazine essay. Goodwin's essay, titled "How I Caused That Story" began by defining her identity and her commitment to her craft. "I am a historian," she began, "With the exception of being a wife and mother, it is who I am. And there is nothing I take more seriously." She went on to say:

> In recent days, questions have been raised about how historians go about crediting their sources, and I have been caught up in the swirl. Ironically, the more intensive and far-reaching a historian's research, the greater the difficulty of citation. As the mountain of material grows, so does the possibility of error.

Goodwin tries to transcend by identifying her values—wife, mother, and historian. She minimizes her offense as well, presenting it as a sourcing challenge common to all historians, one proportional to the intensity and scope of their research. She concedes that fourteen years earlier, she had "failed to provide quotation marks for phrases…taken verbatim," because she mistakenly assumed the words in her notes were her own. Her account again minimizes the offense as error, not theft.

Then she turns to the "larger question" of understanding "how citation mistakes can happen." Goodwin recounts the decade-long process of researching and writing a nine-hundred-page work, which involved sifting through primary sources and taking notes on about three hundred books. She concludes, "If I had had the books in front of me, rather than my notes, I would have caught mistakes in the first place and placed any borrowed phrases in direct quotes." Here she again renames her offense as a set of mistakes.

Goodwin ends her essay with another round of transcendence. She reiterates her pride in proper citation and its importance to historians and describes technological changes she made to her practice—computers, scanners, and "the mysterious footnote key on the computer" shown to her by her son. She concludes that errors are inevitable but should be swiftly corrected when they occur.

Goodwin followed up with corrective action. She had research assistants review the sourcing of *The Fitzgeralds and the Kennedys*. When they discovered additional problems, she promised to have unsold copies destroyed and a new corrected version produced. Goodwin also resigned from the Pulitzer Board and the Harvard University Board of Overseers and took a leave from her role as a PBS commentator. And, while she was disinvited from some speaking engagements, she used others to address the controversy, reiterating the message of her *Time* magazine essay.

Some critics found her account insufficient and euphemistic. Others faulted her settlement with Lynne McTaggart as a cover up. The *Harvard Crimson* cited the university's policy on academic dishonesty and asked why Goodwin was not held to the same standard as students. And Goodwin was charged with hypocrisy because years earlier she herself had accused author Joe McGinniss of copying her works. Goodwin had her defenders as well, including fourteen historians who endorsed her in a letter to the *New York Times* in October 2002. Responding to an article titled "Are More People Cheating?," the historians proclaimed their "high regard for the scholarship and integrity of Doris Kearns Goodwin" and protested her inclusion in an article that cited fraud by executives at Tycho International and Enron, infidelities by Bill Clinton and Kobe Bryant, the corked baseball bat used by Chicago Cub Sammy Sosa, and plagiarism by Stephen Ambrose. The historians wrote:

> Plagiarism is a deliberate intent to purloin the words of another and to represent them as one's own. Ms. Goodwin did not intentionally pass off someone else's words as her own. Her sources in her 1987 book, "The Fitzgeralds and the Kennedys," were elaborately credited and footnoted. Her errors resulted from inadvertence, not intent. She did not, she does not, cheat or plagiarize. In fact, her character and work symbolize the highest standards of moral integrity.

These fourteen historians did not defend Stephen Ambrose.

Let's contrast Goodwin's defense with Ambrose's. Ambrose dismissed the problem and the accusers, even attacking the latter. Ultimately, he was unable to sufficiently correct, bolster, transcend, minimize, apologize, counterattack, or deny. Goodwin, on the other hand, was publically regretful. She confessed to and apologized for embarrassing errors but, like Ambrose, never explicitly conceded intentional wrongdoing. She was nevertheless able to transcend her offenses through her *Time* essay and through reforms and new accomplishments, including a well-received book on Abraham Lincoln. She was no doubt helped too by the inevitable comparison with Ambrose.

Now we'll look at some other examples of accounts that blend with apologies in public perception: a plagiarism response by columnist Maureen Dowd, Ronald Reagan's Iran-Contra statement, Henry Ford's apology for the *Dearborn Independent*, and Lucille Ball's testimony before the House Un-American Activities Committee. In each, the features of self-defense rather than apology dominate.

A Little Help from My Friends

"We're fixing it on the web, to give Josh credit, and will include a note, as well as a formal correction tomorrow."
—*New York Times Columnist Maureen Dowd, 2009*

Pulitzer Prize winner Maureen Dowd joined the *New York Times* in 1983 and moved onto its op-ed page as a columnist in 1995. She writes two columns a week in a signature acerbic style, and she takes particular delight in lampooning presidents, left and right (her Pulitzer was for coverage of the Lewinsky scandal).

In 2009, one of Dowd's columns made her the object of a plagiarism controversy. Dowd's May 17 column contained a paragraph—a forty-two-word sentence—that was virtually identically to one posted by Talking Points Memo editor Josh Marshall a few days earlier. Marshall had blogged that "more and more the timeline is raising the question of why, if the torture was to prevent terrorist attacks, it seemed to happen mainly during the period when we were looking for what was essentially political information to justify the invasion of Iraq." When the apparent copying was pointed out to her, Dowd responded, in an email to the blog, not with an apology but with an account attributing the forty-some borrowed words to a friend's suggestion.

> Josh is right. I didn't read his blog last week, and didn't have any idea he had made that point until you informed me just now. I was talking to a friend of mine Friday about what I was writing who suggested I make this point, expressing it in a cogent—and I assumed spontaneous—way and I wanted to weave the idea into my column. But, clearly, my friend must have read Josh Marshall without mentioning that to me. We're fixing it on the web, to give Josh credit, and will include a note, as well as a formal correction tomorrow.

Readers, including the *Times*'s public editor Clark Hoyt, found her account wanting. Hoyt wrote that "readers have a right to expect that even if an opinion columnist like Dowd tosses around ideas with a friend, her column will be her own words. If the words are not hers, she must give credit." Some questioned how Dowd—or her friend—could get Marshall's quote so exact without plagiarizing.

Dowd survived the episode and even got some credit for—as *Slate*'s Jack Shafer put it—correcting the error and not denying that it was plagiarism. But her implied apology never quite names the transgression either.

Arms for Hostages

"A few months ago I told the American people I did not trade arms for hostages. My heart and my best intentions still tell me that's true, but the facts and the evidence tell me it is not."
—RONALD REAGAN, *March 1987*

In 1982, David Dodge, the president of the American University of Beirut was kidnapped by Lebanese militants. Over the next decade, thirty Westerners would also become prisoners, including the CIA station chief, journalists, academics, and others. US officials believed that the Iranian-backed Hezbollah was behind most of the kidnappings, and the Reagan administration hoped a bargain could be struck to sell military supplies to Iran in return for help in getting hostages released. Congress, however, had banned the sale of weapons to state sponsors of terrorism like Iran. Nevertheless, in 1985, the newly re-elected Reagan administration began to secretly sell arms to Iran. In August and September of 1985, over 2,500 anti-tank missiles were shipped to Iran via Israel. Three American hostages were released: Benjamin Weir, Martin Jenco, and David Jacobson.

Eventually the arms-for-hostages deal came to light. A Lebanese magazine broke the story, which the Iranian government confirmed. Ten days after the story broke, President Ronald Reagan denied it on national television, saying, "We did not—repeat, did not—trade weapons or anything else for hostages, nor will we."

Reagan was wrong.

A Justice Department investigation soon revealed that Colonel Oliver North, a marine working on Reagan's National Security Council staff, had led the operation to trade arms for hostages. And the investigation revealed that the money from the arms sales secretly funded anti-communist Contras in Nicaragua, in violation of a Congressional ban on such support. North was fired, National Security Council director John Poindexter resigned, and Reagan's approval rating dropped twenty-one points in just one month. Reagan was silent on the Iran-Contra scandal for several months, while a special commission headed by former senator John Tower investigated.

In the late winter of 1987, Reagan was ready to address the public to take responsibility. On March 4, he gave a 1,900-word address explaining his silence on the Iran-Contra scandal, which he attributed to a need to get all the facts. Reagan opened with the language of accountability.

First, let me say I take full responsibility for my own actions and for those of my administration. As angry as I may be about activities undertaken without my knowledge, I am still accountable for those activities. As disappointed as I may be in some who served me, I'm still the one who must answer to the American people for this behavior. And as personally distasteful as I find secret bank accounts and diverted funds— well, as the Navy would say, this happened on my watch.

Let's start with the part that is the most controversial. A few months ago I told the American people I did not trade arms for hostages. My heart and my best intentions still tell me that's true, but the facts and the evidence tell me it is not. As the Tower board reported, what began as a strategic opening to Iran deteriorated, in its implementation, into trading arms for hostages. This runs counter to my own beliefs, to administration policy, and to the original strategy we had in mind. There are reasons why it happened, but no excuses. It was a mistake.

Reagan went on to discuss the Lebanese hostages, the diversions of funds, his management style, and the changes he was making in personnel and process. He said that he hoped to move forward, observing, "Now, what should happen when you make a mistake is this: You take your knocks, you learn your lessons, and then you move on. That's the healthiest way to deal with a problem."

Reagan's account—his admission of error and responsibility—was treated by the media as an apology. It was also criticized as confusing. In part, this comes from Reagan's shifts in message. He speaks at length about taking responsibility ("I take full responsibility," "I am still accountable," "I'm still the one who must answer to the American people," "This happened on my watch,"), but at the same time avoids that responsibility. He states, "My heart and my best intentions still tell me that's true, but the facts and the evidence tell me it is not." He reports that he "didn't know about any diversion of funds to the Contras." He refers to a failing memory, saying that "no one kept proper records of meetings or decisions," which "led to my failure to recollect whether I approved an arms shipment before or after the fact. I did approve it; I just can't say specifically when." And he cites a concern for the hostages that clouded his judgment.

It's clear from the Board's report, however, that I let my personal concern for the hostages spill over into the geo-political strategy of reaching out to Iran. I asked so many questions about the hostages' welfare that I didn't ask enough about the specifics of the total Iran plan.

Reagan himself is strangely absent from his account. His thoughts and actions are often reflected as reports from the Tower commission rather than as his own reactions to what happened. He presents things almost as a narrator, and he takes responsibility as the symbolic watch officer. But his statement falls short of an apology. It is a report of mistakes unremembered.

The Dearborn Independent

"Had I appreciated even the general nature, to say nothing of the details of these utterances, I would have forbidden their circulation without a moment's hesitation."
—HENRY FORD, *1927*

Henry Ford was an industrial innovator, a champion of affordable mass production, an authoritarian boss who wanted discipline and ambition in his workers, and a pacifist who financed the Peace Ship to sail to Europe to try to end the first World War. He was also an anti-Semite who published the fraudulent *Protocols of the Elders of Zion* and whose ghost-written articles on "The International Jew" appeared in nearly one hundred issues of a newspaper he ran.

Ford's anti-Semitism became evident when he purchased his hometown newspaper, the *Dearborn Independent* in 1918. Articles were written under Ford's byline by staffer William Cameron and approved by Ford's personal secretary E. G. Liebold. The articles covered many topics—self-improvement, independent thinking, the dangers of large corporations, and the evils of communism. But many of Ford's articles—at one point nearly one hundred consecutive ones—were anti-Semitic screeds, with such titles as "The Scope of Jewish Dictatorship in the U.S.," "Jewish Supremacy in Motion Picture World," and "Jewish Gamblers Corrupt American Baseball."

In 1921, after boycotts and criticism by Jewish leaders and others, the anti-Semitic columns became less frequent. But they resumed in 1924 in response to farming cooperative work led by a lawyer named Aaron Sapiro. The *Dearborn Independent* warned that "a band of Jews—bankers, lawyers, moneylenders, advertising agencies, fruit-packers, produce buyers, professional office managers, and bookkeeping experts—is on the back of the American farmer."

Aaron Sapiro fought back. In the first hate crimes lawsuit in US history, Sapiro sued Ford for libel against him personally and against his race. Writer William Cameron testified that Ford was never consulted about the contents of the article, and Ford himself was conveniently under a doctor's care when he was called to testify. Eventually, the lawsuit was settled out of court, and Ford issued a public apology and retraction. According to the apology, dated June 30, 1927, Ford was surprised to learn what was being published under his name. He was simply too busy, he said, "to devote personal attention to their management or to keep informed as to their contents." Ford's apology goes on to say, "Had I appreciated even the general nature, to say nothing of the details, of these utterances, I would have forbidden their circulation without a moment's hesitation."

It strains credulity to imagine that Ford did not know what was being published under his name in a newspaper he required all Ford dealers to subscribe to. His assertion of ignorance was disputed, widely disbelieved, and belied by reports of his private anti-Semitic comments. Ford's statement is much more an account than an apology. He was "deeply mortified," in his words, not by anything he had done but by the actions of his journal. Had he known, he would have forbidden the publications. And Ford asked forgiveness for harm he "unintentionally committed." Ford's statement repudiated the articles and made excuses for Ford's involvement, but it did not apologize.

The *Dearborn Independent* shut down for good at the end of 1927, and for a time Ford's views fell into the background. But *The International Jew* was translated into German and came to the attention of Adolph Hitler, and in 1938 Hitler's regime awarded Ford the Grand Service Cross of the Supreme Order of the German Eagle for his work in mass production. Ford died in 1947.

The Only Thing Red About Lucy

"I am aware of only one thing I did that was wrong, and that at the time wasn't wrong, but apparently now it is, . . . "
—LUCILLE BALL, *September 4, 1953*

The House Committee on Un-American Activities (HUAC) held its first hearing on the entertainment industry in 1938 when it investigated the New Deal Federal Theater Project. In 1947, HUAC held hearings on communists in Hollywood and communist themes in movies, interviewing forty-one witnesses, ten of whom were blacklisted for refusing to testify. By the 1950s, HUAC interrogations were in full swing, routinely calling on Hollywood figures with past leftist associations to testify, inform on others, and account for their past politics. Hundreds were named by friendly witnesses and called to testify in hearings that lasted from 1951 to 1958.

One of those named was comedienne Lucille Ball, whose television program *I Love Lucy* had begun in 1951. Ball was accused by a former communist named Rena Vale, who testified that she had been at a new members' class for Communist Party members at Ball's home. And records also showed that Ball had listed her party affiliation as Communist for a time in the 1930s. She was even on record as being a member of the State Central Committee of the Communist Party of California, though she claimed not to know of the appointment.

It turned out that Ball's grandfather, Fred Hunt, was a socialist who supported the Communist Party. In her twenties, Ball had agreed to register as a Communist to please her grandfather. On September 4, 1953, Ball met privately with HUAC investigator William Wheeler in Hollywood and testified for two hours. In her testimony, she said:

> I am very happy to have this opportunity to discuss all the things that have cropped up, that apparently I have done wrong. I am aware of only one thing I did that was wrong, and that at the time wasn't wrong, but apparently now it is, and that was registering because my grandfather wanted us to.

She went on to explain that her family knew that "at the time it was very important because we knew we weren't going to have daddy with us very long. If it made him happy, it was important at the time."

The fictional Lucy Ricardo was known for her signature teary television apologies for domestic mishaps, but here the real Lucy simply gives an account without apology. She characterizes her registration as something that "at the time wasn't wrong, but apparently now it is." She characterized her actions as a mistake that could happen to anyone:

> How we got to signing a few things, or going among some people that thought differently, that has happened to all of us out here in the last 10 or 12 years, and it is unfortunate, but I certainly will do anything in the world to prove that we made a bad mistake by, for one week or a couple of weeks, trying to appease an old man.

The HUAC investigator, William Wheeler, concluded that there was "no activity that would warrant her inclusion on the Security Index." Public tension grew when influential columnist Walter Winchell reported two days later that "the top television comedienne has been confronted with her membership in the Communist party." When the chairman of HUAC later reiterated that she had "no role in the Communist Party," Winchell was forced to correct his story.

National Apologies

"To All Persons of Japanese Ancestry"

After the 1941 attack on Pearl Harbor, xenophobia swept the United States and was especially prevalent on the West Coast. California attorney general Earl Warren began urging federal action after warnings that ethnic Japanese in that state might be loyal to Emperor Hirohito. In early 1942, President Franklin Roosevelt signed an executive order enabling the military to designate exclusion zones—areas from which any person might be barred or removed. Roosevelt's order was soon put to use.

Beginning in March, a series of exclusion zones and curfews were established. Civilian Exclusion Order No. 34 applied to most of the West Coast, ordering all those of Japanese ancestry, citizens and non-citizens, to report for assignment to War Relocation Authority camps. Eventually 117,000 Japanese-Americans and Japanese living in the West were interred in ten main camps. Challenged in the Supreme Court, the exclusion orders were upheld in December of 1944 in *Korematsu et al. v. United States*, but the related decision *Ex parte Endo* ruled that the government could not detain a loyal citizen. On January 2, 1945, the exclusion order was rescinded and Japanese-Americans tried to rebuild their lives. They were given a train ticket and twenty-five dollars. Many had sold their homes, farms, and businesses at a loss or had faced economic ruin trying to pay bills and taxes while interred. And the returning Japanese-Americans were often unwelcome in their former communities and jobs. They encountered incalculable hardship, suffering, and loss.

Forty-three years after internment ended, the US Congress apologized. In 1988, legislation sponsored by Wyoming senator Alan Simpson and California congressman Norman Mineta acknowledged that internment had been caused by prejudice and hysteria. Congress authorized redress payments, eventually totaling over $1.6 billion, to internees and their heirs. Five US presidents were directly involved with the eventual apology. In 1976, President Gerald Ford rescinded Executive Order 9066, explaining that history required an understanding of a nation's errors:

> In this Bicentennial Year, we are commemorating the anniversary dates of many great events in American history. An honest reckoning, however, must include a recognition of our national mistakes as well as our national achievements. Learning from our mistakes is not pleasant, but as a great philosopher once admonished, we must do so if we want to avoid repeating them.

Ford went on to talk about the wartime sacrifices and loyalty of Japanese-Americans and the "setback to fundamental American principles." He called for an "American Promise...that this kind of action shall never again be repeated."

Four years later, President Jimmy Carter signed legislation appointing a commission to report on internment. The seven-member Commission on Wartime Relocation and Internment of Civilians was designed, in Carter's words, "to expose clearly" what happened during internment. Carter also noted that the commission would assess whether previous compensation efforts had been adequate and would "reconfirm our Nation's commitment to basic human rights." Together Ford and Carter helped initiate the apology process that would lead to a naming of the offenses.

From July to December of 1981, the commission heard the testimony of more than 750 witnesses, from former internees to an assistant secretary of war during the 1940s. The commission found that internment was not based on military need but on "race prejudice, war hysteria, and a failure of political leadership." The 467-page report released in 1983 recommended a national apology and compensation of twenty thousand dollars to each internee. When the Democrats regained control of the Senate in 1987, the commission recommendations were taken up and eventually passed as the Civil Liberties Act of 1988, signed by President Reagan on August 10 of that year.

The National Apology Process

The initial call to apologize that led to the Civil Rights Act of 1988 came largely from the efforts of a group called the Japanese American Citizens

League (JACL). The JACL had formed in California in 1929 to fight discrimination and later evolved into a national civil rights organization. As the xenophobia of World War II faded and the Japanese-American middle class rebuilt itself, the JACL began to pursue the question of redress, first in a resolution at its national convention in 1970. Eight years later, JACL leaders met with four Japanese-American legislators: senators Daniel Inouye and Spark Matsunaga and congressmen Norman Mineta and Robert Matsui. Inouye, the first ever Japanese-American member of Congress, proposed the strategy of a commission, and that same year a grassroots National Coalition for Redress and Reparations was also established.

A national apology of this scope was unprecedented and came with many obstacles. Some politicians were in principle opposed to apologizing for past acts, and others questioned the cost. Some veterans groups opposed the idea of apology and redress. Some denied internment all together. The transition from Jimmy Carter to Ronald Reagan proved to be particularly challenging. As historian Timothy Maga has noted, Reagan initially opposed the apology and redress legislation, describing the commission as a "left-over Carterism." Reviewing declassified documents, Maga explored the complexity of Reagan's initial opposition. In part, it was based in fiscal conservative ideology and concern about the cost. In part too, it was based on legal concerns about the wording of the legislation. And in part, it was philosophical, based in the belief that sufficient apology and redress had already been provided by the 1948 American-Japanese Evacuation Claims Act and by Ford's proclamation.

Reagan's concerns were also rooted in international politics. Japanese prime minister Yasuhiro Nakasone supported the redress legislation and had chided the United States for not passing it quickly. According to Maga, Reagan became convinced that Nakasone's position was a "back-handed slap" at the United States. In the end, however, Reagan supported the apology and redress legislation. He was swayed by a combination of pragmatic political concerns—the bipartisan support for the legislation and the demonstrated strength of the Japanese-American community—and by an end-of-term sense of fairness and legacy. In his remarks signing the bill, Reagan noted that "it's not for us today to pass judgment upon those who may have made mistakes while engaged in that great struggle. Yet we must recognize that the internment of Japanese-Americans was just that: a mistake." And Reagan de-emphasized redress and stressed the symbolic nature of the apology:

… no payment can make up for those lost years. So, what is most important in this bill has less to do with property than with honor. For here we admit a wrong; here we reaffirm our commitment as a nation to equal justice under the law.

The legislation created a special office to manage the claims process, the Office of Redress Administration, which oversaw more than 82,000 claims in its ten years of operation. George H. W. Bush and Bill Clinton also wrote apology letters to internees, which we return to at the end of the chapter.

Writing History and Having Standing

The US apology for internment is a good example of how nations apologize for their past bad actions. The Civil Liberties Act and the statements of the presidents are the expression—the performance of the apology. The work of the internment commission interpreting testimony and other documentary evidence was crucial. It placed a name on a historic injustice, just as a personal confession places a name on an individual harm.

That creation of an official record often shapes the later expression of the apology. Sociologist Nicholas Tavuchis, one of the first to distinguish the characteristics of group and individual apologies, talks about group apologies as involving "collectivities." When the call to apologize comes from a collectivity like the Japanese-American community of the 1970s and 1980s, the group's overriding interest is "a public, chronicled recantation of the offense." In the apology for internment, official discourse created by the Commission on Wartime Relocation and Internment of Civilians served this role. It was essential to the process, as Daniel Inouye had predicted.

As Tavuchis notes, a public record can be double-edged. Official documentation creates privileged discourse, and "what does not appear on the record is questionable, dubious, or disqualified." In naming the injustice, the historical record also defines the extent of the harm and creates "a public representation of the collectivity's moral self-image." And as national officials and the victims (or their descendants) negotiate the details of the transgression, the offense is nationalized rather than personalized. In the end, the historical record is condensed and inevitably reshaped as it is written into legislative language and executive pronouncements.

Once a transgression has been named, or historicized, there is the further question of standing. Who is empowered—or obligated—to apologize on behalf of a collection of individuals? For internment, the apology came jointly from the legislative and executive branches, apologizing on behalf of the American people. The apology was made even though some citizens, some legislators, and even some actors involved in the original offense disagreed. Congress and the president have the authority—and obligation—to speak for the nation. They have standing. But what exactly does this mean?

Philosopher Nick Smith points out that standing requires some authority in a collective body. Thus, I cannot apologize for the action of my government, my profession, or my university because I do not speak for those entities. But presidents, cabinets, congresses, executive committees, boards, and the like can apologize officially because they do speak for a collective entity, by virtue of election or appointment.

The converse is also important: who is empowered to accept or reject an official apology? In the case of internment, this group was the JACL, the members of other grassroots organizations, and the representatives of the Japanese-American community who advocated for an apology. For victims, standing to accept the apology arises from a different kind of authority than that of apologizers. It is a social authority earned by raising the issue of injustice, pursuing a call to apologize, and participating in the naming of the offense. Having this informal authority, as the JACL did, means being recognized as legitimate by other victims and successors of the offenders.

Inheriting Guilt

A further question concerns inherited guilt. Do successors have a responsibility to apologize for the injustices of their predecessors? Some argue they do not. Social critic Camille Paglia, for example, believes that "an apology can be extended only by persons who committed the original offense." This view is also sometimes taken by politicians opposed to apology. North Carolina senator Jesse Helms, opposing the internment redress costs, argued that they should not be borne by citizens of the 1980s:

> ... a very small percentage, relatively, of the American people alive today were even born when Pearl Harbor was virtually destroyed and our fleet was lying on the bottom. I do not know what that percentage is, but I think the percentage is zero of American people alive today who had anything whatsoever to do with the decisions on the relocation of Japanese-Americans.

Paglia and Helms take too narrow a view of the function of apologies. We should not equate responsibility with guilt. Instead, we must view national apology from the perspective of reconciliation, a perspective Paglia and

Helms ignore. As Nick Smith argues, national leaders have a moral duty to remedy past injustices in much the same way that any of us have a moral duty to respond to injustices or harms we did not cause—someone being beaten, a natural disaster, hunger, and homelessness.

Do all citizens have a moral duty to apologize? Should I apologize to my Japanese-American friends for internment and to my African-American friends for lynching, slavery, and Jim Crow laws? It seems to me that *my* moral responsibility is to condemn those acts and to remedy their consequences as I am able. Since I do not speak for my country, it would be infelicitous and incongruous for me to apologize, though it is appropriate for me as a citizen to bear the costs of redress. An apology by me would do little or nothing to remedy the injustice or effect reconciliation. National leaders, however, have responsibilities and authority that I do not. They have a special responsibility not just to condemn but also to remedy historic injustices and promote reconciliation. And they have the authority to speak for the nation.

Of course, national leaders have other, competing responsibilities, such as attention to fiscal constraints, legal precedent, and political issues. Leaders must consider where an apology might lead in terms of cost and liability. Leaders must also assess support, develop a consensus among various constituencies, and craft appropriate language. And leaders need to decide whether apologies are in the national interest, both strategically and historically.

Are national apologies necessary and useful? I believe they are. National apologies can be a beginning or an ending step in reconciliation. As philosopher Brian Weiner explains, at their best, national apologies mean that "the government is able to declare that it now judges these historic acts to be wrong and that it has become the type of government that extends justice to those it has victimized in the past." In other words, the government has become morally different.

The apology process can also have great meaning for victims and their descendants. Weiner sees apology as encouraging those who have been wronged to perceive "their role in the political collectivity differently." Apology can, he suggests, allow more meaningful political relationships between individuals and governments and can help to reconcile the different political identities an individual has. But Weiner also concedes that national apologies may divide us. For offenders, the process means the hard work of documentation, discussion of restitution, and both moral and financial responsibility for their predecessors' actions. For victims, national apologies entail reliving painful history, being open to reconciliation, and reconsidering the moral status of others. Such efforts can generate new resentments. And those who identify neither with transgressors nor victims may also have an opinion—ranging from pride in the effort at reconciliation to disapproval or even envy.

For a further example of the dynamics of national apology, let's look at another recent case—the US Senate apology for lynchings.

Anti-lynching Laws and the Filibuster

When Congress passed the 1968 Civil Rights Act, it gave the federal government the power to take action against lynching. From 1882 to 1968, nearly five thousand people were lynched in the United States, the majority of whom were African-American males. Few of those who committed the lynchings were brought to justice. And despite repeated efforts to make lynching a federal crime, including the introduction of nearly two hundred anti-lynching bills in the House of Representatives, legislation was blocked again and again by southern senators.

In February of 2005, Louisiana senator Mary Landrieu and Virginia senator George Allen introduced a resolution apologizing to the victims of lynching. The bill specifically recognized the failure of the Senate to enact anti-lynching legislation, since it was that institution's unique filibuster tradition that had enabled just a few senators to thwart the will of the majority of Congress.

The text of Senate Resolution 39 follows the linguistic form of a good apology. The "whereas" phrase names the offense—Senate inaction. The resolution

---

EXCERPT FROM UNITED STATES SENATE RESOLUTION 39, 2005

Whereas an apology offered in the spirit of true repentance moves the United States toward reconciliation and may become central to a new understanding, on which improved racial relations can be forged: Now, therefore, be it

Resolved, That the Senate--

(1) apologizes to the victims of lynching for the failure of the Senate to enact anti-lynching legislation;

(2) expresses the deepest sympathies and most solemn regrets of the Senate to the descendants of victims of lynching, the ancestors of whom were deprived of life, human dignity, and the constitutional protections accorded all citizens of the United States; and

(3) remembers the history of lynching, to ensure that these tragedies will be neither forgotten nor repeated.

also explains the present-day Senate's motivation ("true repentance," "reconciliation," "new understanding," and "improved racial relations") and explicitly performs the apology, with separate predicates apologizing to victims, expressing sympathy and regret, and remembering history. The apology was delivered to relatives and descendants of victims, including a man in his nineties who had survived lynching as a teenager.

The call for a Senate apology arose in 2000 when Atlanta antiques dealer James Allen published *Without Sanctuary: Lynching Photography in America*. The book discussed the history of lynching and its glorification in picture postcards. Its impact led to the establishment of the Committee for a Formal Apology, whose members included activists Dick Gregory and C. Delores Tucker and journalist Janet Langhart Cohen. To build support, committee representatives called on senators personally. Mary Landrieu was especially responsive, characterizing lynching as "terrorism in America" and seeing an apology as crucial because "the Senate failed these Americans." Landrieu and George Allen agreed to sponsor a bipartisan resolution.

On June 13, 2005, the measure passed the Senate by unanimous consent. Unanimous consent does not mean that all one hundred senators voted "aye" or even that a roll-call vote was taken; it just means that no senator objected when the resolution was approved. The distinction is important, because a true expression of unanimity would be a way of measuring sincerity—a formal apology with no public reservations. For a time, it appeared that the lynching apology would gain unanimous support—the resolution quickly gained co-sponsors, including many Southern senators. However, when it came to the floor of the Senate for a final voice vote, fifteen senators had still declined to sponsor the bill. After the actual vote, seven of the non-sponsors signed a large display copy of the resolution, but eight—Republicans Trent Lott and Thad Cochran of Mississippi, John Cornyn of Texas, Lamar Alexander of Tennessee, Judd Gregg and John Sununu of New Hampshire, and Michael Enzi and Craig Thomas of Wyoming — still refused to endorse the apology.

Mississippi's Thad Cochran said, "I don't feel I should apologize for the passage of or the failure to pass any legislation by the US Senate. But I deplore and regret that lynchings occurred and that those committing them were not punished." Tennessee's Lamar Alexander said he condemned lynching too, "but, rather than begin to catalog and apologize for all those times that some Americans have failed to reach our goals, I prefer to look ahead. I prefer to look to correct current injustices rather than to look to the past."

Their objections focus on the naming aspect of apology—articulating a series of past transgressions and taking symbolic responsibility for them. But they ignore the role of apologies in reconciliation, failing to consider that an apology by a present-day Senate is a step toward mutual understanding between the descendants of victims and the successors of transgressors. Can a government really "correct current injustices" (as Alexander would prefer) without addressing past transgressions? A commitment to redressing past injustices builds the trust that present-day (and future) injustices will be taken seriously. And given the Senate's investment in tradition, continuity, and historical authority, it is hard to see how a collective body can associate itself with past successes without also owning up to significant past failures.

Is the Senate's apology sincere, even though the apology was not unanimous? Passing the resolution meant that the Senate apologized as a body, even though a few members held back. Using Erving Goffman's idea of selves, we can think of the Senate as a person—a deliberative body. That figurative person can regret the actions of an earlier self just as an individual can. Resolution 39 says, in effect, that the Senate of 2005 is not the same Senate that blocked anti-lynching efforts. It is sorry for the actions of its earlier self.

The apology was controversial outside the Senate as well. Inevitably, there were comparisons to the apology for internment, and critics worried that the apology might lead to calls for compensation. Others saw the Senate as not going far enough because it did not provide reparations. Nicholas von Hoffman, writing in the *New York Observer*, called the apology "worthless," adding, "The survivors and descendants of the lynched—which includes some Jews, some Italians, homosexuals, labor-union organizers, and political dissidents—have paid socially, psychologically and financially for the violence done to their families. They are owed better than a piece of paper embossed with the Senate's letterhead." And *Black Commentator* publishers Glen Ford and Peter Gamble suggested that many African-Americans saw the apology as "a scam, with no substantial benefits, and less good faith."

The NAACP was more generous. It viewed the apology as "long overdue" and "a good first step toward reconciliation and the official acknowledgment of a dark period in US history," adding that it hoped Congress would establish a commission to investigate the full extent of the damage. The descendants of victims were divided as well. "Someone is finally recognizing our pain," said one. Another added, "I have to let God be the judge because I don't know if they meant it out of their heart or they're just saying it out of their mouth." The responses suggest something about the way people view national apologies. For some, the naming and expression of regret, even if imperfect, are important first steps in being heard and coming to a shared understanding of a harm. To others, such expressions will be incomplete and insincere without reform or redress.

Bewitched

In Chapter 1, we looked at the apology of Samuel Sewall, one of the nine judges at the Salem Town Court of Oyer and Terminer. Now let's take a look at how Massachusetts responded. Recall that in 1692, colonial Massachusetts experienced witchcraft hysteria. It all began with the convulsions and contortions of the daughter of a new minister and several other young women. Cotton Mather had recently published his *Memorable Providences*, about a witch in Boston, and a local doctor suggested witchcraft might be the problem in Salem Town as well.

The first to be accused were three socially marginalized women—a slave, a beggar, and an old woman known for avoiding church. Soon the accusations spread, with reports of spectral visions and women flying on broomsticks. Some women even confessed to being witches and then accused others.

Dominated by followers of Cotton Mather, the Court of Oyer and Terminer admitted as evidence reports of spectral visitations, a "touching test" (in which suspected witches were called upon to touch the afflicted persons to see if the contortions ended), and physical examination for moles (which were considered "witches' marks"). Twenty-six people in Salem Town were tried and convicted of the capital crime of witchcraft. Nineteen were hanged. Others died in prison, and one man in his eighties was crushed to death by stones piled on his chest, an interrogation technique known as pressing.

By late 1692, the tide had begun to turn against the trials and hangings. Increase Mather, Cotton's father, published *Cases of Conscience Concerning Evil Spirits*, which repudiated spectral evidence, and Governor Phips soon banned its use by courts. Most of the last trials ended in acquittals and, in May 1693, Phips released the remaining accused witches. By 1696, the colony was fully aware of its mistakes and the Massachusetts legislature designated January 14, 1697, as a day of atonement. That was when Samuel Sewall apologized.

In the early eighteenth century, the relatives of many of the accused petitioned for pardons. In 1711, two decades after the trials, many accused witches were exonerated and their relatives offered redress. Several other women who were hanged were not included. Their families, out of fear or embarrassment, had not petitioned for exoneration.

Ann Greenslade Pudeator was one of those not pardoned. A septuage-narian twice-widowed midwife with her own inherited land, Pudeator pro-claimed her innocence and insisted that her accuser was a known liar. None of her five children rose to her defense, but nearly 250 years later, one of her descendants did. Lee Greenslit, a Midwestern textbook publisher and amateur genealogist, began a campaign to have her exonerated. Bills were proposed in 1945, 1946, and 1953 but met opposition in the Massachusetts legislature. As you might expect, some opponents of a pardon worried that relatives would file damage suits. Others argued that twentieth-century Massachusetts didn't need to apologize because it wasn't even a state when the witch trials occurred. And one even worried that if the witches were all cleared, Salem's tourist trade would suffer. But in August 1957, a resolve (as Massachusetts laws are called) was finally passed. It named the state's transgressions, declared the old laws "shocking" and "long since abandoned," and implied an apology by admit-ting the error of the state's predecessors, saying that "no disgrace or cause for distress attaches to the said descendants or any of them by reason of said pro-ceedings."

The most coherent and interesting opposition came from the long-serving and influential secretary of the Massachusetts Bar Association, Frank W. Grin-nell. Grinnell wrote that "the witchcraft tragedy cannot be wiped out by any futile paper resolutions." He noted that the judges of the time were "enforcing the law not only as they understood it, but as it was," and that the people were motivated by "genuine fear of the devil, inspired and stimulated by the clergy" and by "lurid preachings" (presumably those of Cotton Mather). What was unique about the aftermath of Salem, Grinnell argued, was the later public repentance by many of the principals in the trials. Grinnell suggests that the historic contrition

> was a striking chapter in the history of public morals. Let us not belittle it, or try to weaken it, by abusing them and flattering ourselves that we are better than they were. Let us not try to do over what they did better. We still have strong tendencies to hysteria and I suggest that, if we had lived in those days, most of us would probably have joined them in their hysterical state of mind, but, perhaps, not in the repentance. Let us not be too censorious.

For Grinnell, the 1957 resolve was a matter of changing history not learn-ing from it, and he believed that a further official apology would lessen the impact of that earlier moment.

In 2001, Massachusetts officially exonerated five other women—Bridget Bishop, Susannah Martin, Alice Parker, Wilmot Redd, and Margaret Scott—who had been unnamed in the 1957 resolution. The 2001 resolution, signed by the governor on Halloween, had been the result of lobbying by descendants who felt that it was important to clear the accused by name. State representative Paul Tirone, who helped pass the 2001 act, agreed that the "other persons" of the 1957 resolve should be cleared by name. "These people were victims of hysteria," he explained, "and they paid deeply with their lives."

Internment, lynching, witch trials: the apologies for these indicate the shape of debates over documenting and apologizing for historic collective injustices. For victims and their successors, apologies can be an important naming of a transgression and recognition of a victim, even three hundred years later. For those called upon to apologize, such statements can be moral milestones, ways of exploring and coming to terms with historic injustices and of contributing to repair and reconciliation. Yet there is always the concern that apologies may be empty gestures or misplaced expressions of guilt by later generations. In the case studies that follow, we look again at the apologies for internment, contrasting the letters of George H. W. Bush and Bill Clinton, at two other acts of national historicizing and repentance—those of Germany and Japan after World War II—and at the British government's posthumous apology to mathematician Alan Turing.

Two Letters

"In enacting a law calling for restitution and offering a sincere apology, your fellow Americans have in a very real sense, renewed their traditional commitment to the ideals of freedom, equality, and justice."
—GEORGE H. W. BUSH

"On behalf of your fellow Americans, I offer a sincere apology to you."
—BILL CLINTON

Unlike previous presidents—Ford, Carter, and Reagan—who addressed their proclamations and remarks to Japanese-Americans and to broader audiences, George H. W. Bush and Bill Clinton were writing directly to former internees. In their letters, which accompanied redress payments to former internees, we see two writers apologizing for exactly the same harm, yet their apologies took rather different approaches. It's a good example of the way in which linguistic choice allows different elements of the apology process to come to the forefront.

GEORGE H. W. BUSH'S LETTER

A monetary sum and words alone cannot restore lost years or erase painful memories; neither can they fully convey our Nation's resolve to rectify injustice and to uphold the rights of individuals. We can never fully right the wrongs of the past. But we can take a clear stand for justice and recognize that serious injustices were done to Japanese Americans during World War II.

In enacting a law calling for restitution and offering a sincere apology, your fellow Americans have, in a very real sense, renewed their traditional commitment to the ideals of freedom, equality, and justice.

You and your family have our best wishes for the future.

George Bush

President Bush's apology letter emphasizes that apologies cannot undo actions. It refers first to the inadequacy of both money and words and then moves on to abstractions like "injustice," "rights," and "a clear stand for justice." In Bush's letter, the identification of the moral wrong is passive: "serious injustices were done to Japanese Americans during World War II." And the naming of the harm occurs in a grammatically subordinate position at the end of the first paragraph.

Bush's second paragraph connects "offering a sincere apology" to a renewed commitment to freedom. The structure of the sentence with its opening

---

BILL CLINTON'S LETTER

Over fifty years ago, the United States Government unjustly interned, evacuated, or relocated you and many other Japanese Americans. Today, on behalf of your fellow Americans, I offer a sincere apology to you for the actions that unfairly denied Japanese Americans and their families fundamental liberties during World War II.

In passing the Civil Liberties Act of 1988, we acknowledge the wrongs of the past and offered redress to those who endured such grave injustice. In retrospect, we understand that the nation's actions were rooted deeply in racial prejudice, wartime hysteria, and a lack of political leadership. We must learn from the past and dedicated ourselves as a nation to renewing the spirit of equality and our love of freedom. Together, we can guarantee a future with liberty and justice for all.

You and your family have my best wishes for the future.

Bill Clinton

gerund (*offering*) subordinates the performance of the apology to the renewal of the commitment to freedom, equality, and justice. The construction is figurative as well, since it is Congress—not fellow Americans—that enacts laws. Bush's mild hyperbole broadens the scope of the apology. But Bush himself is absent from the apology—he never uses the first person.

Bill Clinton's letter begins with an active sentence that clearly acknowledges the moral wrong and names the actor and action ("The United States Government unjustly interned, evacuated, or relocated you"). It speaks to the recipient directly with the phrase "you and many other Japanese Americans" and performs the apology with the phrase "On behalf of your fellow Americans, I offer a sincere apology to you for…" The abstractions and reference to values come at the conclusion, and the repetition of "we" ("we acknowledge," "we understand," and "we must learn") culminating in the inclusive "Together, we" rhetorically symbolizes the moral process of an apology.

Germany's Fifty-year Reflection on World War II

"Anyone who closes his eyes to the past is blind to the present."
—GERMAN PRESIDENT RICHARD VON WEIZSÄCKER, *May 8, 1985*

Adolf Hitler's regime caused a world tragedy with fifty million deaths, including eleven million in the Holocaust—Jews, political dissidents, gays, gypsies, and the disabled. The Allied victors in World War II focused attention on accountability and re-education rather than war reparations. The Nuremberg Tribunal, which began in 1945, tried Nazi leaders and sentenced a dozen to death. In addition, occupation leaders Eisenhower and Patton made certain that German citizens confronted the concentration camps, so there would be German witnesses to what had occurred. They also instituted a reform of the education system aimed at both denazification and documentation of atrocities.

Of course, the occupiers could only do so much. West German politicians had to lead the process. The first was Chancellor Konrad Adenauer, who made a modest symbolic opening to a decades-long process of apology in September 1951. Speaking to the Bundestag, Adenauer said that "the overwhelming majority of the German people abominated the crimes committed against the Jews and did not participate in them." The following year, West Germany signed the Luxembourg Agreement, which made three and a half billion Deutschemarks in payments—essentially reparations—available to the new state of Israel, where many Nazi victims had emigrated. Politically, Adenauer tried to balance the repair of international relations with the internal political climate of a defeated, occupied nation. His efforts thus focused on attenuating guilt as much as accepting it, and at one point he said, "The government of the Federal Republic, in the belief that many have subjectively atoned for a guilt that was not heavy, is determined where it appears acceptable to do so to put the past behind us."

Political scientist Jennifer Lind, who has studied German contrition in her book *Sorry States*, refers to the Adenauer period as one of amnesia rather than apology. Lind notes too that for many years, apologies were politicized: liberal groups were most open to apology and remembrance, and conservatives argued against "perpetual guilt" and proposed focusing instead on national pride and postwar accomplishments.

Later chancellors and presidents were able to make stronger apologies, as time passed and the political conditions changed. Eventually West German contrition became more the norm. In December 1970, West German chancellor Willy Brandt went to Poland, where he knelt before the monument commemorating the Warsaw uprising of 1943. His action was widely viewed as a nonverbal apology, and Brandt later explained that he "did what people do when words fail them." By the time German conservatives returned to power in 1982, acceptance of national responsibility was becoming the norm.

In 1985, West German president Richard von Weizsäcker would refer to the German unconditional surrender as a "day of liberation" for Germans. (Adenauer had declined to observe the day, seeing it as a symbol of defeat.) Addressing the Bundestag on May 8, 1985, the fortieth anniversary of VE Day, von Weizsäcker stressed remembrance, saying, "Anyone who closes his eyes to the past is blind to the present. Whoever refuses to remember the inhumanity is prone to new risks of infection." He then delineated Nazi crimes and their effects on victims. A few days earlier, conservative chancellor Helmut Kohl had visited the site of the Bergen-Belsen concentration camp, where fifty thousand Nazi victims had been buried in mass graves. Accompanied by Ronald Reagan, Kohl said, "We are gathered here in memory of the many innocent people who were tortured, humiliated, and driven to their deaths at Bergen-Belsen, as in other camps." He added, "One of our country's paramount tasks is to inform people of those occurrences and keep alive an awareness of the full extent of this historical burden." Kohl's statement was weakened, however, by the fact that he and Reagan also visited the Bitburg cemetery, where Kohl commemorated German soldiers as war victims.

A decade later Kohl, chancellor of a unified Germany, was unambiguously apologetic. In 1995, on the fiftieth anniversary of the liberation of Auschwitz, Kohl issued a statement saying that Auschwitz was "the darkest and most horrible chapter of German history" and that "one of our priority tasks is to pass on this knowledge to future generations so that the horrible experiences of the past will never be repeated." January 27 is now observed in Germany as Holocaust Remembrance Day.

Japan, Fifty Years Later

"In the hope that no such mistake be made in the future, I... express here once again my feelings of deep remorse and state my heartfelt apology."
—JAPANESE PRIME MINISTER TOMIICHI MURAYAMA, *August 15, 1995*

The attack on Pearl Harbor is the atrocity that many Americans associate with Japan's role in World War II, when 353 Japanese planes attacked a US naval base, killing nearly 2,500. The full tragic scope of Japanese militarism—the use of biological weapons like the bubonic plague, the Death March of Bataan, the rapes of Korean comfort women—rivaled that of Nazi Germany.

When the Japanese unconditionally surrendered on September 2, 1945, the American occupation forces arrested war criminals for a Nuremberg-like tribunal. Among them was General Hideki Tōjō, who had attempted suicide as American forces arrived to arrest him. At the Tokyo War Crimes Tribunal, Tōjō took responsibility for the war, and in his final statements before being hanged, he apologized for the atrocities committed by the Japanese military. Tōjō's statements pleased the occupation leaders. General Douglas MacArthur and others in charge of the American occupation hoped to shift war responsibility away from Japanese emperor Hirohito. According to historian Herbert Bix, MacArthur wanted to promote the idea that Hirohito had been misled and to use the emperor's authority to move Japan away from militarism.

MacArthur's approach coincided with the interests of Hirohito's cabinet as well. Hirohito was given immunity from prosecution for war crimes, and the cabinet promoted the perception that just a few militarists were responsible for Japan's actions. Japanese textbooks treated the war gingerly and focused more on the wartime Japanese suffering than on atrocities. And as the Cold War developed, Japan became a crucial American ally, so issues of reconciliation and apology became less important than the rebuilding of the Japanese economy.

Over time, Japan worked to normalize relations with other Asian countries. Japanese officials began to use apologetic language such as the expression of "true regret" and "deep remorse" for an "unfortunate period in our countries' history." That was the language used by foreign minister Shiina Etsusaburô in the 1965 normalization of relations with South Korea and echoed in the 1972 normalization with China. Official statements in Hirohito's lifetime tended to avoid naming Japanese transgressions and framed them instead as mutual misfortunes. When Hirohito met with President

Gerald Ford in 1975, he described the Sino-Japanese war as a situation in which people of both nations "endured a brief, unfortunate ordeal as storms raged in the usually quiet Pacific." In 1978 when Chinese leader Deng Xiao Ping visited Japan, Hirohito simply referred to "unfortunate events between our countries."

After Hirohito's death in 1989, politicians seeking to strengthen Japan's global position began to apologize more remorsefully, choosing specific phrasings that emphasized humility and acknowledged Japan's role as an aggressor. As was the case in Germany, apologies became politicized. Liberal politicians championed apologetic language and recognition of wartime atrocities, and conservative leaders objected to such language and recognitions as unpatriotic and worried that apologies would entail reparation costs.

The culmination of political battling occurred when the Japanese National Diet considered an apology resolution proposed by Tomiichi Murayama, who led a coalition government from 1994 to 1996. Murayama was an apology advocate and the first socialist prime minister since the late 1940s. His initiative, coming on the fiftieth anniversary of the end of World War II, generated such conservative objection that the word *apology* itself was removed. The June 9 resolution read as follows:

> On the occasion of the 50th anniversary of the end of World War II, this House offers its sincere condolences to those who fell in action and victims of wars and similar actions all over the world. Solemnly reflecting upon many instances of colonial rule and acts of aggression in the modern history of the world, and recognizing that Japan carried out those acts in the past, inflicting pain and suffering upon the peoples of other countries, especially in Asia, the Members of this House express a sense of deep remorse.

A month later, Murayama added his own comments, explicitly apologizing.

> During a certain period in the not too distant past, Japan, following a mistaken national policy, advanced along the road to war, only to ensnare the Japanese people in a fateful crisis, and, through its colonial rule and aggression, caused tremendous damage and suffering to the people of many countries, particularly to those of Asian nations. In the hope that no such mistake be made in the future, I regard, in a spirit of humility, these irrefutable facts of history, and express here once again my feelings of deep remorse and state my heartfelt apology. Allow me

also to express my feelings of profound mourning for all victims, both at home and abroad, of that history.

Both Murayama in his expression of "heartfelt apology" and Helmut Kohl in his description of the "most horrible chapter of German history" articulate or imply apologies. Both apologies involved decades of internal political negotiation and required shifts in public attitudes to overcome postwar amnesia. Today both Japan and Germany see themselves as different nations than they were before.

On Behalf of the British Government

"I am pleased to have the chance to say how deeply sorry I and we all are for what happened."
—BRITISH PRIME MINISTER GORDON BROWN, *2010*

Alan Turing was a computer scientist before there were computers. He worked in logic, philosophy, and pure math, and he helped to develop the first computer design. His idea for a hypothetical logical computing machine is today referred to as the Turing machine. Later, he conceived of the influential test of artificial intelligence known to us as the Turing test. And during World War II, he worked for the British government at its Bletchley Park code-breaking center, where he helped to decode the Enigma Machine. For his efforts, the British government repaid him with chemical castration.

In 1952, Turing was robbed by Arnold Murray, a man he had picked up at a movie theater. When Turing spoke with police, he acknowledged that the two had had a sexual relationship. Both Turing and Murray were charged with indecency under an 1885 law. Turing's conviction cost him his security clearance and his job as a cryptographer. He was also given a choice of going to prison or undergoing estrogen hormone treatment to reduce his sex drive. He chose the chemical castration. Two years later, at the age of forty-one, Turing poisoned himself with cyanide.

Over the years since his death, Turing has been honored and recognized in many ways as a scientist, patriot, and victim of intolerance. In 2009, a British computer scientist began a campaign for an official apology to Turing and a posthumous knighthood. That year, after an internet petition gained over thirty thousand sponsors, Prime Minister Gordon Brown issued an apology to Turing. Brown said:

> Thousands of people have come together to demand justice for Alan Turing and recognition of the appalling way he was treated. While Turing was dealt with under the law of the time and we can't put the clock back, his treatment was of course utterly unfair and I am pleased to have the chance to say how deeply sorry I and we all are for what happened to him.
>
> Alan and the many thousands of other gay men who were convicted as he was convicted under homophobic laws were treated terribly. Over the years millions more lived in fear of conviction.
>
> This recognition of Alan's status as one of Britain's most famous victims of homophobia is another step towards equality and long overdue.

But even more than that, Alan deserves recognition for his contribution to humankind...It is thanks to men and women who were totally committed to fighting fascism, people like Alan Turing, that the horrors of the Holocaust and of total war are part of Europe's history and not Europe's present.

So on behalf of the British government, and all those who live freely thanks to Alan's work I am very proud to say: we're sorry, you deserved so much better.

Brown's apology is interesting in two ways. His statement names the offense for which the government apologizes: "Alan and the many thousands of other gay men who were convicted...under homophobic laws were treated terribly." But the apology is only directed explicitly to Turing. We are left to infer that the British government is also sorry for the effect of its homophobic laws on others. The apology is only implied—certainly Brown could have been more explicit.

Brown's statement also highlights the sense in which earlier governments and later ones are continuous yet distinct. He says that he is "pleased" and "proud" to apologize. How can someone be proud to apologize, when apology involves accepting shame and embarrassment? This again illustrates the split-self idea central to national apologies. Representing a nation that is a new moral self, Brown is able to be both sorry for the acts of a previous government and pleased and proud to be apologizing.

8

International Apologies

Protocol

In the last chapter, we explored apologies from nations and states for historic transgressions against their own people or against humanity more broadly. In this chapter, we take up the complementary theme of apologies from one nation to another. We begin at the ballpark.

The 1992 World Series was the first played outside of the United States, with the Toronto Blue Jays facing the Atlanta Braves. Before game two in Atlanta's Fulton Stadium, a US Marine color guard carried the Canadian flag into the stadium. The problem was that the flag was upside down, the red maple leaf pointing to the ground. The Marines had been given the flag only moments before going on the field and, in their hurry, mounted it incorrectly.

Canadians were understandably angry, and Marine commandant General Carl Mundy, Jr. apologized formally to the Canadian ambassador. President George H. W. Bush also apologized. At a campaign town hall meeting in Atlanta, Bush discussed "the flag situation."

> If that had happened in Canada and we'd have seen the United States flag flown upside down, every American would have been very, very upset. This was a mistake. Certainly, nobody would ever do anything like that on purpose.
>
> So what I wanted to use your program for is to say how badly I feel about it, how badly all the American people feel about it, how much we value our friendship with Canada. They are our strongest trading partner in the whole world, and we would do nothing to hurt the national pride of Canada. So, on behalf of all Americans, I simply wanted to

apologize to the people of Canada and suggest we try to keep this now, from now on, out of the marvelous baseball rivalry between Atlanta and Toronto. And that's all I want to say.

There had been concerns that Canadians would retaliate at the third game of the Series, to be played in Toronto, by flying American flags upside down. But at the start of game three, officials read a statement from General Mundy saying that the Marine Corps had asked to make amends by carrying the Canadian flag again—correctly—and had asked the Canadian Mounties to present the American flag.

Bush's statement expressed his regrets, reiterated the value of the US-Canadian friendship, performed the apology, and suggested a path to forgiveness by focusing on the game. His apology restored face to the Canadians by showing contrition and respect—and restored face to the United States by admitting its error. The transgression was a relatively minor one—harm to national pride by incorrectly displaying a national symbol. The offender and the offended enjoyed a good relationship that both governments wanted to preserve, and the fault was clear. The quick actions—a formal apology by the Marine commandant and a presidential statement "on behalf of all Americans" restored face to the Canadians by showing both contrition and respect. And Toronto won the 1992 World Series, four games to two.

"Come to Japan and Apologize"

In January of 2001, the Japanese fishing ship Ehime Maru set off for Hawaii on an educational voyage. Along with its twenty crew members, the 191-foot trawler carried two teachers and thirteen high-school students from the Uwajima Fishery High School. On February 9, both the Ehime Maru and the USS Greeneville, a 362-foot Los Angeles-class nuclear submarine, were nine miles south of Oahu. With some civilian visitors on board, the Greeneville was demonstrating an emergency surfacing maneuver when a main ballast tank blew. As it rose, the submarine struck the Ehime Maru, sinking it and killing nine of those on board, including four high-school students and both teachers. In addition to the human tragedy, the sinking of the trawler and its aftermath focused attention on a number of issues, including the competence and diligence of the US Navy, liability and compensation, and the perception that Americans did not value the lives of Japanese.

President George W. Bush, just inaugurated, apologized by telephone to Prime Minister Yoshiro Mori, and he discussed the accident on national television, stating, "I want to reiterate what I said to the prime minister of Japan: I'm deeply sorry about the accident that took place; our nation is sorry." On February 11, secretary of state Colin Powell and secretary of defense Donald Rumsfeld also publicly apologized, and the US ambassador to Japan, Tom Foley, met with both Prime Minister Mori and Emperor Akihito to apologize. And when the families of the victims arrived in Hawaii, Admiral Thomas Fargo, commander of the US Pacific Fleet, met with them to apologize as well. But the person that many Japanese wanted to hear from—Scott Waddle, the submarine's commander—was silent at first.

In his memoir, Waddle recounts that he had asked to accompany Fargo to apologize but was ordered not to by the Navy public affairs office. However, Waddle's absence became a symbol of American insincerity and lack of remorse. The *Japan Times* reported on the families' reactions when they arrived in Honolulu. One father described the accident as "inexcusable," remarking of Waddle, "If you're a man, you should fall on your knees and ask for our pardon!" Waddle's attorney released a statement which said, "It is with a heavy heart that I express my most sincere regret to the Japanese people and most importantly, to the families of those lost and injured in the collision between the USS Greeneville and the Ehime Maru." The survivors and families rejected the statement as insincere and impersonal. The Japanese families came to question whether Waddle would take responsibility for his actions and be held accountable.

The Navy disciplined Waddle—he was reprimanded for dereliction of duty and negligent hazarding of his ship—but he was allowed to retire with an honorable discharge and full benefits. After receiving the reprimand, Waddle apologized again in a statement.

My heart aches for the losses suffered by the families of those killed aboard the M/V Ehime Maru and the grief that this accident unfairly has thrust upon them. I think about those lost at sea every day and I grieve for the families. To those families, I again offer my most sincere apology and my hope that our government will promptly and fairly settle all claims made by the families against the United States as a result of this accident.

Despite his statement, the perceived leniency of his punishment exacerbated Japanese anger. One family member explained that "this has ended as a farce," and some observers wondered whether the punishment would have been more severe had it been a European trawler that was sunk. The principal of the Ehime fishing school announced that "the students are seeking a direct apology from [Commander Waddle]. We want him to come to Japan and apologize, not as a civilian but as a member of the United States Navy." The US government eventually reached a $16.5 million financial settlement with the victims and survivors and a separate settlement with the prefecture of Ehime, and it raised the Ehime Maru from the ocean floor at a cost of $60 million. The compensation and efforts helped to repair national relations, but many Japanese remained dissatisfied.

Scott Waddle was dissatisfied too. He was angry with the Navy for ordering him not to apologize in person. After his discharge, Waddle traveled to Ehime in December 2002. He apologized in person to the ship's survivors and victims' families. He also placed a wreath at the Ehime Maru monument at Kakaako Waterfront Park and, after a moment of silence, read the victims' names aloud.

The apologies for the Ehime Maru tragedy highlight the way in which a direct, face-to-face apology and an institutional one may be at odds yet intertwined. To many Japanese and to Waddle himself, it was important that he apologize directly to the survivors and families. To the Navy, it was important to maintain control of the situation and not admit negligence, which could be a basis for further claims. Maintaining control over what is said is also especially important to lawyers, and Waddle's March visit to the families was against his attorney's advice. There is a difference between the needs of institutions and advocates, which are often instrumental, and the needs of individuals, which often involve face-to-face moral expression as a step to forgiveness.

Apology in Japan and in the United States

Scott Waddle's initial apologies did not meet the cultural expectations of the victims of the Ehime Maru tragedy and their families for a direct personal apology. Why not? Much has been written about the cross-cultural differences in apologies between American and Japanese cultures—so much in fact that it might take an entire book to do the topic justice. Anthropologist Ruth Benedict famously overreached by characterizing Western society as having a "guilt culture" in contrast to Japan's "shame culture." And Nicholas Tavuchis insightfully warns us not to take the idea that Japanese apologize more than Westerners too seriously. He points out that the different social use of apologies in Japan—when responding to a favor or gift, for example—make simple frequency comparisons suspect. Of course, we should expect to find cultural differences in the language and social context of apologies, in what requires an apology, and in the response to apologies. And when the practices of cultures differ and expectations are violated, misunderstandings and disappointment result. That was certainly the case in the aftermath of the Ehime Maru accident.

What are some of these differences? From her study of how apology is described in Japanese and American etiquette guides, researcher Naomi Sugimoto proposes a contrast between the Japanese concept of *sunao* in apologies and the American emphasis on sincerity. *Sunao* is "selfless surrender," and Sugimoto suggests that Japanese apologizers defer to the other party's "perception of the situation" and put themselves at "the mercy of the victim." American apologies, by contrast, emphasize sincere and truthful remorse when an apologizer is responsible. To an American, a Japanese apology may seem too self-castigating. To a Japanese, an American apology may seem reticent and self-serving. And in another study involving apologies by American and Japanese college students, Sugimoto found that Japanese students simply admitted fault in apology situations while Americans tended to blend their apologies with accounts.

Other researchers have stressed the importance of shared responsibility in Japanese apologies. One explains that a Japanese speaker "is always expected to apologize in any awkward situation, regardless of the degree of actual personal responsibility." This contrasts with an American style of apology that often seems more individualistic and connected to personal responsibility for a harm. Perhaps the notion of shared responsibility helps to explain why the families of the Ehime Maru victims apologized to the people of Hawaii. In a March 20, 2001, letter they thanked the people of Hawaii for their kindness and help and added:

> The resentment with regard to this accident is definitely not something which is aimed toward the people of Hawaii and the American people. We are worried that, in our grief, we might have been somewhat thoughtless and impolite. If that is the case, we would like to deeply apologize.

Nation to Nation or Person to Person?

An apology from one nation to another is not the same as an apology from one person to another. As we saw in the previous chapter, nations are collectives like corporations, universities, or a local food coop. As collectives, their work is carried on by individual actors (presidents, cabinet secretaries, ambassadors, submarine captains, etc.), but the collective has its own history and identity (as does, for example, the United States). That means that those who apologize on behalf of a collective do not speak for themselves, as do individuals who apologize to express sorrow for some transgression. Their words are fashioned for the permanent diplomatic or public record and are presented in measured, formal, unemotional, and even somewhat artificial language. Nicholas Tavuchis explains:

> In contrast to unmediated interpersonal relations, where ephemeral words have the power to seal an apology, and thus put an end to something that alienates, unrecorded representative speech has no meaning or authority. Consequently, the apology is fashioned for the record and exists only by virtue of its appearance on the record.

As important as Scott Waddle's face-to-face apology was to the families and residents of Ehime, it had no national authority. That came from the admirals, ambassadors, and President Bush.

In the last chapter, we discussed how national apologies, which establish an official record of a transgression, are aimed at reconciliation. Like national apologies, public diplomatic apologies are for the record. But they differ in an important way. Diplomatic apologies are political statements between presumed international equals, so defending national honor is often balanced against reconciliation. It helps to view diplomatic apologies in terms of the face of collectives rather than as the contrition of nations. One nation loses face—or honor—by admitting and apologizing for a transgression while the other nation gains face by being apologized to. Such negotiated facework affects the symbolic power relationships between nations (or collectives)—one apologizes and one accepts.

An official apology also establishes a focal point for reaction among the constituencies of apologies (usually citizens of nations). Many Japanese, for example, thought that the US apology for the Ehime Maru was incomplete because Captain Waddle had not apologized personally. Other Japanese saw it as lacking because the bodies had not been recovered. Some Americans, in turn, complained that the United States was apologizing too much. We saw this reaction earlier in the example of the Thomson-Urrutia Treaty (discussed in Chapter 4), which the Senate declined to ratify if the expression of regret to Colombia was included. When a nation apologizes, some of its citizens will inevitably see the apology as a loss of face and prestige. And when a nation receives or accepts an apology, some of its citizens will inevitably criticize it as insufficient or insincere. Sometimes, however, insincerity is the only diplomatic solution, as we will see in the next example.

The Pueblo Incident: Duress and Insincerity

On January 23, 1968, at the height of the war in Vietnam and just two days after an assassination attempt on South Korean president Park Chung Hee, North Korean forces boarded the USS Pueblo. One crew member was killed and eighty-two captured. The Pueblo had been collecting intelligence near the fifty-mile territorial limit, and North Korea claimed that the ship had strayed inside the limit. The United States maintained it had not, and President Lyndon Johnson ordered nearly fifteen thousand Air Force and Navy reservists to active duty on January 25. The crew was held for eleven months, during which time they were beaten, tortured, and forced to sign "confessions," which were reported on North Korean radio.

The North Koreans wanted an apology. In March, they sent Johnson an open letter supposedly written by Pueblo crewmen. It asked the United States to frankly admit the vessel had violated North Korean territory. Later that month the North Koreans circulated more letters and warned that if the United States did not apologize the crew might be killed. While the propaganda war played out in public, negotiations with Major General Pak Chung Kuk were taking place in Panmunjom, on the border of the two Koreas. The meetings, nearly thirty in all, were led first by Rear Admiral John Victor Smith and, after April, by Army major general Gilbert Woodward. The North Koreans insisted that the United States admit fault, apologize, and assure the regime that there would be no further violations—these became known as the "three As." In May, Pak gave Woodward a document to sign as the basis for a settlement. The document included the three As, and provoked discussion within the Johnson administration about whether or not to accept the terms. Finally the debate was settled by Johnson himself, who decided to continue the negotiations rather than accept the North Korean document.

In late summer, US officials proposed that rather than signing the document they might simply acknowledge receipt of the crew on the document. This became known as the overwrite strategy—the United States would write on the document but not actually sign it. At the October 10 meeting, Pak rejected

Woodward's suggestions as "sophistries and petty stratagems," and the next two meetings were stalled over this issue. The State Department did not want to sign the document and then turn around and announce that the United States had lied. That was too high a level of insincerity. In early December, the State Department came up with another option. Woodward could announce prior to signing that he was signing a false document, thereby removing the element of deception. This became known as the prior refutation strategy.

Both sides were becoming anxious to end the standoff. Johnson wanted to have the crew reunited with their families at Christmas. And, after the November 5 election, it was clear to the North Koreans that they would soon have to deal with a new administration. Pak agreed to the plan on December 17.

On December 22, General Woodward reiterated that the United States was blameless. He ended his remarks saying, "The paper which I am going to sign was prepared by the North Koreans and is at variance with the above position, but my signature will not and cannot alter the facts. I will sign the document to free the crew and only to free the crew." The eighty-two crew members were released on December 23, 1968. Exactly eleven months after their capture, they walked across the "Bridge of No Return" separating the two Koreas. The North Koreans excised the final sentence of the written document ("Simultaneous with the signing of this document, the undersigned acknowledges receipt of 82 former crew members of the Pueblo and one corpse.") and used the apology for propaganda purposes. They also moved the Pueblo to Pyongyang and converted it to an anti-American museum. It remains there today.

In this intentionally insincere apology, both countries acted instrumentally rather than with any moral rapprochement in mind. The North Koreans wanted the US government to lose face. In order to save face, General Woodward made it clear that he was signing a false document under duress. Thanks to the prior refutation strategy, both sides were able to reach closure and the crew of the Pueblo was repatriated. But the apology itself was devoid of contrition or reconciliation.

The three examples in this chapter have shown the different ways in which nations save face and preserve control while apologizing to other nations, and how those strategies succeed or fail (sometimes simultaneously). We look now at four examples in which relations are similarly tense: the Iraqi apology for bombing the USS Stark, the US apology for blowing up an Iranian passenger jet, the US apologies for the Abu Ghraib prison scandal, and US regrets after an airline collision with a Chinese fighter.

Stark Reality

"I would like to express to you my deepest regret over the painful incident that has happened to the U.S. frigate Stark and to the victims lost in it."
—SADDAM HUSSEIN, *May 19, 1987*

Launched in the fall of 1980, the nearly decade-long war between Iran and Iraq led to a million deaths. Even more were wounded or became refugees. Iraq had hoped for a quick victory against an isolated and disorganized neighbor, but by mid-1982, the invasion was repulsed and Iraq was on the defensive.

The war continued for the next six years as the Ayatollah Khomeini's forces tried to overthrow Iraq, and Saddam Hussein's army used its advantage in weaponry to resist. Fighting spilled over to the Persian Gulf, with Iraq and Iran attacking one another's oil tankers and Iran imposing a naval blockade. The Iranian blockade also included attacks on Saudi and Kuwaiti tankers. In response to this tanker war, the United States increased its naval presence in the region. It was officially neutral but was selling arms to both sides (covertly in the case of the Iranians) and had a strategic interest in protecting the flow of oil from the Persian Gulf states.

Tragedy struck on the night of May 17, 1987, when an Iraqi F-1 Mirage jet attacked a US ship. The USS Stark was a 3,500-ton frigate deployed to the Persian Gulf. An Iraqi pilot, approaching in a radar blind spot, was about ten miles from the frigate when it fired two missiles at the same time that the Stark was sending its warning message. The missiles went undetected until the last seconds and struck the Stark's hull in the crew quarters. Thirty-seven sailors were killed and twenty-one others were injured.

Some suspected that the attack might have been retaliation for the covert sale of US arms to Iran (discussed in Chapter 6). The official Iraqi explanation was that the Stark had been misidentified by the pilot as an Iranian ship. Iraq's president, Saddam Hussein, apologized to Ronald Reagan the day after the attack. His letter expressed regret (in the first paragraph), denied intent and shifted blame (in the second), expressed hopeful good intentions (in the third), placed the attack in the context of the larger war (in the fourth), and offered condolences (in the fifth).

Excellency:
I would like to express to you my deepest regret over the painful incident that has happened to the U.S. frigate Stark and to the victims lost in it.

I am confident of your certainty that the Iraqi planes which were operating in an area where they are used to attack enemy targets had no intention whatsoever to strike at a target belonging to your country or to any country other than Iran, which continues to commit aggression against our country and which bears fully the responsibility of disturbing the security and stability of the region as a whole.

I hope that this unintentional incident will not affect the relation between our two countries, which we wish to remain cordial on the basis of mutual respect, the rules of international conduct and our common interest in the preservation of peace and stability in the region.

This tragic incident emphasizes once again the urgent necessity that efforts should be brought together in order to bring the war to an end and to force the Iranian regime to accept peace in accordance with the rules of international law and the resolution of the (U.N.) Security Council with a view to sparing the region further bloodshed and losses. In this respect, we follow with great interest the effort made by your government in the Security Council.

I shall be grateful, Mr. President, if you kindly convey to the families of the victims of the incident my personal condolences and feeling of sympathy. I have instructed our ambassador to Washington to do the same and to explain our position to the American public opinion while reaffirming the wish of the Iraqi people to preserve the friendship with the people of the United States.

Accept, please, Mr. President, assurances of my highest consideration.

Saddam Hussein, President of the Republic of Iraq

The Reagan administration pursued reparations for the deaths but otherwise accepted the Iraqi account of mistaken ship identity. It also used the incident to strengthen its engagement in the region and began to escort Kuwaiti tankers that registered under the American flag. And it redefined the rules of engagement, allowing American ships in the region to attack any Iraqi or Iranian aircraft that approached on a threatening path. The following year, those rules would lead to the downing of an Iranian civilian plane.

Flight 655

"We deeply regret any loss of life."
—PRESIDENT RONALD REAGAN, *July 3, 1988*

"I will never apologize for the United States of America, ever. I don't care what the facts are."
— VICE PRESIDENT GEORGE H. W. BUSH, *August, 1988*

The Strait of Hormuz is a narrow shipping channel separating Iran from the tiny tip of Oman, between the Persian Gulf and the Arabian Sea. On July 3, 1988, as the United States prepared to celebrate Independence Day, the crew of the USS Vincennes, a Ticonderoga-class guided missile cruiser, made a tragic error. It shot down a passenger aircraft, Iran Air flight 655.

The war between Iran and Iraq was in its eighth year, and the Vincennes was stationed in the Persian Gulf to escort US-registered Kuwaiti oil tankers and to enforce the embargo against Iran. The Vincennes had been engaged with Iranian gunboats and had pursued them into Iran's territorial waters.

Flight 655 was on its short twenty-eight-minute flight from Bandar Abbas to Dubai when it was misidentified as an attacking F-14 Tomcat. At 10:24, after attempts to contact the ship on a military frequency went unanswered, the captain of the Vincennes ordered his crew to fire two antiaircraft missiles at the plane. Flight 655 crashed into the Persian Gulf killing all 290 people on board.

The first accounts of the attack by Admiral William Crowe, chairman of the Joint Chiefs of Staff, reported that the airliner was outside its prescribed air corridor and descending in an attack profile. President Reagan issued a statement saying,

> I am saddened to report that it appears that in a proper defensive action by the USS Vincennes this morning in the Persian Gulf an Iranian airliner was shot down over the Strait of Hormuz. This is a terrible human tragedy. Our sympathy and condolences go out to the passengers, crew, and their families. The Defense Department will conduct a full investigation.
>
> We deeply regret any loss of life. The course of the Iranian civilian airliner was such that it was headed directly for the USS Vincennes, which was at the time engaged with five Iranian Boghammar boats that had attacked our forces. When the aircraft failed to heed repeated warnings, the Vincennes followed standing orders and widely publicized procedures, firing to protect itself against possible attack.

The only U.S. interest in the Persian Gulf is peace, and this tragedy reinforces the need to achieve that goal with all possible speed.

Iran protested to the United Nations Security Council, and the United States took the unusual step of sending Vice President George H. W. Bush to present its response. On July 14, Bush argued that Iran shared responsibility for failing to divert passenger traffic from a war zone. A few days later the Security Council unanimously adopted a resolution of "deep distress," but it assigned no blame. A month-long Navy investigation concluded that the Vincennes did not purposely attack a civilian airliner and judged that its captain acted prudently under the circumstances. The United States offered compensation to the families of the victims. Iran insisted that the compensation be accompanied by an admission of wrongdoing and took the issue to the International Court of Justice. In 1996, a financial settlement was reached in the suit.

Beyond Reagan's statement of regret, however, no US apologies were offered, and it is difficult to interpret Reagan's words as an apology. He offers condolences and sympathy and regret for "any loss of life," a phrasing which can suggest generalized regret for death that was unconnected to the downing of flight 655. His administration treated the shooting of the ship as a justifiable error, offering an account that fell short of apology.

It was also an election year, and Vice President Bush was trying to distinguish himself from his opponent, Michael Dukakis, in terms of unapologetic patriotism. At an August campaign stop, Bush told a crowd that as president he would "never apologize for the United States of America, ever. I don't care what the facts are." It was a theme Bush had used before and would repeat throughout his 1988 campaign.

And what was the feeling in Iran? The shooting down of flight 655 probably hastened the end of the Iran-Iraq War, as Iranian leaders worried anew that the United States might openly join Iraq in the hostilities. But among the Iranian people, the US reaction represented American disregard for Iranian lives and arrogance even in error. It remains an important symbol to Iranians to this day.

A Few Bad Apples

"So to those Iraqis who were mistreated by members of the U.S. armed forces, I offer my deepest apology."
—DEFENSE SECRETARY DONALD RUMSFELD, *May 2004*

In early 2004, the world learned of a startling military investigation. A group of seventeen American soldiers at the Abu Ghraib Prison in Iraq were being investigated for abuse of Iraqi detainees. By March, charges of dereliction of duty, maltreatment, aggravated assault, and battery had been filed against six soldiers. More would be charged, and eleven soldiers were eventually convicted. By late April, the media was covering the story in full, showing graphic photos of hooded prisoners being psychologically and sexually abused. Domestic and international audiences saw pictures of smiling US soldiers holding prisoners on leashes and forcing them to masturbate, and of prisoners hung from the wrists. They heard accounts of rape and other sexual abuses, and of torture and murder.

As the military investigated the abuses, the government struggled to find the words to respond. When Brigadier General Mark Kimmitt appeared on CBS's *Sixty Minutes* on April 27, he began to address the call to apologize. Asked by journalist Dan Rather, "What can the Army say specifically to Iraqis and others who are going to see this and take it personally?" Kimmitt said that he and others were "appalled," and that the Abu Ghraib guards had "let their fellow soldiers down." He added,

> So what would I tell the people of Iraq? This is wrong. This is reprehensible. But this is not representative of the 150,000 soldiers that are over here. I'd say the same thing to the American people…Don't judge your army based on the actions of a few.

Here Kimmitt acknowledged the moral harm but did not apologize. On May 5, President George W. Bush reiterated that sentiment in an interview with Al Hurra, an Arabic-language satellite television channel.

> First, people in Iraq must understand that I view those practices as abhorrent.
> They must also understand that what took place in that prison does not represent America that I know. The America I know is a compassionate country that believes in freedom. The America I know cares about every individual. The America I know has sent troops into Iraq to

promote freedom; good, honorable citizens that are helping the Iraqis every day.

It's also important for the people of Iraq to know that in a democracy everything is not perfect, that mistakes are made. But in a democracy as well those mistakes will be investigated and people will be brought to justice.

Bush here gives an account, speaking of American values, shifting blame away from "the America I know," and promising accountability for "mistakes." He went on to contrast the US response to that of Saddam Hussein, whose "trained torturers were never brought to justice." Spokesman Scott McClellan characterized Bush's statement this way: "The president is sorry for what occurred and the pain it has caused."

Also speaking on Arabic television, national security advisor Condoleeza Rice explained, "We are deeply sorry for what has happened to these people and what the families must be feeling. It's just not right. And we will get to the bottom of what happened." And, a few days later, in testimony before Congress, Donald Rumsfeld, who had at first minimized the seriousness of the misconduct, apologized directly. He opened his statement with the language of accountability, obligation, and right versus wrong, saying, "These events occurred on my watch. As secretary of defense, I am accountable for them and I take full responsibility." He explained that the United States failed to meet its obligations and ended by saying:

So to those Iraqis who were mistreated by members of the U.S. armed forces, I offer my deepest apology. It was inconsistent with the values of our nation, it was inconsistent with the teachings of the military to the men and women of the armed forces, and it was certainly fundamentally un-American.

But Rumsfeld also tried to minimize the damage by stressing the inconsistency with American values. He added, "It's important for the American people and the world to know that while these terrible acts were perpetrated by a small number of U.S. military, they were also brought to light by the honorable and responsible actions of other military personnel." He ended with a statement of the American values of life, liberty, and the rule of law and invited the world to "watch how a democracy deals with wrongdoing and with scandal and the pain of acknowledging and correcting our own mistakes and our own weaknesses."

The Bush administration's apologies acknowledged harm, offered regret, provided accounts, asserted American values, and promised accountability. Yet they failed to repair the damage because they placed the administration and military outside of the offenses—the transgressions were the work of a few bad apples and the administration and military were victims as well. Engaged in a struggle for world opinion and domestic support in a time of war, the Bush administration may have felt that expressions of consolation and promises of accountability were the best that could be offered. Officials thus minimized the offenses, shifted blame, and offered little in the way of explanation of how the offenses happened. The result was that the United States seemed unable to accept moral responsibility for the actions of its bad apples and could only say that those actions did not represent the American self. Ultimately, the United States gave up some of its moral authority in the war on terror with a weak apology for a very serious transgression.

Two Sorries

"We're sorry that that happened, but it can't be seen as an apology."
—SECRETARY OF STATE COLIN POWELL, *April 8, 2001*

On April 1, 2001, a US Navy reconnaissance plane with a crew of twenty-four was collecting intelligence about seventy miles from Hainan Island, in the South China Sea. The plane, a 117-foot long EP-3E ARIES II, with a wingspan of one hundred feet, was intercepted by a pair of Chinese J-8 fighters. The fighters were smaller, single-person interceptors and one of them was piloted by a top-gun risk-taker named Wang Wei.

Flying just twenty feet from the US plane, Wang Wei collided with the larger craft, damaging it and losing control of his own plane. Wang's plane crashed into the ocean killing him. The US plane was severely damaged as well, losing cabin pressure and one of its propeller engines. As the crew destroyed sensitive intelligence information and equipment, the pilot regained enough control to make an emergency landing on Hainan Island, a tropical island province of China. The crew was detained and interrogated by the Chinese, who demanded an American apology.

The two governments disputed the cause of the collision. The American account was that Wang Wei had bumped the wing of the EP-3. The Chinese account, based on the testimony of the other interceptor pilot, was that the American plane had veered into Wang's fighter. The situation was complicated by disagreement over airspace and reconnaissance flights. The Chinese foreign ministry called on the United States to apologize, using the word *dao-qian*, which translates as "apologize" and which had traditionally been used for affronts to national interest or honor. The US position, articulated by Secretary of State Powell, was that the United States had regrets but would offer no apology. On April 8, Powell spoke on *Face the Nation*:

> There is a widow out there. And we regret that. We're sorry that her husband was lost no matter what the fault was. We do acknowledge that we violated their airspace, but look at the emergency circumstances that that pilot was facing. And we regret that. We've expressed sorrow for it, and we're sorry that that happened, but it can't be seen as an apology, accepting responsibility.

On April 11, Joseph Prueher, the US ambassador to China, sent a letter of regret, with mutually agreed-upon wording in English to show regret and sorrow without an apology. The first half of the short letter set the context and expressed regret:

> On behalf of the United States Government, I now outline steps to resolve this issue.
>
> Both President Bush and Secretary of State Powell have expressed their sincere regret over your missing pilot and aircraft. Please convey to the Chinese people and to the family of pilot Wang Wei that we are very sorry for their loss.
>
> Although the full picture of what transpired is still unclear, according to our information, our severely crippled aircraft made an emergency landing after following international emergency procedures. We are very sorry the entering of China's airspace and the landing did not have verbal clearance, but very pleased the crew landed safely.

The remainder of the letter outlined future meetings and discussion, acknowledged that the issue of reconnaissance flights would be discussed, and stated the understanding that the aircrew would be released. The sorries in this letter report on the Bush administration's regret about Wang Wei's death and about the lack of verbal clearance for the emergency landing. The Chinese Foreign Ministry statement acknowledging the letter treated this as an apology.

> As the U.S. Government has already said "very sorry" to the Chinese people, the Chinese Government has, out of humanitarian considerations, decided to allow the crew members to leave China after completing the necessary procedures.

The earlier drafts of Ambassador Prueher's letter did not include the adverb *very* and were unacceptable to the Chinese negotiators. It was only when Prueher changed the two instances of *sorry* to *very sorry* that the letter was acceptable. The Chinese translation rendered *very sorry* as *shenbiao qianyi*, which indicates profound regret and acceptance of wrongdoing and the Chinese government referred to the letter as an American *daoqian*. Each government got what it wanted.

9

Why We Apologize, or Don't

I Shall Resign the Presidency Effective at Noon Tomorrow

In the 2008 film *Frost/Nixon*, Richard Nixon, played by Frank Langella, is interrogated about the Watergate scandal by interviewer David Frost, played by Michael Sheen. The fictional Nixon expresses remorse after being pressed by Frost.

> And the American people? I let them down. I let down my friends. I let down the country. And worst of all, I let down our system of government. And the dreams of all those young people that ought to get into government, but now they think, "It's all too corrupt," and the rest. Yeah. I let the American people down, and I'm gonna have to carry that burden with me for the rest of my life.

Ben Bradlee, the executive editor of the *Washington Post* when it broke the story, saw this comment as a fictionalized apology. Bradlee complained that the filmmakers "never should have let him apologize in the film. Nixon never was sorry for what he did." Did the real Richard Nixon ever apologize?

Nixon turned the word *gate* into a synonym for scandal. Things began with a bungled break-in of the Democratic National Committee offices at the Watergate office building and reached their climax on August 8, 1974, with Nixon's resignation. The investigation of the five-man break-in revealed that the burglars—"plumbers" as they were known—had been hired by the Committee for the Re-election of the President. Nixon and his aides became involved in an extensive cover-up, revealed in a nationally televised Senate investigation. The investigation led to the release of Oval Office audiotapes showing Nixon's personal involvement. The House Judiciary Committee recommended impeachment.

Having lost the support of the people and key members of his own party, Nixon chose to resign rather than face the impeachment vote and Senate trial. Announcing his resignation, Nixon emphasized that he was resigning against his will for the good of the country—he tried to transcend—and he expressed some conditional regret.

> I regret deeply any injuries that may have been done in the course of the events that led to this decision. I would say only that if some of my judgments were wrong, and some were wrong, they were made in what I believed at the time to be the best interest of the Nation.

Nixon's resignation speech was a regretful account of his situation, not an apology for his transgressions. His expression of regret was vague, hypothetical, and conditional; he admitted wrong judgments but denied wrong intent. A month later, President Gerald Ford pardoned Nixon. The day after the pardon, Nixon's office released a statement. He was more contrite but still unapologetic.

> No words can describe the depth of my regret and pain at the anguish my mistakes over Watergate have caused the nation and the Presidency, a nation I so deeply love and an institution I so greatly respect...
>
> That the way I tried to deal with Watergate was the wrong way is a burden I shall bear for every day of the life that is left to me.

Here Nixon admits mistakes and speaks of anguish and burdens. He treats himself as a victim of his own mistakes and frames his mistakes as managerial, not criminal. Three years later, in the transcripts of the actual 1977 Frost-Nixon interviews, Nixon is defiant. He says:

> When I resigned, people didn't think it was enough to admit mistakes; fine. If they want me to get down and grovel on the floor, no. Never. Because I don't believe I should.

Over the years, asked if he was sorry or would apologize to the American people for Watergate, Nixon repeatedly said no. Asked again in April 1984, in a television interview with a former aide, Frank Gannon, he replied:

My answer to that question and to those who say, "Will you apologize?" "Are you sorry?" is simply a fact: There's no way that you could apologize that is more eloquent, more decisive, more finite, or to say that you are sorry, which would exceed resigning the Presidency of the United States. That said it all. And I don't intend to say any more.

Ben Bradlee was right. Nixon never saw himself as apologizing, only as regretting mistakes. He framed his resignation as a sacrifice greater than any apology. Nixon's refusal to apologize was a combination of face-saving and silence that served his self-image and pride. And it grew stronger over the years.

Why We Refuse to Apologize

Why do some individuals (or collectives) ignore the call to apologize? Why is it sometimes hard to name a transgression and say you are sorry? Psychological and cultural issues surely enter into this. In the next chapter, we discuss "the John Wayne Code," which holds that men should never apologize because it is a sign of weakness. Did Nixon see himself as following such a code of never apologizing? Initially of course, he had legal reasons for not apologizing, but after the pardon, those were no longer an issue. Perhaps he wanted to avoid giving his political enemies—and he thought of them as enemies—the satisfaction of seeing him "grovel," as he puts it. For Nixon, to apologize was to give in.

Some refusals to apologize come from a conviction that one has done no wrong. But often, as with Richard Nixon, a harm is apparent, and it is a sense of pride that prevents an apology. People feel that apologizing will cause them to lose respect—to lose face. In such instances, an offender may know that he or she has done wrong but is not able to face his or her transgression. In other instances, the refusal to apologize may come not from misplaced pride or honor but from concerns about legal liability. Here is a sad and tragic example.

Union Carbide and Bhopal

In early December 1984, a water leak developed at the Union Carbide pesticide plant in Bhopal, the capital of the state of Madhya Pradesh. The leak created a reaction that increased the temperature and pressure of the forty-two-ton underground reservoir until the tank vented gases into the atmosphere. Bhopal had a population of nine hundred thousand at the time, with many workers and others living in housing near the plant. As northwesterly winds spread the heated gas, hundreds of thousands of people were exposed to the leaked methyl isocyanate. In low concentrations, methyl isocyanate can cause coughing, chest pain, irritation of the eyes, nose and throat, and skin damage. At higher concentrations, it causes lung disease, hemorrhaging, blindness, pneumonia, and death. Nearly ninety-three thousand pounds of gases leaked from the tank, killing thousands immediately and leading to tens of thousands of deaths over time and hundreds of thousands of injuries. It was the worst industrial accident in history.

The Indian government arrested the plant manager, Jaganathan Mukund, on charges of homicide. And when the chairman of the board of Union Carbide arrived in India on December 7 to inspect the site, he was also arrested, though held only briefly. Chairman Warren Anderson was charged with "negligence and criminal corporate liability" and "criminal conspiracy" but was released on two-thousand-dollars' bail and given protective custody during his inspection of the site. Anderson had felt it was important to visit the site personally to assess the situation, provide relief, and even discuss compensation. When he returned to the United States, Anderson said, "Union Carbide has a moral responsibility in this matter, and we are not ducking it."

Trained as a lawyer, Anderson would not concede that Union Carbide was legally responsible for the disaster. His statement left moral responsibility vague, but it seemed clear that he meant that Union Carbide had only a responsibility to provide aid and some compensation. For Union Carbide, accepting moral responsibility did not extend to accepting guilt, since guilt might imply negligence and damages. If it was merely morally responsible, then compensation could be discussed separate from damages.

The matters of blame and compensation were complicated by the fact that, under Indian law, the Bhopal plant was an independent subsidiary of Union Carbide, with 49.1 percent of its shares Indian-owned—it was known as Union Carbide India Limited. The Bhopal plant had been operating at a loss for some time, with cost-cutting and layoffs impacting both safety and morale. Did the blame lie with the Indian subsidiary or the parent company?

The government of Prime Minister Rajiv Ghandi quietly accepted five million dollars in disaster aid from Union Carbide. In 1989, Union Carbide, Union Carbide India Limited, and the Indian government reached a further settlement of $470 million. In the years to follow, Union Carbide India and Union Carbide itself were purchased by other corporations. Eveready Industries India, Ltd., a battery maker, purchased Union Carbide India in 1994, and in early 2001, Dow Chemical purchased Union Carbide. This raised a further question: would the moral responsibility be inherited by the new owners?

On the eighteenth anniversary of the gas leak, Dow was challenged by Greenpeace to assume more responsibility for Bhopal, whose citizens continued to suffer. In response, CEO Michael D. Parker posted an open letter to employees that read in part: "Without a doubt, the tragedy changed our industry forever as companies across the globe collectively took on the moral responsibility to prevent anything like it from ever happening again." Parker explained the inherited 1989 settlement and reiterated Dow's view that "we clearly have no legal obligations in relation to the tragedy," while also noting that Dow had been exploring philanthropic initiatives. And he emphasized that, regardless of protests, "what we cannot and will not do...is accept responsibility for the Bhopal accident." Parker stressed the generalized responsibility of "companies across the globe" but rejected any legal obligations for Dow.

Both Union Carbide and Dow chose not to apologize for the Bhopal disaster. The combination of liability fears, reputation management, insufficient public outcry, scope of the tragedy, and murkiness surrounding the actual causes led Union Carbide to choose its more limited, defensive course. The company opted for a legalistic compensation agreement—an instrumental solution that ended legal responsibility—rather than an apology and open-ended process of reconciliation and reparation. Dow in turn considered the legal issue closed when it took over Union Carbide and chose to pursue only more general philanthropic activities. For Dow, the question of apology had been settled as well: there was no obligation beyond the collective moral commitment of corporations.

Some apologies did result from Bhopal. In 2004, on the twentieth anniversary of the disaster, the BBC reported that Dow was taking full responsibility for the disaster and liquidating Union Carbide to establish a compensation fund for Bhopal victims. The statement turned out to be a hoax, perpetrated by the activist group known as The Yes Men. The BBC apologized for the reporting. The Indian government also apologized for its handling of the removal of toxic material from the site. And, as several ex-employees of the Union Carbide India plant were tried and convicted in 2010, there were calls for a state apology for letting Warren Anderson leave the country decades earlier.

Thus far in this chapter, we've seen how some individuals or collectives resist apologizing. They may argue that apology is implied in some other action, as Richard Nixon suggested, and that articulating it amounts to groveling before adversaries and being publically shamed. They may worry that apology creates liability rather than resolution, as Union Carbide and Dow seemed to. Refusals to apologize do not entail the conviction that one is in the right. They are simply the resistance to admitting having done wrong. And of course, refusals to apologize may blend account strategies: actors may concede that something bad has happened and even note their involvement but not take responsibility. So, why *do* people apologize? That is our next topic.

Naked Cruelty

Political strategist Lee Atwater was—depending on your perspective—hard-edged and aggressive or vicious and mean-spirited. Atwater cut his teeth in South Carolina, working with Governor Carroll Campbell and Senator Strom Thurmond. Among other tricks, Atwater used push polling to present negative information in the form of survey questions and planted fake reporters in his opponents' press conferences. Atwater's reputation grew. He served as the deputy director for Ronald Reagan's re-election in 1984 and became the campaign manager for George H. W. Bush in 1988. As Bush's campaign manager, he helped to develop an aggressive media campaign contrasting Bush and his opponent, Governor Michael Dukakis, on wedge issues. One of these was crime, and Atwater ruthlessly exploited the Massachusetts governor's opposition to the death penalty.

Dukakis had supported an existing prison furlough plan and had also vetoed a proposed ban on furloughs for murderers. Atwater commissioned a commercial highlighting an African-American convict named Willie Horton. Horton had stabbed a boy to death during a robbery and had been serving a life sentence for first-degree murder. On weekend furlough from prison, Horton kidnapped a young couple, tortured the man, and raped the woman. The ad linking Dukakis and Willie Horton never actually ran, but it was reported and shown on the national media, producing the same effect. An ad with the same message but without Willie Horton's picture did run, so Atwater was able to make the attack in two ways. Atwater also encouraged and exploited rumors that Dukakis had received treatment for mental illness and that his wife had once burned a flag at a protest. These efforts helped George Bush to overcome a seventeen-point deficit in early polling.

After Bush's election, Atwater became chairman of the Republican National Committee. But midway through the Bush administration, Atwater—still in his thirties—was diagnosed with brain cancer. As it became clear that he had only a short time to live, Atwater had an apparent religious conversion, and he privately apologized to many old political victims. He also wrote a public apology to Michael Dukakis.

> In 1988, fighting Dukakis, I said that I "would strip the bark off the little bastard" and "make Willie Horton his running mate." I am sorry for both statements. The first for its naked cruelty and the second because it makes me sound racist, which I am not.... Mostly I am sorry for the way I thought of other people.

Atwater died in March of 1991, at the age of forty.

Why Do We Apologize?

What made Atwater apologize? Some assumed that Atwater was merely continuing to manipulate the media. Others believed that his deathbed apologies were sincere and that he had had a change of heart. It may be that Atwater's apologies were not easily characterizable—part instrumental, part sincere, and part "emotional damage control," as one observer put it. The time between Atwater's initial collapse while speaking at a Republican fundraising breakfast to his last breath was just over a year, much of that spent on morphine.

Determining why an apology happened is difficult because the call to apologize so often arises from within. Motivations may be aimed at changing others' perceptions or even changing one's self-perception. Or they may be ethical, arising from a new realization of empathy and shame. For Lee Atwater, we may never know how much was calculation and how much was moral attachment. The best we can do is infer possible motivations from text and context.

One possibility is that the call to apologize arose from the imminence of death and the wish to not be remembered for his lowest behavior. Atwater said he was "sorry for the way [he] thought of other people," and "for the naked cruelty" of his treatment of Dukakis. This suggests, or at least expresses, empathy. And his observation that the Willie Horton ad made him appear racist conveys embarrassment as well. Yet guilt for his actions did not enter into his apology, and he maintained that tough comparative advertising (as he called it) was a necessary political tool. His remorse was for his attitude, for his former glee in meanness.

Not everyone accepted Atwater's apology, but Michael Dukakis did. When Atwater died Dukakis said: "We obviously were on opposite sides of a tough and negative campaign, but at least he had the courage to apologize. That says a lot for the man." Perhaps that is what Lee Atwater wanted as well—to be remembered as having the courage to apologize.

Not a Day Goes By

William Calley was a lieutenant and platoon leader in the US Army during the Vietnam War. He joined the army in 1966 and was commissioned a second lieutenant in the infantry. Calley was young, just twenty-three when he joined up. At five foot three and 130 pounds, he was short and thin, with red hair that had earned him the nickname Rusty. Before joining the army, he had graduated high school, given college an unsuccessful try, and knocked around in a variety of jobs. He was widely described as average. On March 16, 1968, he would become something else.

Calley was in Charlie Company, which arrived in Vietnam in December 1967. The Tet Offensive, a wave of surprise attacks by Viet Cong forces, began in late January 1968, and a number of hamlets in the village of My Lai were thought to be harboring the Viet Cong. Several platoons of US forces began offensive action against those hamlets, with Calley's First Platoon at the center. No regular Viet Cong soldiers were found, but many civilians were wounded and killed in the initial attack. As the attack progressed more noncombatants—women, children, the elderly—were forced into ditches and shot. At one point, a group of over seventy people was herded into the center of the village and executed. In all, hundreds of villagers were killed.

A helicopter flying over the area witnessed the killings, intervened, and later reported the situation to higher officers. After an initial cover-up, in which it was claimed that 128 Viet Cong had been killed in addition to the twenty-two civilians, the My Lai massacre, as it would be called, become known to higher military and political leaders. In September 1969, Calley and twenty-five others were charged with premeditated murder and other crimes. My Lai became a national story two months later when reporter Seymour Hersh documented the events in the November 12, 1969, edition of the *St. Louis Post-Dispatch*.

Calley's trial began just over a year later, on November 17, 1970. Military prosecutors argued that Calley had illegally ordered his men to murder everyone in the village, in defiance of the rules of engagement. Calley's defense was that he was acting under orders from Captain Ernest Medina. The case hinged on whether Medina had ordered the soldiers to kill everyone in the village or to kill all the enemy soldiers. Medina, who was tried separately and acquitted, denied giving an order to kill everyone in the village. According to Calley at the time:

> I was ordered to go in there and destroy the enemy. That was my job that day. That was the mission I was given. I did not sit down and think in terms of men, women and children. They were all classified as the same, and that's the classification that we dealt with over there, just as the enemy. I felt then and I still do that I acted as I was directed, and I carried out the order that I was given, and I do not feel wrong in doing so.

On March 29, 1971, a six-officer jury convicted Calley of the premeditated murder of twenty-two Vietnamese civilians, and he was sentenced to life imprisonment at Fort Leavenworth. The trial and sentence pleased virtually no one, from those who thought that troops should be supported unconditionally to those who thought that higher ups should have been held accountable. Calley was viewed as both a murderer and a scapegoat. His sentence was reduced twice, first to twenty years and then to ten years, and, as legal challenges continued, President Nixon commuted Calley's sentence to time served. Calley was released in late 1974. He married and, for the next thirty years, worked at his father-in-law's jewelry store in Columbus, Georgia. He didn't speak publically about My Lai until 2009.

On August 19, 2009, a friend of his from Columbus, a former broadcast journalist named Al Fleming, invited Calley to speak at the Kiwanis Club of Greater Columbus. There, before a friendly and familiar hometown audience, Calley got something off his chest. He told the Kiwanis:

> There is not a day that goes by that I do not feel remorse for what happened that day in My Lai. I feel remorse for the Vietnamese who were killed, for their families, for the American soldiers involved and their families. I am very sorry.

Fleming, with Calley's agreement, had arranged the Kiwanis meeting as a question-and-answer session. Asked whether obeying an unlawful order is itself unlawful, Calley responded:

> I believe that is true. If you are asking why I did not stand up to them when I was given the orders, I will have to say that I was a 2nd Lieutenant

getting orders from my commander and I followed them—foolishly, I guess.

Calley said that he did not want to have his comments interpreted as an excuse but merely as what happened. His words meet some of the criteria of an apology: Calley expresses empathy—remorse for Vietnamese victims and his fellow soldiers—and some shame for his actions as well. But his apology fails in some ways, too. He delivered it to a service club rather than addressing it to any of the victims, so he is not apologizing to those actually harmed. He names his transgression only as "what happened that day." And he hedges in expressing his own guilt, maintaining still that he was "foolishly" following orders.

Why did William Calley apologize? And why did he wait until 2009? Had remorse developed and grown over the years in which he reflected on the events of March 1968? Had he wished to apologize earlier and simply not known of an appropriate way to do so? The need to say something about his feelings was evidently present in Calley by 2009 or he would have refused Al Fleming's invitation to speak. Once he did speak, it was impossible for him not to express remorse.

In his book *On Apology*, psychiatrist Aaron Lazare explores the psychology of apology. We apologize, Lazare says, for external and internal reasons. External reasons include hopefulness: the opportunity to repair a breech and restore one's reputation. Internal reasons involve empathy, guilt, and shame: we feel for another person, we understand the need to punish ourselves, and we are embarrassed by our failure to live up to our best self-image. Our conscience, Lazare suggests, is the combination of empathy, guilt, and shame we feel when we know we are wrong. We can see glimpses of this in the apologies of Lee Atwater and William Calley. We fail to apologize, he suggests, from fear. We may fear ostracism and punishment. We may fear other people's response to the transgression or to the apology. We may fear the social or emotional damage to self-image created by an apology—that expressing weakness, fault, shame, or embarrassment causes us to lose face.

For both Lee Atwater and William Calley, apologies seem motivated by a need to express empathy and shame. Accepting guilt was a harder, separate element in each instance. Their calls to apologize arose not in the immediacy of a transgression but impending death in one instance and daily reflection in another. Such internal calls to apologize have a psychological and moral complexity that requires us to assess the balance of instrumental and ethical motivations in others. Of course, not all calls to apologize come from within.

External calls to apologize are in a sense simpler, because the instrumental motivations often far outweigh the ethical. We end with an example of a baldly instrumental, coerced apology. Curiously enough, it is an apology for making an apology.

Shakedown

Each day from late April to mid-July 2010, thousands of barrels of oil leaked into the Gulf of Mexico from the Deepwater Horizon explosion. On June 16, after meeting with British Petroleum (BP) officials in the White House, President Barack Obama announced an agreement that many saw as a step toward accountability. The company would establish an independently run compensation fund of twenty billion dollars for the victims of the oil spill. Representative Joe Barton was not pleased. Barton was a former oil company consultant and Republican congressman representing Arlington, Texas. And he was the ranking Republican on the House Energy and Commerce Committee. As that committee prepared to hear from BP chief Tony Hayward, Barton offered this opening statement:

> I apologize. I'm ashamed of what happened in the White House yesterday. I think it is a tragedy of the first proportion that a private corporation can be subjected to what I would characterize as a shakedown—in this case a $20 billion shakedown.

Democrats and Republicans condemned Barton's remarks. The House Republican leadership ordered Barton to apologize. He did later that day, saying that he thought BP should be held responsible, and "if anything I have said this morning has been misconstrued in opposite effect, I want to apologize for that misconstruction." A later statement apologized explicitly, without the conditional "if":

> I apologize for using the term "shakedown" with regard to yesterday's actions at the White House in my opening statement this morning, and I retract my apology to BP. I regret the impact that my statement this morning implied that BP should not pay for the consequences of their decisions and actions in this incident.

The irony, of course, is that Barton's first apology—to BP—reflected his true sentiments. (It was also infelicitous, since Barton was not in a position to apologize for the Obama administration or the United States.) His second set of apologies failed in a different way. They were forced and vague, regretting a "misconstruction" and the implication of the earlier apology. In the morning session, Barton's call to apologize came from anger within him. Later in the day a different sort of call to apologize came from Barton's leadership, resulting in an instrumental, but much less sincere, apology.

We look next at some additional responses to external calls to apologize: from President Dwight Eisenhower (and candidates Richard Nixon and John F. Kennedy) during the U2 incident, from President Jimmy Carter during the Iran hostage crisis, and from General George Patton for slapping supposed malingerers. And we end with Vice President Dick Cheney's refusal to apologize after shooting a fellow hunter.

Distasteful Necessity

"The position of the United States was made clear with respect to the distasteful necessity of espionage."
—PRESIDENT DWIGHT EISENHOWER, *May 16, 1960*

Before there were satellites and Google Earth images, governments used spy planes for intelligence gathering. In the 1950s, the Eisenhower administration worked with Lockheed engineers in California to develop a stealth spy plane. The U2, a long-winged, large glider powered by a jet engine, was able to fly at seventy thousand feet, presumably above the range of Soviet ground-to-air missiles.

President Eisenhower authorized the first U2 flights in July 1956. Soviet radar could track the flight—their radar reached higher than US analysts had thought—but interceptor planes could not reach the U2 at its altitudes. Khrushchev protested, but Eisenhower continued to cautiously authorize flights. Neither Eisenhower nor Khrushchev made the spy plane issue public.

By 1960 the Soviets had developed missiles that could reach the altitudes where the U2 spy planes were flying. However, the CIA underestimated their range and failed to inform Eisenhower of the potential risk. On May 1, a U2 piloted by Francis Gary Powers left from a secret base in Pakistan only to be shot down in central Russia. The Eisenhower administration at first claimed that the U2 was a weather plane whose pilot had become unconscious and strayed into Russia on autopilot. But when Khrushchev announced that the pilot was alive and displayed the wreckage to the media, Eisenhower revealed the U2 program.

Khrushchev and Eisenhower met a few days later at a long-planned summit in Paris to discuss a nuclear test ban treaty. At the opening session, Khrushchev demanded that Eisenhower personally apologize for the flights. Eisenhower refused to apologize and responded by discussing "the distasteful necessity of espionage activities in a world where nations distrust each other's intentions." He offered an account, not an apology:

> ...these activities had no aggressive intent but rather were to assure the
> safety of the United States and the free world against surprise attack by
> a power which boasts of its ability to devastate the United States and
> other countries by missiles armed with atomic warheads.

Khrushchev left the Paris conference, withdrew his invitation that Eisenhower visit the Soviet Union, and the two never again met face to face. Francis Gary Powers was tried and received a ten-year prison sentence from a

Soviet military tribunal. He was in a Soviet prison for almost two years until exchanged for Soviet spy Rudolf Abel in 1962.

Some US senators had urged Eisenhower to make a statement of regret to save the Paris summit. Among them was John F. Kennedy, and the question of whether Kennedy urged Eisenhower to apologize came up in the 1960 presidential campaign and in the second Nixon-Kennedy debate. Kennedy explained that he had "suggested that if the United States felt it could save the summit conference it would have been proper for us to express regrets." Kennedy claimed that opponents were distorting his position, and he argued that an expression of regret was the sign of a strong country, saying "It's not appeasement. It's not soft." Rather than lie, Kennedy said, "it would have been far better for us to follow the common diplomatic procedure of expressing regret and then trying to move on."

In the debate, Vice President Nixon responded by agreeing that an apology was a sign of strength but denied that regrets were appropriate: "The United States is a strong county. Whenever we do anything that's wrong, we can express regrets. But when the President of the United States is doing something that's right, something that is for the purposes of defending the security of this country against a surprise attack, he can never express regrets or apologize to anybody, including Mr. Khrushchev."

Eisenhower's and Nixon's responses are based in the view that a country shows strength by not apologizing when it is "doing something that's right." Kennedy's position is more instrumental. The diplomatic thing to do is express regrets and move on.

We can see too the politicization of international apology in Kennedy's complaints about political attacks. As president, Kennedy took this lesson to heart in 1961, when Operation Zapata, the invasion of Communist Cuba by US-armed Cuban exiles, failed. At his April 22 press conference, Kennedy had this response: "There's an old saying that victory has 100 fathers and defeat is an orphan." He closed the topic for further discussion by adding that:

> I've said as much as I feel can be usefully said by me in regard to the events of the past few days. Further statements, detailed discussions, are not to conceal responsibility because I'm the responsible officer of the government but merely because I—and that is quite obvious—but merely because I do not believe that such a discussion would benefit us during the present difficult situation.

There is no regret expressed and no forgiveness asked for the failure. Yet his simple statement that he was accountable quelled the issue.

America Held Hostage

"The United States is not going to apologize."
—PRESIDENT JIMMY CARTER, *September 18, 1980*

On November 4, 1979, Iranian militants took over the US embassy in Tehran. For 444 days, they held Americans inside the embassy hostage, while the Carter administration and the Iranian government negotiated their release. Among the Iranian demands: an admission of US guilt and an apology for past US actions against Iran.

Mohammad Reza Pahlavi, the recently deposed Shah of Iran, had just come to the United States for cancer treatment. The Shah had been in power since 1941 and had survived a 1953 power struggle with his prime minister, Mohammad Mosaddegh, who briefly nationalized the oil industry, only to be ousted in a CIA-supported coup. As a Cold War ally, the Shah westernized Iran and provided the United States with a steady supply of oil in return for military and other support. The Shah's repressive regime eventually collapsed, and in mid-January 1979, Pahlavi fled Iran.

The new leader was the Shiite fundamentalist Ayatollah Ruhollah Khomeini, who had been exiled in 1964. Khomeini consolidated power by fomenting anti-Americanism, and when the Shah entered the United States on October 22, Khomeini-inspired militants attacked the embassy and took fifty-two hostages. As it became clear that the hostage crisis would not be quickly resolved, Carter embargoed Iranian oil and froze Iranian assets. Eventually, he severed diplomatic relations after initial negotiations for the hostages' release failed, and he launched a failed rescue operation in April 1980.

Carter and his negotiators had ruled out the idea of an apology as a matter of national honor. At a September 18 news conference, Carter explained his administration's two goals:

One is to preserve the honor and integrity of our Nation and to protect its interests. That's never changed. And the second goal has also never changed, and that is not to do anything here in this country that would endanger the lives or safety of the hostages nor interfere with their earliest possible release back to freedom.

Asked whether national honor ruled out an apology, Carter replied, "The United States is not going to apologize."

The invasion of Iran by Iraq on September 22, 1980, created new opportunities to resolve the hostage crisis. Iran urgently needed its assets released. And after the 1980 elections, it was clear that Iran would soon have to deal with a new administration that had promised never to pay "ransom for people who have been kidnapped by barbarians."

In continued negotiations between Deputy Secretary of State Warren Christopher and Algerian intermediaries for Iran, what became known as the Algiers Accords was developed. The United States agreed to three key Iranian demands— unfreezing assets, a US pledge not to intervene in Iran's internal affairs, and a mechanism to adjudicate claims for American business losses—but not to an apology. Once the essential points had been agreed to, the remainder of the negotiations concerned the amounts of the funds and whether they would be in gold or currency. After negotiations concluded on January 19, 1981, the United States released 7.9 billion dollars in Iranian assets, and the Iranians set aside a billion dollars in escrow to pays claims to American businesses. The hostages were finally released just hours after Carter left office on January 20, 1981.

A Slap in the Face

"In my dealings with you I have been guilty on too many occasions, perhaps, of criticizing and of loud talking."
—GENERAL GEORGE S. PATTON, *August 1943*

General George S. Patton did not believe in battle fatigue. A West Point graduate, Patton had joined the army in 1909, served as an officer in the Tank Corps in World War I, and commanded troops in North Africa, Sicily, and the European Theater of Operations before taking command of the Third Army in 1944.

When Patton was commanding troops in Sicily, he visited the 15th Evacuation Hospital on August 3, 1943. There, Patton slapped and cursed at a soldier he believed to be malingering. Patton found Private Charles Kuhl resting on a box of supplies. When Kuhl did not salute, Patton asked him what his problem was. Kuhl replied, "I guess I just can't take it," and Patton slapped Kuhl's face with his gloves. A week later, on August 10, Patton slapped another American soldier, Private Paul Bennett, at the 93rd Evacuation Hospital.

It is a court-martial offense for an officer to strike an enlisted man, and the slapping incidents were reported to General Dwight Eisenhower, the supreme commander of the Allied Expeditionary Force. Eisenhower wrote that the allegations caused him to question Patton's judgment and self-discipline and "raise serious doubts in my mind as to your future usefulness." The future president wrote that he expected a confidential reply from Patton, and he "strongly advise[d]" Patton to apologize or make "other such personal amends to the individuals concerned" if the charges were true. Patton apologized to the soldiers and hospital staff. He also made a tour of his units and gave a speech in which he offered his regrets:

> In my dealings with you I have been guilty on too many occasions, perhaps, of criticizing and of loud talking. I am sorry for this and I wish to assure you that when I criticize and censure I am wholly impersonal...for every man I have criticized in this army I have probably stopped, talked to and complimented a thousand, but people are more prone to remember ill-usage than to recall compliments; therefore I want you officers and men who are here to explain to the other soldiers, who think perhaps I am too hard, my motives and to express to them my sincere regret.

In his speech, Patton does not explicitly apologize for the slapping incidents, although they had been featured in the media when reporter Drew Pearson highlighted them and suggested an army cover-up. And in the film version of the story, George C. Scott's Patton is more contrite and explicit:

> I can assure you that I had no intention of being either harsh or cruel in my treatment of the…soldier in question. My sole purpose was to try to restore in him some sense of appreciation of his obligations as a man and as a soldier. "If one could shame a coward," I felt, "one might help him to regain his self-respect." This was on my mind. Now, I freely admit that my method was wrong, but I hope you can understand my motive. And that you will accept this explanation…and this…apology.

The Quail Hunt

"Ultimately, I am the guy who pulled the trigger."
—VICE PRESIDENT DICK CHENEY, *2006*

After a Senate argument with Patrick Leahy, Vice President Dick Cheney chose not to apologize for a particularly coarse response—he told Leahy to go fuck himself. In his 2011 autobiography, Cheney offered no apologies for his advice and actions during the George W. Bush administration. Some individuals simply find it difficult to apologize. Cheney seems to be one of them.

Here is a case in point. In February 2006, while on a quail hunt on a fifty-thousand-acre ranch in south Texas, Cheney turned quickly, took aim at a bird, and fired his twenty-eight-gauge shotgun. The birdshot hit a fellow hunter named Harry Whittington in the face, neck, and chest. Whittington, a seventy-six-year-old lawyer, lost consciousness immediately and was rushed to a hospital in nearby Kingsville and then taken by helicopter to Corpus Christi. He had suffered a heart attack and collapsed lung.

Initially a spokeswoman from the ranch blamed Whittington for stepping into the vice president's line of fire. Cheney himself spoke with investigators after the shooting and later in the week discussed it on Fox News. "I turned and shot at the bird," Cheney said, "and at that second, saw Harry standing there. I didn't know he was there." Asked about the responsibility for the shooting, Cheney replied:

> Well, ultimately, I am the guy who pulled the trigger, that fired the round that hit Harry. And you can talk about all of the other conditions that existed at the time, but that is the bottom line. And there is no—it's not Harry's fault. You can't blame anybody else. I'm the guy who pulled the trigger and shot my friend. And I say that's a day I'll never forget.

Cheney provides an account and accepts responsibility but expresses no remorse and offers no apology. When he was released from the hospital, Whittington told reporters, "My family and I are deeply sorry for all that Vice President Cheney and his family have had to go through this past week." Whittington, who described Cheney as an acquaintance, later clarified that his statement was not meant to suggest that he was admitting fault. "I didn't intend it that way," Whittington said. "It was more of a sense of disappointment that it happened at all. I'm sure it must have been difficult for Mr. Cheney and his family."

Did Cheney ever apologize privately to Harry Whittington? In 2010, *Washington Post* staff writer Paul Farhi asked Whittington that question. According to Farhi, Whittington paused and responded, "I'm not going to go into that." Farhi ended his report by saying that Whittington was "still waiting for Dick Cheney to say he's sorry."

Apology in American Culture

The John Wayne Code

In *She Wore a Yellow Ribbon*, Captain Nathan Brittles is a veteran cavalry officer on one last patrol before compulsory retirement. The 1949 film is a John Ford western, set in the post-Little Big Horn America of 1876, with John Wayne as Nathan Brittles. His mission is to prevent an attack by the Arapahos. After overcoming a number of obstacles, he eventually prevents the attack by stampeding the Indians' horses. As Garry Wills has suggested, the film emphasizes post-Civil War unity under a strong and selfless leader, an implicit message for the post-World War II United States.

Brittles's mission is complicated by another, gender-laden assignment. He has to escort the wife and the niece of his commanding officer to the stagecoach station at Sudrow's Wells. To protect the women from the war parties, Brittles approaches Sudrow's Wells indirectly, arriving too late to save the outpost or to intervene as war parties take a shipment of repeating rifles. When they reach the station and discover the massacre, the commander's niece, Olivia Dandridge, says to Brittles: "You don't have to say it, Captain. I know all this is because of me; because I wanted to see the West; because I wasn't—I wasn't 'Army' enough to stay the winter."

Brittles replies with the now-famous line: "You're not quite 'Army' yet, miss ... or you'd know never to apologize ... it's a sign of weakness." She again tries to take the blame by responding, "Yes, but this was your last patrol and I'm to blame for it," leaving Wayne to shoulder the responsibility; "Only the man who commands can be blamed. It rests on me ... mission failure!"

"Never apologize" is Nathan Brittles's motto as a soldier, and he invokes it two other times earlier in the film. When Lieutenant Ross Pennell apologizes for planning a picnic with Olivia out by the waterfall, Brittles tells him, "Never apologize, mister. It's a sign of weakness." And when his aide, Sergeant

Quincannon says "Sorry," Brittles snaps, "Never apologize, mister, it's a sign of weakness." Quincannon mimics the phrase as Brittles says it, an indication that it is a familiar refrain from his captain. (And later, in a rush when Pennell again apologizes, Brittles simply replies, "Oh, shut up.")

Yet Nathan Brittles is not always intolerant of apologies. When Olivia apologizes for causing friction between his lieutenants, he does not chastise her. She says, "I'm sorry I made such a fool out of myself at the gate today." Brittles replies, "You made a fool out of a couple of army lieutenants." "Then I'm forgiven," she asks, and Brittles responds, "There's nothing to forgive." Later Lieutenant Flint Cohill apologizes to Olivia, saying, "The old man says don't ever apologize, it's a sign of weakness. But I'm sorry for everything I've said and done." And when Cohill and Pennell almost come to blows over Olivia, only to be interrupted and scolded by Brittles, they apologize to each other after he has left. "Sorry, Ross," says Cohill. And Pennell replies, "I'm sorry, Flint."

Although his own men ignore the advice, Nathan Brittles's saying has been handed down, proverb-like, as the folk wisdom that real men never apologize. In the process, its attribution and meaning have evolved as well. The sentiment is routinely attributed to John Wayne, the larger-than-life folk figure, not Nathan Brittles, the fictional cavalry officer. Brittles used it as shorthand for accepting responsibility for one's duty and actions. Over time, though, it has become associated with a certain type of masculinity that denies regret, empathy, and responsibility rather than the stoic who quietly bears them.

What Is "a Sign of Weakness"?

The John Wayne code can be seen in behavior of postwar presidents at crucial junctures—Kennedy after the Bay of Pigs, Nixon in his resignation, Carter during the hostage crisis, Reagan during the Iran-Contra scandal, George H. W. Bush saying that he'd never apologize for America. And some officials at the Pentagon, State Department, and White House intelligence community reportedly invoked *She Wore a Yellow Ribbon* during 2005 discussions in the Bush administration about apologizing for desecration of the Koran. The apology theme has worked the other way as well, with some Democratic presidents portrayed by opponents as too quick to apologize for the United States. We saw this with Woodrow Wilson in the Thomson-Urrutia Treaty and with candidate John F. Kennedy during the U2 incident. When Bill Clinton acknowledged it was wrong that "European-Americans benefited from the slave trade," he was criticized as "a flower child with gray hairs doing exactly what he did back in the '60s...apologizing for the actions of the United States." And in 2012, a supposed apology tour by Barack Obama was one of the themes of Mitt Romney's unsuccessful presidential campaign (Romney even titled his campaign biography *No Apologies*). This political framing suggests that for a president to apologize is to deny American exceptionalism—to deny that the United States is the John Wayne of nations.

What does John Wayne's motto really mean? We know that as a speech act, an apology is an expression of regret and acceptance of responsibility for a transgression. As a moral act, an apology is an acceptance of blame that seeks to restore moral balance to a relationship by naming the transgression and articulating regret and responsibility. And as a social act, an apology restores face to an offended party. If we consider "Never apologize, it's a sign of weakness" in that context, we can see its potential for semantic drift. What is the sign of weakness that one should never make: expressing regret, making excuses, accepting responsibility, restoring face to an offended party, or re-establishing a moral balance by one's words and actions?

Nathan Brittles is not averse to accepting responsibility or duty, nor is he blind to the moral balance he must preserve. He orders his men to shoot over the heads of the Indians and wins by stampeding the Indians' horses so they must walk away from the planned attack. And he understands the value of face as well. For Nathan Brittles, "Never apologize. It's a sign of weakness" means that one should never make excuses for actions. But he demonstrates through his actions that accepting blame or preserving another's face is not weakness. Talking too much about it is. The sentiment is part of the strong, silent stereotype, that actions speak more loudly than words. Brittles's motto actually should be *Excuses are signs of weakness*. But it is often taken to mean that error and empathy cannot be acknowledged.

We Think You Should Apologize

Apology also plays a significant role in the 1991 film *Thelma and Louise*, which blends a feminist critique of male behavior with the road film. Housewife Thelma Dickinson and her waitress friend Louise Sawyer set off on a two-day road trip in which they become crime victims and then outlaws, and finally drive into the Grand Canyon to their deaths. At the start of their trip, they stop at a cowboy bar where Thelma is attacked by a man she had been dancing with. Louise thwarts the attack, but then kills the attacker when he insults them. Thelma and Louise head west aiming for Mexico. Along the way,

Thelma has a sexual awakening with a hitchhiking robber on parole. When the robber steals Louise's savings, Thelma makes restitution by robbing a convenience store. Their crimes escalate and Thelma and Louise are cornered by police near the Grand Canyon where, like Butch Cassidy and the Sundance Kid, they choose death over capture.

As in *She Wore a Yellow Ribbon*, apology is a recurring theme. Thelma begins as a housewife who apologizes as a matter of course. She ends up demanding apologies at gunpoint. In an early scene, for example, we find Thelma cutting out recipes and talking with Louise on the phone. She finishes the call and shouts up the stairs to her overbearing husband Darryl. Hungover, Darryl chastises her, "Dammit, Thelma, don't holler like that!" Thelma responds with a routine apology and explanation: "I'm sorry, Doll, I just didn't want you to be late."

Later, after Thelma has robbed a convenience store, a highway patrolman stops the women for speeding. As he begins to check Louise's license plate number, Thelma puts a gun to his head and tells him to drop the radio.

THELMA: Officer, I am so sorry about this. Could you let go of that? I really, really apologize, but please put your hands on the steering wheel. See, if you get on that radio, you're gonna find out that we're wanted in two states and probably considered armed and dangerous, at least I am, then our whole plan would be shot to hell. Louise, take his gun.
LOUISE: I am really sorry about this.

Louise shoots the police radio and Thelma instructs the patrolman to get in the trunk. As they drive away, Thelma and then Louise each shout "Sorry!" to the trunk of the car. They recognize their transgression and apologize in language replete with the intensifiers (*so sorry; really, really apologize*) of stereotypical women's speech.

Finally, in the obligatory pyrotechnic scene, the women come roaring up to a tanker truck driver whom they have encountered several times before. Each time they passed on the highway, he made sexual gestures and catcalls from his cab. This time, Thelma and Louise pull over and the trucker stops as well. Thelma tells him to follow her off the highway onto a dirt road. He follows, parks, and expectantly walks up to Thelma and Louise's car with a shirt pocket full of condoms. Thelma tells him, "We think you have really bad manners," and says, "We think you should apologize." The trucker responds with expletives:

TRUCKER: I'm not apologizing for shit!
LOUISE: Say you're sorry.
TRUCKER: Fuck that.
LOUISE (pulls her gun): Say you're sorry or we'll make you fuckin' sorry.

Louise gives the trucker one final chance, which he declines with a further expletive. Then Thelma and Louise shoot the truck's tires and fire their guns into the tanker itself, blowing it up. Apologies are important, the film tells us, and the consequences of not apologizing—and of not treating women right—are serious.

Apology and Gender

In these two films, viewers are offered two gendered stereotypes: the John Wayne model of "never apologize" as a salient theme for males and Thelma and Louise as a counter-narrative of women coming more naturally to apology. Casual observers of culture take it as a given that males and females have different approaches to apology. Linguist Deborah Tannen sees this perception of apology as a problem. In her book *Working 9 to 5*, she writes:

> Many women are frequently told "Don't apologize" or "You're always apologizing." The reasons "apologizing" is seen as something they should stop doing is that it seems synonymous with putting oneself down. But for many women, and a fair number of men, saying "I'm sorry" isn't literally an apology; it is a ritual way of restoring balance to a conversation.

As we discussed earlier (in Chapter 4, when we looked at first lady Hillary Clinton's *sorry*s for her role on a health-care task force), saying "I'm sorry" does not mean admitting fault or accepting blame. It can be a routine way of taking another person's feelings into account—of showing the empathy that maintains relationships. Tannen's concern is that empathy can be misconstrued as apology. Our speaking styles vary. Some of us employ these non-literal *sorry*s frequently (the stereotypical female style) while others do not (the stereotypical male style). According to Tannen, those who are not accustomed to the high-empathy style may misunderstand speakers of that style as always apologizing. In other words, if you say "sorry" a lot to show empathy, listeners who share that style may understand what you are doing, but those who don't may misunderstand empathy as apology.

Being seen as apologizing too much can have social consequences. Susan Solovic, author of *The Girls' Guide to Power and Success* links apology with blame: "Ritual or not, when you say you are sorry all the time it becomes a form of self-deprecation." She adds, "By accepting blame even when you are not at fault, you are giving away your power and jeopardizing your professional image." As for men, Solovic generalizes that they "like to deflect blame whenever they can. So when you say you are sorry they are more than happy to oblige you and let you take the blame." In work and social situations, her reasoning goes, a speech style heavy with apologies will be to a woman's disadvantage every time.

Popular imagery reinforces the idea of apology as social weakness and self-deprecation. The premises of that argument are not beyond challenge, and the underlying cultural assumptions and logic suggest further questions. Do men really see apology as a weakness? (All men, many men, some men?) Are men usually willing to let women take the blame? Do only women see "sorry" as an expression of ritual empathy? Let's look briefly at some of the research which confirms a more complicated picture.

Linguist Janet Holmes, studying a corpus of 183 apologies made by New Zealanders, found that women used more apologies than men, giving about three-fourths of the apologies in Holmes's data. But she also found that the apologies were distributed in interesting ways. Women tended to apologize more to other women, particularly to female friends, than to men, while men apologized more to women than to other men. In fact, women received about three-fourths of the apologies (73 percent), and among the apologies given by men, about two-thirds of them were apologies to women. Holmes concludes that women use apologies (and compliments) more than men and she suggests that the sexes perceive apologies differently. Men see apologies as "face-threatening acts ... to be avoided where possible," and women see them "primarily as 'other-oriented' speech acts aimed at facilitating social harmony." Presumably, then (given the numbers Holmes found) men feel less loss of face in apologizing to women than to other men.

More recently, a University of Waterloo study asked students to keep a journal about offenses they had committed or experienced and apologies they had made or received. Men reported offering fewer apologies than women. But they also reported committing fewer offenses, and the ratio of offenses to apologies was the same for both sexes. The Waterloo researchers interpreted this to mean that men have a higher threshold for what counts as an offense and thus offer fewer apologies. A second Waterloo study asked subjects to rate both imaginary and remembered offenses. Men rated offenses as less severe than women did, again suggesting a threshold difference.

Such complexities suggest that the simple generalization that women apologize more than men is too coarse. But the stereotype has cultural traction more salient than facts or complexities. Images, assumptions, and stereotypes shape the ways in which we think and talk about apology. Gender stereotypes often reframe empathy as apology (think back to how Hillary Clinton's regrets were interpreted as an apology). Consider the following example: At the 2011 Australian Open, Belgian tennis star Kim Clijsters handed her opponent Dinara Safina a harsh defeat not usually seen in professional tennis. Clijsters shut the Russian out in two straight sets, 6–0, 6–0. Safina, the number one ranked player at the time, had just days before lost 6–0, 6–1 to Marion Bartoli. After winning, Clijsters expressed empathy for her opponent's slump saying, "I do feel bad for her." Clijsters noted that she was pleased when Safina briefly appeared to rally but was not going to give her any mercy. Clijsters was expressing a tough competitive spirit—no quarter given—along with empathy for an opponent's embarrassment.

Reuters headlined its story: "Kim Clijsters says sorry for Safina 'double bagel'" ("double bagel" is the tennis term for a 6–0, 6–0 result). Other sports commentators recycled the Reuters story with headlines that "Clijsters apologizes for handing Safina historic loss" and "Should Clijsters have apologized for winning mentality?" But of course, Clijsters was not apologizing—she was expressing empathy. "Feeling bad" for an opponent was quickly reimagined as saying "sorry" and then as apologizing.

Apology and Power

The theme of gender differences in apology and the recurring image of weakness (à la the John Wayne code) bring us to the issue of power. Do those with less social power and social status feel a greater need to apologize, regardless of gender? A CEO who is late to a meeting might not feel the need to apologize. But a staff member who arrives late is likely to apologize. A student who turns in a paper late might apologize, while a professor who returns work late will feel less need to do so. Power itself can be viewed in a fairly uncomplicated way. In many relationships, there is a person or group that holds authority and commands deference. For subordinates, failure to apologize challenges the power relationship and can lead to ostracism, loss of status, punishment, or other negative consequences. Janet Holmes noted this in her analysis of apologies in New Zealand, observing, "In general, one would expect that, where participants differ in power or status, apologies upwards to those of higher status or greater power would be more frequent than apologies downwards to those of lower status or less power." However, Robin Tolmach Lakoff, in her *Language and Power*, suggests that the speech of the more powerful is often constrained by its own gravitas. "Everything a powerful person says is taken seriously," Lakoff explains, "So the powerful person is powerless in this respect."

As an example, Lakoff reports on a 1983 phone conversation between Ronald Reagan and Coretta Scott King, the widow of Martin Luther King, Jr. Reagan had initially opposed the idea of a national holiday recognizing Martin Luther King, Jr., but when a bill passed with a veto-proof majority, he signed it into law. At a news conference in 1983 just prior to signing the bill, Reagan was asked by a reporter whether he agreed with Senator Jesse Helms of North Carolina that King had been "a communist sympathizer." Reagan dodged with a question of his own. "We'll know in about 35 years, won't we?" he said, referring to the date when FBI files would be unsealed. Reagan later called King's widow to ask her not to be offended by his comment. According to Mrs. King, Reagan characterized it as "a flippant remark made in response to what he considered a flippant question." Mrs. King, and the news media, reported Reagan's telephone call as an apology. Reagan's staff framed it as an explanation.

Lakoff suggests that there are two things going on in this example. Reagan's power made it important that he apologize, since he had used his authority to cast doubt on King's allegiances. In effect, Reagan sent a message diametrically opposed to the bill he was signing. But Reagan also wanted to save face by not apologizing publically and naming his offense, so he made a private, indirect, implied apology to Mrs. King. The power differential allowed him to name the offense as merely a flippant answer and to blend account and apology to suit his needs. Mrs. King was free to characterize Reagan's call as an apology, while his staff could characterize it as an explanation, bringing the matter to a conclusion.

Reagan was not the only president to experience this paradox of power. As president-elect, Barack Obama offered a flippant remark at his first post-election press conference. Asked about his meetings with former presidents, Obama said, "In terms of speaking to former presidents, I've spoken to all of them that are living." Recognizing the oddness of that sentence, he added, "I didn't want to get into a Nancy Reagan thing about, you know, doing any séances," referring to the former first lady's consultations with an astrologer. Obama called Mrs. Reagan later that day to, as his spokesperson characterized it, "apologize for the careless and off-handed remark he made." A few months later, Obama also apologized for an offhand reference to the mentally ill. Discussing his poor bowling score on *The Tonight Show*, he joked that "it was like the Special Olympics or something." After the show's taping, Obama telephoned the chairman of the Special Olympics, Tim Shriver, to apologize.

Reagan's predecessor, Jimmy Carter, apologized to another former first lady, Lady Bird Johnson. In a pre-election interview with *Playboy* magazine, Carter had tried to contrast himself with presidents Richard Nixon and Lyndon Johnson, saying, "I don't think I would ever take on the frame of mind that Nixon or Johnson did, lying, cheating, or distorting the truth." Mrs. Johnson told the media that she was "distressed, hurt, and perplexed" by the remark, and Carter called her to apologize.

As one commentator later put it, frankness can be a pitfall for candidates and new presidents who must learn that "every offhand word, every spontaneous remark, every comment informed more by emotion than calculation risks profound consequences." So, while the powerful may not need to apologize for some things, their prominence and social authority sometimes make their apologies all the more crucial. I offer two final examples of the use of power in apology, one a quiet apology of historical significance and the other public face-work between a sitting president and a news icon.

The Quiet Apology

Though the 1954 case of *Brown v. Board of Education* outlawed segregation in public schools, other forms of segregation remained—in bus and restaurant seating, barbershops and housing, public accommodations and university admissions, even churches and cemeteries. Segregation was not just shameful within the United States, it was also embarrassing internationally. In the 1950s, Africa and Asia were celebrating their independence and rising in importance as the nonaligned Third World. The United States and the Soviet Union were competing for the attention and allegiance of developing African and Asian nations led by Nehru, Nasser, Nkrumah, and Sukarno.

When Komla Agbeli Gbedemah, the Ghanaian finance minister, was refused service at a Howard Johnson's restaurant, the incident underscored the international consequences of segregation. How could the United States compete internationally for the allegiance of people of color when we discriminated against their diplomatic representatives? In early October 1957, Gbedemah, a close ally of President Kwame Nkrumah, was traveling with an assistant from New York to Washington. The two stopped for orange juice at a Howard Johnson's near Dover, Delaware. The waitress gave them the thirty cent juices to go, explaining that they could not sit in the restaurant. Gbedemah reportedly told the manager, "You can keep the orange juice and the change, but this is not the last you have heard of this."

The incident became headline news around the world. Noting that he had entertained Richard Nixon on the vice president's 1957 African tour, Gbedemah said, "If the Vice President of the U.S. can have a meal in my house when he is in Ghana, then I cannot understand why I must receive this treatment at a roadside restaurant in America." The US State Department apologized, calling the incident "exceptional and isolated." And on October 10, President Eisenhower, who had recently ordered federal troops to desegregate schools in Little Rock, Arkansas, invited Gbedemah to breakfast at the White House. There is no transcript of the meeting, but Gbedemah later told the press that the presidential breakfast made amends for the incident, adding, "I hope that the people of Ghana understand that there are very few people in the U.S. who act that way."

Eisenhower himself did not go on record or issue a statement. He allowed the invitation to imply the public apology, in effect making amends for the slight with a breakfast of his own. Americans and Africans could infer Eisenhower's values and attitudes from the breakfast meeting, which included a White House tour and an offer of help to find funding for the Akosombo Dam. The quiet, implied apology was an effective use of Eisenhower's authority both ethically and instrumentally. Eisenhower symbolically apologized on behalf of the country. And he did so without having his wording become the story, nationally or internationally.

Good Night, David

David Brinkley was a newscaster for fifty-four years—from 1943 to 1997. From the mid 1950s to 1970 he co-anchored *The Huntley–Brinkley Report* and, beginning in 1981, hosted *This Week with David Brinkley*. From 1970 onward, he was often a commentator on the news as well as a reporter, and he grew increasingly used to expressing his own views. Brinkley was often wry and incisive, but on election night in 1996, he made a series of open-mike slips. Brinkley commented on Bill Clinton's victory speech as "one of the worst things [he had] ever heard" and as "totally unnecessary."

That was just the beginning. As ABC wrapped up its election coverage at 12:30 a.m. eastern time, Peter Jennings complimented the seventy-six-year-old Brinkley on his long career. Brushing off the compliments, Brinkley praised his colleagues' creativity and contrasted them with Clinton. "Bill Clinton has none of it," Brinkley said, "He has not a creative bone in his body. Therefore, he's a bore, and will always be a bore." Brinkley added, "We all look forward with great pleasure to four more years of wonderful, inspirational speeches full of wit, poetry, music, love and affection, plus more goddamn nonsense." Jennings interjected, "You can't say that on the air, Mr. Brinkley." Brinkley replied, "Well, I'm not on the air." But he was.

Brinkley, who had previously arranged to tape an interview with Clinton for his Sunday show, realized his offense. Clinton might have canceled his appearance, but instead chose to go ahead with the interview with Brinkley. The program began with an apology by the newsman.

> Before we begin I am reminded of something I wrote years ago. "It may be impossible to be objective," I said, "But we must always be fair." Well, after a long day election day, and seven hours on the set, what I said at the end of our election night coverage was both impolite and unfair. And I'm sorry. I regret it.

Brinkley identifies his offense and characterizes it as wrong. And he says he is sorry. Clinton initially looked stern at the taping but immediately softened and accepted Brinkley's apology. His response was this:

> Well, thank you.... You know, let me just say, I accept that. I've said a lot of things myself late at night when I was tired. And you had really been through a rough day. I always believed you have to judge people on their whole work. And if you get judged based on your whole work, you come out way ahead.
>
> ...Beside that, one person loved it. The vice president was very happy when you said I was boring.... You've made me very popular in the White House.

Clinton accepts the apology, establishes a context, compliments Brinkley, and makes a joke. He uses his power—the power to accept or reject the apology—to assert values and repair a social breach. What happened between Brinkley and Clinton could happen to any of us. Like David Brinkley, we might make an ill-conceived comment at the end of a long day or in a moment of intemperate candor. Or, like Bill Clinton, we might learn of such a comment directed at us. If we are to repair the breach our actions cause, we must apologize. And if we are the victim of an offense, we are often wise to acknowledge and accept the apology and be a partner in restoring the balance. The ability to apologize, in the end, is one of the things that make us human. As we have seen, we are at our most human when we exercise the ability to apologize.

The Scope and Meaning of Apologies

The apologies in this book, from those of James Frey and Oprah Winfrey to Dwight Eisenhower's breakfast invitation and David Brinkley's concise regrets, show us the range and complexity of apology. We have seen the moral work of apology: how we name harms and express regret. We have seen too the social work of apologies, from serving as the simplest rituals for minor transgressions (such as calling someone the wrong name) to profound expressions aiming to repair historic offenses (such as lynching or internment). And we have seen how the purpose and motivation of an apology can range from calculatingly instrumental to heartfelt and sincere. The goal has not been to prescribe a single right way to apologize but rather to describe how apologies function, how they succeed, and how they fail. In part, this is because description must always precede prescription. In part too it is because each situation is unique and because different transgressions call for different apologies. And while it would be high-minded to prescribe sincerity over instrumentality, that prescription would not reflect either reality or utility. Instrumentality and sincerity are not, I believe, mutually exclusive. Some apologies arise both from an instrumental desire for closure and from an honest moral understanding and regret. We humans are, after all, complicated, sometimes contradictory beings.

Language has been a central concern of this book. The language of apologies both mirrors and enables these complicated purposes. Our language may be formal, literal, and performative ("I apologize for"), or it may imply apology by reporting on internal states ("I'm sorry for," "I regret"). But, of course, the set of words that sometimes implies apologies need not always do so. Sometimes *sorry* and *regret* just offer empathy or diplomacy. The language of apologies also includes requests for forgiveness and expressions of fault and responsibility which may, more weakly, be used to imply apologies, when we say "Forgive me," "I'm responsible," "I was wrong," or "My bad."

Beyond the choice of predicate, the resources of grammar—complement types; formal and informal style; and the use of passives, pronouns, abstract nouns, adverbs, and subordination—allow a range of explicitness in naming transgressions and directing apologies. A careful reading of grammatical choice and detail helps us understand speakers' attitudes toward their words. Is the language an expression of a sincere apology, an insincere one, a mere report of internal states, an excuse, or even an insult? The analysis of language ideally includes the larger context—a paragraph, letter, press release, interview, or dialogue—which allows for a fuller understanding of intentions and implications. Often, especially in corporate or state apologies, the sentence with the apologetic predicate is only the first part of the story, with explanations, future plans, and elaboration of the harm following.

An apology is not just a linguistic act but a larger social and moral process that can break down at different points. Over and over, we have seen how apologies succeed and how they fail, sometimes simultaneously. The most successful apologies effect a reconciliation in which the offended and offender reaffirm common values and mutual worth. Each party has some self-esteem or face restored—the offended by having their moral wrong acknowledged and the offender by re-entering the moral community. And when a grievance is resolved instrumentally, without reconciliation, there is only the agreement to put an end to the dispute. When apologies fail, however, neither reconciliation nor resolution occurs. The parties may have ignored the call to apologize, the apology itself may have been hopelessly flawed, or the offended party may have been unable or unwilling to accept the apology.

Why do we apologize? We apologize because we feel embarrassment, guilt, shame, and a desire to make things right. We want to take responsibility and reconcile. Of course, our self-interest competes with these feelings and nudges us to the instrumental side of apology—to reconcile without responsibility or embarrassment. We resist apologizing because we believe it signifies weakness or loss of status—"groveling" as Richard Nixon put it. We may even believe—or convince ourselves—that we have nothing to apologize for. Coming to terms with a transgression requires reflection, analysis, courage, and maturity. Some of us are simply more open psychologically than others to apology and reconciliation.

In the end, apologies are like the language that constitutes them. They may be casual or formal, public or private, sincere or manipulative, precise or vague. To attempt to apologize is to choose a language and a purpose for addressing an offense. We hear a call to apologize; name an offense; articulate remorse; and imbue the whole with a cultural, contextual meaning.

A Reader's Guide to Analyzing Apologies

AS I HAVE discussed the examples in this book with friends and colleagues, I have been struck by their recurring dismay at insincere public apologies. Such apologies are "self-serving," "cynical attempts to seek forgiveness," that "insult our intelligence," and "only encourage that sort of bad behavior if they are accepted." The answer to a culture of imperfect apology is not to stop apologizing. It is instead to reflect on the contexts and purposes of apologies (and speech acts more generally) that go beyond generalizations and stereotypes. If we can develop a sensitivity and curiosity about process, language, and purpose, we will all be able to recognize and respond to the different uses of apologetic language, whether instrumental or heartfelt, routinely social or historically significant.

How do you analyze an apology in practice? The preceding chapters have established some key questions—sets of questions, really—that can be used to think through what is going on in any apology. These questions are not meant as moral rules but rather as social and linguistic diagnostics with which to figure out an apology. The end of this book is thus a starting point for you as readers to a take your own fresh look at apologies.

1. What is the call to apologize? (Does it come from an internal realization or from external demands? Do all parties see the need to apologize in the same way?)
2. Is the harm named? (Has the apologizer confessed to violating a moral or social expectation? Is the confession just an anti-rhetorical assertion of the speaker's inner goodness and repentance, or is there a public chronicling of the transgressions?)
3. What is the language of the apology? (Is it explicit or implied? Is it conditional, ambiguous, or vague? How much work is done by conversational implicature? What grammatical devices shape the nuances of the apology? Is there enough information?)

4. Is the apology really an account? (Do clarification, explanation, and excuses overwhelm the language of apology?)
5. Does the apology lead to reconciliation? To resolution? Or to neither?
6. Is the apology felicitous? Is the apologizer in a position to make the apology?

Now here is an opportunity for you to give this a try.

We Will Meet Our Obligations

Ten days after the *Valdez* oil spill in 1989, Exxon published a three-paragraph "Open Letter to the Public" from Chairman and CEO Lawrence Rawl as a full-page ad in major newspapers.

> On March 24, in the early morning hours, a disastrous accident happened in the waters of Prince William Sound. By now you all know that our tanker, the Exxon *Valdez*, hit a submerged reef and lost 240,000 barrels of oil into waters of the Sound.
>
> We believe that Exxon has moved swiftly and competently to minimize the effect this oil will have on the environment, fish and other wildlife. Further, I hope you know that we have already committed several hundred people to work on the clean up. We will also meet our obligations to all those who have suffered damage from the spill.
>
> Finally, and most importantly, I want to tell you how sorry I am that this accident took place. We at Exxon are especially sympathetic to the residents of Valdez and the people of the state of Alaska. We cannot, of course, undo what has been done. But I can assure you that since March 24th, the accident has been receiving our full attention and will continue to do so.

Do you think the Exxon statement is an effective apology? What's present and what's missing? What considerations do you think went into the writing of the open letter?

We Will Make This Right

On April 20, 2010, the Deepwater Horizon, a mobile offshore drilling platform, exploded forty miles off the Louisiana coast. Eleven men were killed and seventeen others injured in the blast and its fiery aftermath. The blast also began a three-month long oil spill—the largest oil industry accident in history—releasing a total of nearly five million barrels of oil before it was successfully capped in mid-July.

BP offered its apologies through a television commercial launched on June 1. In the commercial, BP's CEO Tony Hayward was filmed with the Gulf Coast as a backdrop. He said,

> The gulf spill is a tragedy that never should have happened. I'm Tony Hayward. BP has taken full responsibility for cleaning up the spill in the gulf. We've helped organize the largest environmental response in this country's history. More than two million feet of boom, thirty planes, and over 1,300 boats are working to protect the shoreline. Where oil reaches the shore, thousands of people are ready to clean it up. We will honor all legitimate claims, and our clean-up efforts will not come at any cost to taxpayers.
>
> To those affected and your families, I am deeply sorry. The Gulf is home for thousands of BP's employees and we all feel the impact. To all the volunteers and for the strong support of the government, thank you. We know it is our responsibility to keep you informed. And do everything we can so this never happens again. We will get this done. We will make this right.

Do you think BP did a better job of apologizing than Exxon? What's different, if anything?

A Botched Joke

In the waning days of the 2006 midterm election, Senator John Kerry, the 2004 Democratic presidential candidate, was talking about the importance of education and aiming to get in a dig at his old rival George W. Bush. Kerry said, "If you make the most of it, you study hard, you do your homework and you make an effort to be smart, you can do well. And if you don't, you get stuck in Iraq." It sounded like he was insulting American troops. The text of his remarks, released by his office the following day, read, "I can't overstress the importance of a great education. Do you know where you end up if you don't study, if you aren't smart, if you're intellectually lazy? You end up getting us stuck in a war in Iraq. Just ask President Bush." Kerry misspoke his prepared line. Initially he refused to apologize, arguing that he had simply misspoken and that his intent was being distorted for political ends. But soon, he issued a written statement saying:

I sincerely regret that my words were misinterpreted to wrongly imply anything negative about those in uniform and I personally apologize to any service member, family member or American who was offended.

Is Kerry's apology effective? Should he have apologized?

More Than Enough Responsibility

In early 1967, Senator Robert Kennedy was struggling with Vietnam. As the attorney general in his brother's administration, and for a time in the Johnson administration, Kennedy had been involved in many of the early decisions about the war. He was personally close to Robert McNamara and to Averell Harriman, the US ambassador-at-large and later chief negotiator at the Paris peace talks. But for some time he had been convinced that a negotiated settlement was the only way to end the war. By late February, he had made up his mind to call for a halt to the bombing, and on March 3, Kennedy addressed the Senate.

Kennedy opened his speech by noting that he did not favor unilateral withdrawal from Vietnam and that the United States should remain in Vietnam until it had fulfilled its commitments. But, he suggested, the United States should "test the sincerity" of the Soviets and others by halting the bombing campaign and pursuing negotiations. In his speech, he said:

Three presidents have taken action in Vietnam. As one who was involved in many of those decisions, I can testify that if fault is to be found or responsibility assessed, there is more than enough to go around for all—including myself.

Was Senator Kennedy apologizing?

References

INTRODUCTION

What follows is a listing by chapter and section of the works that have been quoted or paraphrased in the text. URLs have been verified as of January 5, 2013.

1. James Frey's note to readers appeared as a letter in the *New York Times*, February 1, 2006. For Winfrey's interviews with Frey, see "James Frey and the *A Million Little Pieces Controversy*" and "James Frey Five Years Later," http://www.oprah.com/showinfo/James-Frey-and-the-A-Million-Little-Pieces-Controversy and http://www.oprah.com/oprahshow/James-Frey-Five-Years-Later-Part-1.

CHAPTER 1

1. Harry Truman's apology to General Cates can be found at *The American Presidency Project* website, http://www.presidency.ucsb.edu/ws/?pid=13607. Original media coverage appeared in the *New York Times* in September 1950 (William S. White, "President Likens 'Propaganda' of Marines to Stalin Set-Up," September 5, 1; Paul Kennedy, "Truman Apology to Marines: Says He Regrets Words," September 7, 1; Paul Kennedy, "President Talks the Marines into Forgiveness and Cheers," September 8, 1). The incident is reviewed in Franklin D. Mitchell's "An Act of Presidential Indiscretion: Harry S. Truman, Congressman McDonough, and The Marine Corps Incident of 1950," *Presidential Studies Quarterly* (1981): 565–575.

2. For background on Karla Faye Tucker's crime, punishment, and apology, see Beverly Lowry's article "The Good Bad Girl," *New Yorker*, February 9, 1998, 60–77, and Lowry's later book *Crossed Over: A Murder, A Memoir* (New York: Vintage, 1992). For media coverage, see Sam Howe Verhovek, "Texas, in First Time in 135 Years, Is Set To Execute Woman," *New York Times*, February 3, 1998, A1, and Larry King, *Karla Faye Tucker: Live from Death Row*, CNN Transcript # 98011400V22, 1998. The remarks by Tucker's lawyer are cited in Mary Sigler, "Mercy, Clemency, and the

Case of Karla Faye Tucker," *Ohio State Journal of Criminal Law* 4, no. 455 (2007). Pat Robertson's comments appeared as "Transcript of Speech on Religion's Role in the Administration of the Death Penalty," *William & Mary Bill of Rights Journal* 9, no. 215 (2000).

3. Erving Goffman's approach was articulated in his 1959 book *The Presentation of Self in Everyday Life* (New York: Anchor Books, 1959). His approach to apologies is further developed in the section "On Face Work" *Interaction Ritual: Essays on Face-to-Face Behavior* (New York: Anchor Books, 1967), 5–12, and "Remedial Interchanges," *Relations in Public: Microstudies of the Public Order* (New York: Basic Books, 1971), 112–113, 144.

4. The account of John McCain's POW years appeared first in "How the POW's Fought Back," *U.S. News & World Report*, May 14, 1973, 46 52, 110–115, and is retold in his *Faith of My Fathers* (New York: Random House, 1998). See also Dan Nowicki and Bill Muller, "McCain Profile: Prisoner of War," *The Arizona Republic*, March 1, 2007, http://www.azcentral.com/news/election/mccain/articles/2007/03/0 1/20070301mccainbio-chapter3.html.

5. The quotes from Lionel Trilling are from *Sincerity and Authenticity* (Cambridge, MA: Harvard University Press, 1972), 2, 10–11.

6. The quote from Nicholas Tavuchis's book *Mea Culpa: A Sociology of Apology and Reconciliation* (Stanford, CA: Stanford University Press, 1991) 7, 12, 27 and 36. Quotes from Nick Smith, *I Was Wrong: On the Meanings of Apologies* (Cambridge: Cambridge University Press, 2008), 113, 142–145, and 63–65.

7. Bill Clinton's apology for the Tuskegee study can be found at http://clinton4. nara.gov/textonly/New/Remarks/Fri/19970516-898.html. For a summary of press coverage, see "News Coverage of the Presidential Apology" at Tuskegee's web site: http://www.tuskegee.edu/Global/story.asp?S=1211608.

8. Samuel Sewall's story is documented in Richard Francis, *Judge Sewall's Apology* (New York: HarperCollins, 2005) and Mary Adams Hilmer, "The Other Diary of Samuel Sewall," *The New England Quarterly* 55, no. 3 (September 1982): 354–365.

9. "Apology for Margaret," *Time*, January 11, 1943, 70–71.

10. "Dear Tom Jefferson," *Harford Courant*, April 13, 1993, http://articles.courant. com/1993-04-13/news/0000103420_1_feared-courant-church-and-state.

CHAPTER 2

1. The Wilson-Harvey affair is discussed at length by Alexander George and Juliette George, *Woodrow Wilson and Colonel House: A Personality Study* (New York: Dover, 1956), 96–98 and Josephy Tumulty, *Woodrow Wilson as I Knew Him* (Literary Digest, 1921), 82–93. For news reports of the time, see the *New York Times* articles "Wilson Ashamed He Tells Harvey," January 31, 1912; "'Marse Henry' Disgusted," February 1, 1912; and "Colonel Harvey Urges Election of Hughes," October 1, 1916.

2. Nicholas Tavuchis's explanation of the moral syllogism of *call-apology-forgiveness* can be found on page 20 of *Mea Culpa*; his critique of Goffman is from note 41, pp. 136–38. Tavuchis seems to be using *syllogism* here to mean a process of reasoning consisting of three parts, not in the sense of formal logic where it refers to a pair of premises supporting a conclusion.

3. News coverage of Joe Biden's apology included Adam Nagourney, "Biden Unwraps His Bid for '08 With an Oops!" *New York Times*, January 31, 2007, A1; Fredreka Schouten, "Biden Burned by 'Clean' Language," *USA Today*, January 31, 2007; and an MSNBC report titled "Sen. Biden Apologizes for Remarks on Obama: White House Hopeful's Racially Tinged Comment Stirs Controversy." For Eugene Robinson's view, see "An Inarticulate Kickoff," *Washington Post*, February 2, 2007, A15. Biden's earlier comment about Indian-Americans is reported in "Biden Explains Indian-American Remarks," MSNBC, http://www.msnbc.msn.com/id/13757367/. Biden boasting about his support among Indian-Americans on the C-SPAN program "The Road to the White House," said, "I've had a great relationship. In Delaware, the largest growth in population is Indian-Americans moving from India. You cannot go to a 7-Eleven or a Dunkin' Donuts unless you have a slight Indian accent. I'm not joking." In the MSNBC interview, Biden said his comment "was meant as a compliment."

4. Materials related to Mel Gibson's arrest and apologies can be found at the Anti-Defamation League website, www.adl.org/: "ADL Says Mel Gibson's Anti-Semitic Tirade Reveals His True Self; Actor's Apology 'Not Good Enough,'" July 30, 2006; "Mel Gibson's Apology to the Jewish Community," August 1, 2006; "ADL Welcomes Mel Gibson's Apology to the Jewish Community," August 1, 2006. Media coverage includes Allison Hope Weiner, "Mel Gibson Apologizes for Tirade after Arrest," *New York Times*, July 30, 2006.

5. On George Wallace's apologies, see Stephen Lesher, *George Wallace: American Populist* (Reading, MA: Addison Wesley, 1994); Dan Carter, *The Politics of Rage: George Wallace, the Origins of the New Conservatism, and the Transformation of American Politics* (New York: Simon & Schuster, 1995); Colman McCarthy, "George Wallace–From the Heart," *Washington Post*, March 17, 1995, A27; Rick Bragg, "Emotional March Gains a Repentant Wallace," *New York Times*, March 11, 1995, 2; and "Wallace Gives Apology and Award to Black Woman He Tried to Keep Out of Univ. of Alabama," *Jet*, October 28, 1997, 6.

6. Jeff Zeleny, "Kerrey Apologizes to Obama," *New York Times*, The Caucus [blog], December 20, 2007.

7. Sources for the Tiger Woods-Fuzzy Zoeller controversy are "Zoeller Apologizes for Woods Comments," *New York Times*, April 22, 1997, B12; "Apology Accepted by Woods," *New York Times*, April 25, 1997, B9; "Golfer says Comments about Woods Misconstrued," CNN.com, April 21, 1997; "Kmart Drops Zoeller," *New York Times*, April 23, 1997, B8; Joe Drape, "Woods Has Empathy for Zoeller And a Rebuke for the President," *New York Times*, May 14, 1997, B11; and Joe Drape, "Woods Meets

Zoeller For Lunch," *New York Times*, May 21, 1997, B13. For Aaron Lazare's discussion, see *On Apology* (New York: Oxford University Press, 2004), 94–96.

8. The Lincoln-Shields correspondence appears in Herbert Mitgang, *Abraham Lincoln: A Press Portrait* (New York: Fordham University Press, 2000), 39. During the Civil War, Lincoln appointed Shields a Union general.

CHAPTER 3

1. For coverage of George H. W. Bush's Nightline interview, see Merrill Hartson, "By George, Is it Ted or Dan?" *Lawrence Journal-World*, June 10, 1988, 3C, and Maureen Dowd, "Bush Traces How Yale Differs from Harvard," *New York Times*, June 11, 1988, 10.

2. The "macaca" incident is reported in Tim Craig and Michael D. Shear, "Allen Quip Provokes Outrage, Apology: Name Insults Webb Volunteer," *Washington Post*, August 15, 2006, A1. For the Bunning comment, see Ariane de Vogue, " 'I Am Alive': Justice Ginsburg Fires Back at Sen. Bunning's Death Prediction," ABC News, March 24, 2010, http://abcnews.go.com/Politics/Supreme_Court/justice-r uth-bader-ginsburg-takes-dig-senator-bunning/story?id=10188167. Mike Huckabee's apology is reported in Sarah Wheaton, "Huckabee Jokes about Obama Ducking Gunfire," *New York Times*, The Caucus [blog], May 16, 2008.

3. For an exposition of speech acts, see J. L. Austin's *How To Do Things with Words* (Cambridge, MA: Harvard University Press, 1962), especially pages 14–15, 45–47 and 53–55. Austin calls *apologize* an "explicit performative." An extended discussion of the verb *promise* appears in John Searle's 1969 book *Speech Acts* (pp. 54–71) and his later articles "A Taxonomy of Illocutionary Acts," *Language, Mind and Knowledge* edited by Keith Gunderson (Minneapolis: University of Minnesota Press, 1975), 344–369 and "Indirect Speech Acts," *Syntax and Semantics, 3: Speech Acts*, ed. Peter Cole and Jerry L. Morgan (New York: Academic Press, 1975, 59–82). Linguist Jenny Thomas, in her book *Meaning in Interaction* (London: Longman, 1995), 99ff, builds out Searle's approach this way with the four criteria mentioned in the text.

4. H. Paul Grice's theory of conversational implicature was developed in the paper "Logic and Conversation," *Speech Acts*, ed. Peter Cole and Jerry L. Morgan (New York: Academic Press, 1975), 41–58.

5. The Amazon-Orwell situation is described in Deborah Gage, "Amazon Apologizes for Kindle Flap," *InformationWeek*, July 24, 2009, and Thomas Claburn, "Amazon Settles Kindle Deletion Lawsuit For $150,000," *InformationWeek*, October 2, 2009.

6. The McDonald's apology is described in "McDonald's to Settle Suits on Beef Tallow in French Fries," *New York Times*, March 9, 2002, 11; Simon Davis, "McDonald's Admits Using Beef Fat for 'Vegetarian' French Fries," *The Telegraph*, May 25, 2001, /www.telegraph.co.uk/news/worldnews/asia/india/1331625/McDonalds-admits-u sing-beef-fat-for-vegetarian-french-fries.html. See also a 2006 case study by Alex

van der Zwart and Rob van Tulder of Erasmus University titled *Where's The Beef?* *It's In Your Fries!* (H. B. Bharti and Vegetarian Legal Action Network (VLAN) versus Mcdonald's, www.ib-sm.com/CaseMcDonalds.pdf).

7. For the "Text of Father Coughlin's Address to Townsendites," see the *New York Times*, July 17, 1936, 6. For his apology, see "Coughlin Apology Made to Roosevelt," *New York Times*, July 24, 1953, 1. For background on Coughlin, see "Coughlin Silenced," *Time*, October 18, 1937, 64, and Donald Warren, *Radio Priest: Charles Coughlin, the Father of Hate Radio* (New York: Free Press, 1996).

8. Bill Meyer, "Captain of Exxon Valdez Offers 'Heartfelt Apology' for '89 Oil Spill in Alaska's Prince William Sound," *Cleveland Plain Dealer*, March 5, 2009. Writer Sharon Bushell interviewed Hazelwood, who argued that he was wrongly blamed in *The Spill: Personal Stories from the Exxon Valdez Disaster* (Fairbanks, AK: Epicenter Press, 2009), 282.

9. Sharon Otterman and Robery Mackey, "Bin Laden's Reading List for Americans," *New York Times*, The Lede [blog], September 14, 2009; Eric Pfeiffer, "Carter Apologizes for 'Stupid' Book Passage," *Washington Times*, January 25, 2007, A12; and "Jimmy Carter Apologizes to Jewish Community," *Chicago Sun-Times*, December 24, 2009.

10. The NRA verbiage is from a "special report" titled "The Final War Has Begun" in the June 1994 edition of *The American Rifleman*, written by Wayne R. LaPierre, Jr., and cited in Fox Butterfield, "Terror In Oklahoma: Echoes Of The N.R.A.," *New York Times*, May 8, 1995, A17. According to the *Times*, the portrayal of the ATF as fascists goes back to a 1981 NRA-produced documentary called "It Can Happen Here." LaPierre's apology is cited in Richard Keil, "NRA Apologizes for 'Jack Boot' Letter," *Seattle Times*, May 18, 1995, and the quote from Fraternal Order of Police president Dewey Stokes is from Michael Kramer, "That Was No Apology," *Time*, May 29, 1995, 23.

CHAPTER 4

1. Hillary Clinton's lunch with journalists was reported in Michael Sneed, "Hillary 'Sorry' About Health Care," *Chicago Sun Times*, January 10, 1995, 1; *The Arkansas Democrat-Gazette*, "First Lady Says She's Sorry, But Insists She Won't Hide For Next Years," January 10, 1995, A6; and Marian Burros, "Hillary Clinton Asks Help in Finding a Softer Image," *New York Times*, January 10, 1995, A15. Deborah Tannen's discussion of Clinton's comments occurred in the *New York Times Magazine* ("I'm Sorry, I Won't Apologize," July 21, 1996, 34). Tannen saw Clinton's expression as "clearly…an expression of regret" that was mistaken for an apology, but as I note, Clinton's language blends regret and apology. The comment "That is the woman trying to take all the burdens on herself" was from Joan Bray, a Missouri state representative cited in the *St. Louis Post-Dispatch* (Christine Bertelson, "Some Helpful Hints on the Image Thing," January 12, 1995, 1B).

2. Martha Stewart's apology is reported in Brooke A. Masters, "Martha Stewart Sentenced to 5 Months in Prison," *Washington Post*, July 16, 2004.

3. "Prince Harry Apologizes for Nazi Costume," *New York Times*, January 13, 2005, A12.

4. Dan Rather's apology appeared as a CBS News story: http://www.cbsnews.com/stories/2004/09/20/politics/main644546.shtml. The accompanying CBS statement can be found at http://www.usatoday.com/news/politicselections/nation/president/2004-09-21-cover-guard_x.htm, and the *Report of the Independent Review Panel* conducted by Dick Thornburgh and Louis D. Boccardi is available at www.cbsnews.com/htdocs/pdf/complete_report/CBS_Report.pdf.

5. The apologies by John Yates and Tiger Woods are reported in Cherry Wilson, "John Yates Expresses 'Massive Regret' over Phone Hacking Investigation," *The Guardian*, July 9, 2011, and "Injured Woods Ruled out of British Open," *CNN World Sports*, July 5, 2011.

6. Eisenhower's press statement was reported by William J. Jorden, "President Voices Regret at Ruling," *New York Times*, August 20, 1960, 1. John F. Kennedy's "Report to the Nation on the Situation at the University of Mississippi, September 30, 1962," is available at the American Presidency Project website: http://www.presidency.ucsb.edu/ws/?pid=8915.

7. The language of the initial Thomson-Urrutia treaty was reported in "Planning to Bare Whole Panama Deal," *New York Times*, June 19, 1914, 3. The quotes from Teddy Roosevelt, Senator George Perkins, and the *Times* editors are from "Quotes Roosevelt in Fighting Treaty," *New York Times*, April 14, 1921, 14; "To Fight Adoption of Colombia Treaty," *New York Times*, April 19, 1914, 1; and "Colombia's Treaty," *New York Times*, June 13, 1914. The comments from James T. Du Bois, Woodrow Wilson, and Senator Gilbert Hitchcock were also from the *New York Times*: "Tells Roosevelt Treaty is Right," June 26, 1914; "Say Regret Isn't Apology," April 18, 1914, 1; and "Sincere 'Regret' in Colombia Treaty," April 18, 1914, 1.

8. The negotiations between Asa Philip Randolph and the Roosevelt administration are discussed in Jervis Anderson's *A. Philip Randolph: A Biographical Portrait* (Berkeley: University of California Press, 1973). The War Department statement on segregation and the telegram sent by Randolph, White, and Hill were printed in "White House Blesses Jim Crow," *The Crisis*, November 1940, 350–351, 357, as was Roosevelt's response: "Roosevelt Regrets that Army Policy was 'Misinterpreted,'" *The Crisis*, December 1940, 390. In their response, Randolph, White, and Hill noted that Roosevelt's letter was issued on the same day that the Senate killed an anti-lynching bill.

9. John McCain's statement was reported in Ann Gerhart and Annie Groer, "The Reliable Source," *Washington Post*, June 12, 1998, B3.

10. Ben Zimmer's discussion is at the *Visual Thesaurus* site: http://www.visualthesaurus.com/cm/wordroutes/2327/.

11. On the Kent State shootings, see "Kent State: In Memory of 4 Slain, 1970," *New York Times*, May 5, 1990, 11; "Ohio Approves $675,000 to Settle Suits in 1970 Kent State Shootings; "Governor Rhodes and 27 National Guardsmen Offer Their Regrets for Deaths of 4 and Injuries to 9," *New York Times*, January 5, 1979, A12; and "Nation: A Late Apology," *Time*, January 15, 1979, 12.

12. Jane Fonda's apologies appear in her biography *My Life So Far* (New York: Random House, 2005) and at The Pacifica Radio/UC Berkeley Social Activism Sound Recording Project: Anti-Vietnam War Protests in the San Francisco Bay Area & Beyond, available at http://www.lib.berkeley.edu/MRC/pacifica-viet.html#fonda88. Her apologies were discussed in "Top 10 Celebrity Protesters," *Time*, March 19, 2012, http://www.time.com/time/specials/packages/article/0,28804,2109301_2109302_2109305,00.html; in Dexter Lehtinen's "Fonda's Pseudo-Apology," *National Review Online*, September 22, 2009, http://www.cbsnews.com/2100-215_162-692015.html; and in "Did Jane Fonda Really Apologize for Vietnam? Oliver North Weighs In," www.foxnews.com/story/0,2933,152763,00.html.

13. For the description of the experiments, see Gretchen Reynolds, "The Stuttering Doctor's 'Monster Study,'" *New York Times Magazine*, March 16, 2003, 36–39, 83–84. For Mary Tudor's reflections, see Jim Dyer, "Ethics and Orphans: 'The Monster Study,'" *San Jose Mercury News*, June 10–11, 2001, A1. The "Statement by Dr. David Skorton, University of Iowa Vice President for Research and Interim Vice President for University Relations" was a press release issued by the University of Iowa on June 13, 2001.

CHAPTER 5

1. Jimmy Swaggart's February 21, 1988, apology sermon is at AmericanRhetoric.com's Online Speech Bank: http://www.americanrhetoric.com/speeches/jswaggarta-pologysermon.html. The story of his downfall is summarized by David Tell in his article "Jimmy Swaggart's Secular Confession," *Rhetoric Society Quarterly* 39, no. 2 (April 2009): 124–146, and in Richard N. Ostling, Laura Claverie, and Barbara Dolan, "Religion: Now It's Jimmy's Turn," *Time*, March 7, 1988, 46. Tell suggests a broader strategy of silence on the part of Swaggart and the Assembly of God leadership.

2. Quotes from David Tell are from "Jimmy Swaggart's Secular Confession." Quotes from James O'Donnell are from "An Introduction to Augustine's Confessions," which can be found at http://www9.georgetown.edu/faculty/jod/augustine/introconf.html. O'Donnell also notes that writing the *Confessions* seems to have resolved Augustine's period of writer's block. The quotes from Rousseau ("to say what I have to say would…") are from the Appendix to *The Confessions of J. J. Rousseau*, trans. S. W. Orson (London: Aldus Society, 1903), 647 [Penn State University Electronic Edition, 2001]. It is worth noting that Rousseau's view of self-disclosure

was consistent with the views in his *Essay on the Origins of Language*. There Rousseau portrayed language as originating in cries of nature and evolving into speech and writing: in its drift toward more conventional and less spontaneous forms, language gains precision but sacrifices expressivity. The coda to Swaggart's tale and his quote, "The Lord told me it's flat none of your business," are from "Scandals: No Apologies This Time," *Time*, October 28, 1991, 35.

3. Clinton's remarks are from "Testing of a President: In His Own Words; Last Night's Address," *New York Times*, August 18, 1998, A12; "Testing of a President;President Clinton's Address at the National Prayer Breakfast," *New York Times*, September 12, 1998, A12; "Clinton's Rose Garden Statement," *Washington Post*, December 11, 1998, online; John F. Harris, "President Responds with Simple Apology," *Washington Post*, February 13, 1999, A1. For additional discussion, see Keith Hearit's *Crisis Management by Apology* (Mahwah, NJ: Lawrence Erlbaum, 2006), 85–95.

4. Mark Sanford's disappearance and apology are discussed in "Transcript: Mark Sanford's Press Briefing" and "Mysteries Remain after Governor Admits an Affair," both from *New York Times*, June 24, 2009, online, and in Gina Smith, "Sanford Met in Atlanta after Returning from South America," *The State*, June 24, 2006, available at http://www.thestate.com/2009/06/24/838823/sanford-met-in-atlanta-after-returning.html#storylink=cpy.

5. Alexander Hamilton's apology was reprinted in "Foundering Father: A 1797 Confession of Adultery," *Harper's*, November 1, 1998, 51–58.

6. The quotes from Augustine are from *The Confessions of St. Augustine* (New York: Dover, 2002), Book 2, Ch III, pp. 22–23, and Book 3, Ch 1, p. 31.

7. The quotes from Rousseau are from *The Confessions of J. J. Rousseau*, trans. S. W. Orson (London: Aldus Society, 1903), 9–10, 84 [Penn State University Electronic Edition, 2001].

8. Quotes from McNamara's memoir are from *In Retrospect–The Tragedy and Lessons of Vietnam* (New York: Times Books, 1995). The description of McNamara is from "The Particular Tragedy of Robert McNamara," *Time*, July 5, 1971, 23–24. Robert Strassfeld's comments are from "Robert McNamara and the Art and Law of Confession: 'A Simple Desultory Philippic (or How I was Robert McNamara'd into Submission),'" *Duke Law Journal* 47, no. 491 (1997). Quotes from *The Fog of War* are from "The Fog of War: Transcript," http://www.errolmorris.com/film/fow_transcript.html.

CHAPTER 6

1. Packwood's statement, "If any of my comments or actions have indeed been unwelcome," appeared in Florence Graves and Charles Shepard, "Packwood Accused of Sexual Advances," *Washington Post*, November 22, 1992, 1. His November 27 apology ("I never consciously intended to offend any women. I, therefore, offer my deepest apologies") is reported in *Senate Report 352-6, 104th Cong., 1st Sess. Documents*

Related to the Investigation of Senator Robert Packwood (1995), volume 3, 662. Packwood's December 10 news conference ("I am here today to take full responsibility for my conduct") and other quotes, including the question and answer session, are available through the Federal News Service, FNS Regular Package Broadcast Interview, 1993, December 10, *Federal News Service* 202-347-1400. It was discussed in Martin Tolchin, "Packwood Offers Apology without Saying for What," *New York Times*, December 11, 1992, A24.

2. B. L. Ware and Wil A. Linkugel's article, "They Spoke in Defense of Themselves: On the Generic Criticism of Apologia," appeared in the *Quarterly Journal of Speech* in 1973. The quote "succeeds in restructuring" is from Erving Goffman's discussion of accounts in "Remedial Work," *Relations in Public: Microstudies of the Public Order* (New York: Harper & Row, 1971), 245. William Benoit's typology is discussed in *Accounts, Excuses, Apologies: A Theory of Image Restoration Discourse* (Albany: State University of New York Press, 1995). See especially pages 63–95. The quote from Keith Hearit ("present a compelling counter description") is from his *Crisis Management by Apology* (Mahwah, NJ: Lawrence Erlbaum, 2005), 115.

3. Packwood's resignation speech was excerpted in "The Packwood Case; Excerpts from Packwood's Statement of Resignation," *New York Times*, September 8, 1995, 16. For more background see Mark Kirchmeier, *Packwood: The Public and Private Life from Acclaim to Outrage* (New York: HarperCollins West, 1995).

4. Materials on Stephen Ambrose can be found in Fred Barnes, "Stephen Ambrose, Copycat," *Weekly Standard*, January 14, 2002, 27, posted online January 4; Fred Barnes, "Ambrose Apologizes," posted online January 6, 2002, http://www.weeklystandard.com/Content/Public/Articles/000/000/000/752brzuv.asp, and at George Mason University's *History News Network*, "How the Ambrose Story Developed," April 2010 update, http://hnn.us/articles/504.html, which contains an extensive summary and links to documents. George McGovern's letter appeared in the January 28, 2002, *New York Times*, 14; Ambrose's attack on journalist Mark Lewis, who had published several articles about Ambrose's writing, was a letter to the editor in the February 6, 2002, *Wall Street Journal*, A19. And his *Los Angeles Times* interview appeared in Megan K. Stack, "For Historian Ambrose, It's Time for a 'Love Song,'" May 11, 2002, 1, 22. Death did not entirely insulate Ambrose. In 2010, Ambrose's claims to have been contacted by Dwight Eisenhower to be his biographer and to have spent hundreds of hours interviewing Eisenhower were called into question by the deputy director of the Eisenhower library who found documents suggesting that it was Ambrose who approached Eisenhower and that the two only spent about five hours together.

5. Doris Kearns Goodwin's account, "How I Caused That Story," appeared in *Time*, January 27, 2002, 69. The original charges appeared in Bo Crader, "A Historian and Her Sources," *Weekly Standard*, January 28, 2002, 12. The Harvard Crimson editorial, "The Consequence of Plagiarism," March 11, 2002, can be found at http://www.thecrimson.com/article/2002/3/11/the-consequence-of-plagiarism-it-seems/. The

letter from the fourteen historians was published in the *New York Times* of October 23, 2003, A18. The historians were Arthur Schlesinger, Jr., John M. Blum, Gabor Borritt, Douglas Brinkley, Catherine Clinton, Robert Dallek, John Diggins, John Gable, David Halberstam, Walter Isaacson, Don Miller, Evan Thomas, Richard Wade, and Sean Wilentz. For more details, see "How the Goodwin Story Developed," George Mason University's *History News Network*, July 13, 2006, http://hnn. us/articles/590.html. For an extended discussion of Goodwin's repair strategy, see Keith Hearit's *Crisis Management by Apology* (Mahwah, NJ: Lawrence Erlbaum, 2006), 105–120.

6. Maureen Dowd's column was called "Cheney, Master of Pain," *New York Times*, May 16, 2009, WK13; Josh Marshall's May 14 blog post, "Bubbling," can be found at *Talking Points Memo*, http://talkingpointsmemo.com/archives/2009/05/bub-bling.php. Marshall had blogged: "More and more the timeline is raising the question of why, if the torture was to prevent terrorist attacks, it seemed to happen mainly during the period when **we were** looking for what was essentially political information to justify the invasion of Iraq." The paragraph that originally appeared in Dowd's column read: "More and more the timeline is raising the question of why, if the torture was to prevent terrorist attacks, it seemed to happen mainly during the period when **the Bush crowd was** looking for what was essentially political information to justify the invasion of Iraq." As Marshall in his response to Dowd said, "Whatever the mechanics of how it happened, I never thought it was intentional" ("Very Briefly on Dowd," *Talking Points Memo*, May 19, 2009). The paragraph in question is now quoted on the *Times* site prefaced by the quote-introducing sentence, "Josh Marshall said in his blog." The quote from the *Times*'s public editor is from Clark Hoyt, "The Writers Make News. Unfortunately," *New York Times*, May 24, 2009, WK8. Jack Shafer's comment is from "Maureen Dowd's Next Step," *Slate.com*, May 18, 2009. For a summary, see Jonathan Bailey, "The Maureen Dowd Plagiarism Scandal," *Plagiarism Today*, May 18, 2009, http://www.plagiarismtoday. com/2009/05/18/the-maureen-dowd-plagiarism-scandal/, and John McQuaid, "Say It Ain't So, MoDo," *Huffington Post*, May 18, 2009, http://www.huffingtonpost. com/john-mcquaid/say-it-aint-so-modo_b_204649.html.

7. The quote ("We did not—repeat, did not—trade weapons or anything else for hostages, nor will we.") is from Robert Pear, "The Reagan White House; Reagan and Panel Differ on Some Points," *New York Times*, March 5, 1987, 19, and the quotes from Reagan's speech are from "The Reagan White House; Transcript of Reagan's Speech," *New York Times*, March 5, 1987, 18.

8. Lucille Ball's testimony is from *Investigation of Communist Activities in the Los Angeles Area*, part 7 of the Hearings of House Committee on Un-American Activities, 83rd Congress, 1st sess., September 4, 1953, 2561–2571, http://www.archive. org/stream/investigationofco7unit/investigationofco7unit_djvu.txt. The quote from Walter Winchell is from Stefan Kanfer, *Ball of Fire: The Tumultuous Life and Comic Art of Lucille Ball* (New York: Knopf, 2004), 168.

9. Henry Ford's letter, published on July 8, 1927, appears in Neil Baldwin's *Henry Ford and the Jews: The Mass Production of Hate* (New York: Public Affairs Press, 2002), 238–240. See also Max Wallace, *The American Axis* (New York: Macmillan, 2004), 29–34, and Victoria Woeste, *Henry Ford's War on Jews and the Legal Battle against Hate Speech* (Stanford, CA: Stanford University Press, 2012), 339. The "Jewish Exploitation of Farmer's Organizations," published under the byline of Robert Morgan, appeared in the *Dearborn Independent*, April 23, 1924.

CHAPTER 7

1. Quotes are from Gerald R. Ford, "Proclamation 4417 – An American Promise," February 19, 1976, *The American Presidency Project*, http://www.presidency.ucsb.edu/ws/?pid=787; Jimmy Carter, "Commission on Wartime Relocation and Internment of Civilians Act Remarks on Signing S. 1647 into Law," July 31, 1980, *The American Presidency Project*, http://www.presidency.ucsb.edu/ws/?pid=44855; Ronald Reagan, "Remarks on Signing the Bill Providing Restitution for the Wartime Internment of Japanese-American Civilians," August 10, 1988, *The American Presidency Project*, http://www.presidency.ucsb.edu/ws/?pid=36240. Timothy P. Maga's "Ronald Reagan and Redress for Japanese-American Internment, 1983–88" appeared in *Presidential Studies Quarterly* 28 (Summer 1998): 606–619. At one point, Reagan even expressed some doubt that internees had not gone willingly to camps. According to Maga (who cites February 6, 1988, Box 2/Japanese American [576683-583999] of the HU 013-22 Collection), Reagan told Thomas Kean that internees had not been "forced into internment" but rather had gone "on their own volition." Reagan also worried that the Civil Rights Bill was politically motivated to embarrass Republicans.

2. Quotes are from Nicholas Tavuchis, *Mea Culpa: A Sociology of Apology and Reconciliation* (Stanford, CA: Stanford University Press, 1991), 71 ("a public, chronicled recantation of the offense") and 103 ("what does not appear on the record is questionable, dubious, or disqualified" and "a public representation of the collectivity's moral self-image").

3. Quotes are from Nick Smith, *I Was Wrong: On the Meanings of Apologies* (Cambridge: Cambridge University Press, 2008), 214–215, and Brian Weiner, *Sins of the Parents: The Politics of National Apologies* (Philadelphia: Temple University Press, 2005), 145. The quote from Camille Paglia ("an apology can be extended") is from "Ask Camille: Camille Paglia's Online Advice for the Culturally Disgruntled," published online in *Salon.com* on July 8, 1997, and reprinted in *When Sorry Isn't Enough: The Controversy over Apologies and Reparations for Human Injustice*, ed. Roy L. Brooks (New York: New York University Press, 1999), 353–354. The quote from Jesse Helms is from the *Congressional Record* ("Senate Debate on April 12, 1988," Senator Helms speaking against S 1009, 100th Cong., 2nd sess.).

4. Mary Landrieu's observation that "the Senate failed these Americans" is from her news release, "Senate Apologizes to Lynching Victims, Families for Failure to Act," June 13, 2005, http://www.landrieu.senate.gov/?p=news&id=799. See also Sheryl Gay Stolberg, "Senate Issues Apology over Failure on Lynching Law," *New York Times*, June 14, 2005, A15; "NAACP Says Lynching Resolution Long Overdue," NAACP news release, June 14, 2005, http://www.naacp.org/press/entry/naacp-s ays-lynching-resolution-long-overdue. Nicholas von Hoffman's comments are from "An Apology for Lynching Does Nothing for Victims," *New York Observer*, August 7, 2005. The comments from publishers Glen Ford and Peter Gamble appear in "The Meaningless Apology on Lynching," *The Black Commentator* 142, http:// www.blackcommentator.com/142/142_cover_lynching.html. Thad Cochran's remarks ("I don't feel I should apologize") were made to the *Clarion-Ledger* in Jackson, Mississippi, and cited in William Raspberry's "A 'Sorry' Excuse from Cochran," *Washington Post*, June 20, 2005, A15. Lamar Alexander's comment is from the *Congressional Record* of June 13, 2005 ("But, rather than begin to catalog and apologize") from the Senate floor debate (151 Cong. Rec. – Apologizing To Lynching Victims and Their Descendants, Cr June 13, 2005, S6364-6387, at S6387).

5. The discussion of the witch trial apologies is based on Daniel Lang, "Poor Ann!" *New Yorker*, September 11, 1954, 89–107, and Zell Rabin, "They Want Their Witches Back," *Sydney Morning Herald*, September 8, 1957. The "resolve relative to the indictment, trial, conviction and execution of Ann Pudeator and certain other persons for witchcraft in the year sixteen hundred and ninety-two" can be found at http://www.mass.gov/anf/research-and-tech/gov-data-and-docs/ state-docs-and-resources/state-docs-online/ma-acts-and-resolves/massachusetts-a cts-and-resolves-1692-to-1959.html. The quotes from Frank W. Grinnell are from "Obscuring American History: Reversing the Salem Witchcraft Convictions," *ABA Journal*, November 1957, 998. The quote from Paul Tirone is from "Massachusetts Clears Five Witches in Salem Trials," *New York Times*, November 2, 2001, A2.

6. George H. W. Bush's letter to internees is in Wendy Ng, *Japanese American Internment during World War II: A History and Reference Guide* (Westport, CT: Greenwood Press, 2002), 163. Bill Clinton's letter can be found at http://www.pbs.org/ childofcamp/history/clinton.html.

7. The quote from Richard von Weizsäcker ("Anyone who closes his eyes...") is reported in James M. Markham, "'All of Us Must Accept the Past,' The German President Tells M.P.'s," *New York Times*, May 9, 1985, A20. Adenauer's apology ("The German people abominated the crimes") can be found in Jennifer Lind's book *Sorry States: Apologies in International Politics* (Ithaca, NY: Cornell University Press, 2008), 110. Willy Brandt's recollection is cited in Dan Fastenberg, "Top Ten National Apologies: The Holocaust," *Time*, June 17, 2010. Helmut Kohl's remarks at Bitburg ("We are gathered here in memory of the many innocent people") can be found in Björn Krondorfer, *Remembrance and Reconciliation: Encounters between Young Jews and Germans* (New Haven, CT: Yale University Press, 1995),

24. Helmut Kohl's later remarks ("the darkest and most horrible chapter of German history" and "one of our priority tasks is to pass on this knowledge to future generations...") are cited in Lind, 143.

8. The quote from Murayama Tomiichi ("In the hope that no such mistake be made in the future, I... express here once again my feelings of deep remorse and state my heartfelt apology") is from Lind, 62. The remarks of the Japanese Diet are also from Lind, 62–63.

9. "Gordon Brown: I'm Proud to Say Sorry to a Real War Hero," *The Telegraph*, September 10, 2009, http://www.telegraph.co.uk/news/politics/gordon-brown/6170112/Gordon-Brown-Im-proud-to-say-sorry-to-a-real-war-hero.html.

CHAPTER 8

1. Sources for the Canadian flag incident are Claire Smith, "Marines Rally 'Round the Maple Leaf, Easing a Flap," *New York Times*, October 21, 1992, B11. President George H. W. Bush's comments can be found in *Public Papers of the Presidents of the United States: George H. W. Bush* (1992–1993, Book II), October 20, 1992 (Washington, DC: U.S. Government Printing Office, 1880).

2. George W. Bush's quote ("I want to reiterate what I said") is archived as *Remarks by the President at Meeting with Republican Members of the House and Senate Budget Committees*, February 15, 2001, http://georgewbush-whitehouse.archives.gov/news/releases/2001/02/20010215-8.html. Scott Waddle's account of the events is in Scott Waddle and Ken Abraham, *The Right Thing* (Nashville, TN: Thomas Nelson, 2003). The quote "If you're a man" is from "Families of Missing Lash out at U.S. Navy," *Japan Times*, February 18, 2001. The statement from Scott Waddle's lawyer was reported in Elaine Sciolino, "Sub's Commander Expresses Regret to Victims' Families," *New York Times*, February 26, 2001, A10. Waddle's statement after the disciplinary hearing is available at "Waddle: 'My Heart Aches' for Victims of Sub Collision," CNN.com, April 23, 2001, http://articles.cnn.com/2001-04-23/us/waddle.statement_1_submarine-collision-uss-greeneville-cmdr-navy-ship?_s=PM:US. The reactions to the disciplinary hearing are reported in "End of Sub Tragedy Called 'Farce': Relatives Criticize Navy Ruling," *Japan Times*, April 25, 2001. For additional details on the Ehime Maru apologies, see Keith Hearit's *Crisis Management by Apology* (Mahwah, NJ: Lawrence Erlbaum, 2006), 170–180.

3. Anthropologist Ruth Benedict's observations about "guilt culture" and "shame culture" are in *The Chrysanthemum and the Sword: Patterns of Japanese Culture* (Boston, MA: Houghton Mifflin, 1946.). Nicholas Tavuchis's observations are from *Mea Culpa: A Sociology of Apology and Reconciliation* (Stanford, CA: Stanford University Press, 1991), 37–44.

4. Naomi Sugimoto's research on manner and etiquette and her discussion of "self-surrender," are from *Japanese Apology across Disciplines* (Nova Publishers, 1999), and the quote "is always expected to apologize in any awkward situation" is

from R. Naotsuka, N. Sakamoto, T. Hirose, H. Hagihara, J. Ohta, S. Maeda, and T. Hara, *Mutual Understanding of Different Cultures* (Tokyo: Science Education Institute, 1981), 166. The letter from Ehime Maru families to Hawaii can be found at "Ehime Maru Victims' Families Thank Hawaiians for Kindness" (*Japan Times*, March 23, 2001).

5. The quote from Nicholas Tavuchis ("In contrast to unmediated interpersonal relations") is from *Mea Culpa*, 102.

6. The quotes from General Pak and General Woodward are from Trevor Armbrister's *A Matter of Accountability* (Guilford, CT: The Lyons Press, 2004), 328, 340.

7. "Iraq Leader's Letter to Reagan: 'Deepest Regret,'" *Los Angeles Times*, May 19, 1987, online.

8. "The Downing of Flight 655; Text of Reagan's Statement," *New York Times*, July 4, 1988, 6. The expression of "deep distress" is from UN Security Council Resolution 616 (Resolution 616 (1988) adopted by the Security Council at its 2821st meeting, on July 20, 1988). The quote from Vice President George H. W. Bush ("I don't care what the facts are") is from *Newsweek* ("Perspectives: Overheard," August 15, 1988, 15).

9. The quote from Donald Rumsfeld is from "'My Deepest Apology' From Rumsfeld; 'Nothing Less Than Tragic,' Says Top General," *New York Times*, May 8, 2004, A8. General Mark Kimmitt's statement can be found at "Abuse at Abu Ghraib," CBS News, http://www.cbsnews.com/2100-500164_162-615781.html. George W. Bush's statement and Scott McClellan's characterization are from David Stout and Terence Neilan, "Bush Tells Arab World that Prisoner Abuse was 'Abhorrent,'" *New York Times*, May 6, 2004, A1. Condoleeza Rice's comment is from Fred Barbash, "'Justice Will Be Delivered' On Arab TV, Bush Decries Prisoner Abuses in Iraq," *Washington Post*, May 5, 2004, [online]. See also Nick Smith's *I Was Wrong* (Cambridge: Cambridge University Press, 2008), 176–186.

10. Secretary of State Colin Powell's *Face the Nation* interview can be found as *FTN Transcript – April 8, 2001* at http://www.cbsnews.com/8301-3460_162-284682. html. Joseph Prueher's letter is at "Text of U.S. Letter to China," http://articles.cnn. com/2001-04-11/us/prueher.letter_1_emergency-landing-china-international-e mergency-procedures?_s=PM:US, and the Chinese response is described in "Careful Language Saves Day for Detained Crew," http://articles.cnn. com/2001-04-11/world/collision.letter.analysis_1_emergency-landing-chinese-cra ft-chinese-fighter-jet?_s=PM:asiapcf. For additional discussion, see Aaron Lazare's *On Apology* (New York: Oxford University Press, 2004), 214–219.

CHAPTER 9

1. The quote from Nixon/Langella is from *Frost/Nixon*, directed by Ron Howard (Los Angeles: Universal Films, 2008). The quote from Ben Bradlee ("Never should have let him apologize in the film. Nixon never was sorry for what he did.")

is from the "Bradlee slams 'Frost/Nixon': 'Nixon never was sorry,'" *Washington Times*, December 2, 2008. Nixon's resignation speech can be found at the "President Nixon's Resignation Speech, August 8, 1974," *Character Above All: Explorations in Presidential Leadership*, PBS NewsHour, http://www.pbs.org/newshour/character/links/nixon_speech.html. Nixon's post-pardon statement can be found in "The Statement by Nixon," *New York Times*, September 9, 1974, A1. His quote, "When I resigned, people didn't think it was enough to admit mistakes," is from *Frost/Nixon: Behind the Scenes of the Nixon Interviews* (New York: HarperCollins, 2007), 24. The quote from Nixon's interview with Frank Gannon is from John Herbers, "Nixon, In T.V. Talk, Shuns Watergate Apology," *New York Times*, April 6, 1984, A17. See also Nicholas Tavuchis's *Mea Culpa*.

2. The quote from Warren Anderson ("Union Carbide has a moral responsibility") and the description of the charges ("negligence and criminal corporate liability" and "criminal conspiracy") are from Peter Stoler, Dean Brelis, and Pico Iyer, "India: Clouds of Uncertainty," *Time*, December 24, 1984, 28–29. Michael Parker's "An Open Letter to All Employees, on the Tragedy in Bhopal, India 18 Years Ago" originally appeared at http://www.dow. com/ dow_news/corporate/2002/20021128a.htm and is archived at http://www.bhopal.net/oldsite/parkermemo.html.

3. Lee Atwater's apology is from "Gravely Ill, Atwater Offers Apology," *New York Times*, January 13, 1991, 16. The characterization "emotional damage control" is from John Brady, *Bad Boy: The Life and Politics of Lee Atwater* (Boston: Addison-Wesley, 1997), 316. Michael Dukakis's comment ("At least he had the courage to apologize") can be found at "Late GOP Strategist Lee Atwater Mourned," *Associated Press AP News Archive*, March 30, 1991, http://www.apnewsarchive.com/1991/Late-GOP-Strategist-Lee-Atwater-Mourned/id-e06614cb56b60a2cf2cabf453a225523.

4. William Calley's quote ("I was ordered to go in there") is from his court-martial testimony in *United States v. Calley*, US Court of Military Appeals (1973) 22 USCMA 534, 48 Cmr 19. Calley's apology and discussion with the Kiwanians ("There is not a day that goes by" and "I believe that is true") is reported in "Calley Expresses Remorse for Role in My Lai Massacre in Vietnam," *Los Angeles Times*, August 22, 2009.

5. Aaron Lazare's discussions of external and internal reasons for apologies can be found in his book *On Apology* (New York: Oxford University Press, 2004), 134–179. We can also fail to apologize, he notes, when we simply do not realize we have committed a harm.

6. Representative Joe Barton's apologies can be found Brian Montopoli, "Rep. Joe Barton Apologizes to BP's Tony Hayward for White House 'Shakedown,'" CBS News, June 17, 2010, http://www.cbsnews.com/8301-503544_162-20008020-503544/rep-joe-barton-apologizes-to-bps-tony-hayward-for-white-house-shakedown-video-/.

7. Dwight Eisenhower, "Statement by the President Concerning the Position Taken by Chairman Khrushchev at the Opening of the Summit Conference," May 16, 1960, *The American Presidency Project*, http://www.presidency.ucsb.edu/ws/index. php?pid=11789. The quotes from Richard Nixon and John F. Kennedy are from their second presidential debate, "Presidential Debate in Washington, DC," October 7, 1960, *The American Presidency Project*, http://www.presidency.ucsb.edu/ ws/?pid=29401. Kennedy's Bay of Pigs remarks are from "Transcript of the President's News Conference on World and Domestic Affairs," *New York Times*, April 22, 1961, 8.

8. Jimmy Carter's comments on Iran are from "The President's News Conference," September 18, 1980, *The American Presidency Project* http://www.presidency.ucsb. edu/ws/?pid=45082. The quote from Ronald Reagan ("ransom for people who have been kidnapped by barbarians") is from Mark Bowden's *Guests of the Ayatollah: The Iran Hostage Crisis: The First Battle in America's War with Militant Islam* (New York: Grove Press, 2006), 563.

9. The quotes from General Eisenhower ("raise serious doubts...") and Patton's apology ("in my dealings") are from Martin Blumenson's *The Patton Papers: 1940–1945* (Cambridge, MA: Da Capo Press, 1974), 329 and 228. The quote from George C. Scott's portrayal is from *Patton*, directed by Franklin J. Schaffner (Los Angeles: Twentieth Century Fox, 1970).

10. Sources for the Dick Cheney shooting episode were "Exclusive Interview with V. P. Dick Cheney," *Special Report with Brit Hume*, February 15, 2006, transcript at http://www.foxnews.com/story/0,2933,185013,00.html#ixzz2FcbiYB1g, and Paul Farhi, "Since Dick Cheney Shot Him, Harry Whittington's Aim has Been to Move On," *Washington Post*, October 14, 2010, C1.

CHAPTER 10

1. The quotes from Nathan Brittles and other characters are from *She Wore a Yellow Ribbon*, directed by John Ford (Argosy Pictures, 1949). Garry Wills's observation is from *John Wayne's America* (New York: Simon & Schuster, 1998), 180.

2. The reported campaign to use *She Wore a Yellow Ribbon* to influence policy is reported in Jack Wheeler, "No Apology," *To the Point News*, June 1, 2005, http:// www.tothepointnews.com/content/view/1350/44/.

3. *Thelma and Louise*, directed by Ridley Scott (Beverly Hills, CA: Metro-Goldwyn-Mayer Studios, 1991).

4. Deborah Tannen, *Working 9 to 5* (New York: HarperCollins, 1994), 45.

5. The quote from Susan Solovic is from *The Girls' Guide to Power and Success* (New York: American Management Association, 2001), 63. Psychiatrist Aaron Lazare sees a benefit to a gender differences in apology behavior, suggesting that women's "overall style of interaction and management of grievance through apologies

can be expected to enhance group cohesiveness and facilitate conflict resolution." Lazare writes that in his psychiatric practice "he has observed a particular kind of apology style in some women who regards their apologies as excessive and even shameful. These women appear to have been intimidated by their parents—particularly their fathers—during childhood." *On Apology*, 28.

6. Janet Holmes's results are described in *Men, Women and Politeness* (London: Longman, 1995), 154–191. For Nick Smith's critique, see *I Was Wrong* (Cambridge: Cambridge University Press, 2008), 109–112.

7. Karina Schumann and Michael Ross, "Why Women Apologize More than Men: Gender Differences in Thresholds for Offensive Behavior," *Psychological Science* 21 (2010): 1649–1655.

8. The quote from Kim Clijsters ("I do feel bad") is from a January 18, 2011 Reuters story: "Kim Clijsters Says Sorry for Safina 'Double Bagel,'" http://uk.reuters. com/article/2011/01/18/uk-tennis-open-clijsters-idUKTRE70H1GL20110118. Chris Chase's article "Clijsters Apologizes after Handing Safina Historic Loss," *Yahoo! Sports*, January 18, 2011, http://sports.yahoo.com/tennis/ blog/busted_racquet/post/Clijsters-apologizes-after-handing-Safina-hist or?urn=ten-309023; "Should Clijsters have apologized for winning mentality?" *Jon Wertheim's Tennis Mailbag, Sports Illustrated.com*, January 19, 2011, http:// sportsillustrated.cnn.com/2011/writers/jon_wertheim/01/19/australian.open. mailbag/index.html.

9. Robin Tolmach Lakoff's quote ("Everything a powerful person says is taken seriously") is from *Talking Power* (New York: Basic Books, 1990), 267; her discussion of Ronald Reagan's apology to Coretta Scott King is recounted in *Language and Power* (Berkeley: University of California Press, 2001), 25–27. Obama's apologies for his séances and Special Olympics comments are reported in Shailagh Murray, "Obama Calls Nancy Reagan," *Washington Post*, November 7, 2008, and David Stout, "Obama Apologizes for Quip about Disabled People," *New York Times*, March 21, 2009, 10. Jimmy Carter's apology to Lady Bird Johnson is reported in Lee Dumbart, "Carter's Comments on Sex Cause Concern," *New York Times*, September 23, 1976, 36, and Christopher Lydon, "Mrs. Johnson Says She was Perplexed by Carter Remarks," *New York Times*, September 24, 1976. The assessment of the danger of speaking one's mind is from Peter Baker, "A Presidential Pitfall: Speaking One's Mind," *New York Times*, July 27, 2009, 13.

10. Gbedemah's retort ("You can keep the orange juice") is reported in Godfrey Mwakikagile's *Relations Between Africans, African Americans and Afro-Caribbeans* (Dar es Salaam, Tanzania: New Africa Press, 2007, 28). Gbedemah's comments ("If the Vice-President" and "I hope") were reported in "From Segregation to Breakfast," *Time*, October 21, 1957, 26. Eisenhower considered sending a follow-up note to Gbedemah, but was advised against it by State Department officials, who cited Nkrumah's wish to downplay the incident in light of his foreign minister's frequent

press statements. Relations between Gbedemah and Nkrumah later deteriorated, and Gbedemah was dismissed in 1961. As for the Delaware Howard Johnson's, it was advised by its corporate office to serve all customers.

11. David Brinkley's comments about Bill Clinton are in Brian Lowry, "Brinkley Gets Up Close and Personal" *Los Angeles Times*, November 7, 1996, online, and John Carman, "David Brinkley Signs Off with Blast at Clinton," sfgate.com, November 7, 1996. The Brinkley-Clinton exchange is from James Bennet, "Brinkley Offers Apology. Clinton Accepts," *New York Times*, November 11, 1996, B8.

A READER'S GUIDE TO ANALYZING APOLOGIES

1. Lawrence G. Rawl, "An Open Letter to the Public," *New York Times*, April 3, 1989, A12.
2. Tony Hayward, "A Message from Tony Hayward," *YouTube*, http://www.youtube.com/embed/KKcrDaiGE2s.
3. David Stout, "Kerry Apologizes for Iraq Remark," *New York Times*, November 1, 2006, online.
4. Robert F. Kennedy, "Speech to the Senate, March 2, 1967," in *Landmark Speeches on the Vietnam War*, ed. Gregory Allen (College Station: Texas A&M Press, 2010), 75–91.

Bibliography

This bibliography contains the main theoretical books and articles consulted in this work.

Austin, J. L. *How to Do Things with Words*. Cambridge, MA: Harvard University Press, 1962.

Benedict, Ruth. *The Chrysanthemum and the Sword: Patterns of Japanese Culture*. Boston: Houghton Mifflin, 1946.

Benoit, William. *Accounts, Excuses, Apologies: A Theory of Image Restoration Discourse*. Albany: State University of New York Press, 1995.

Brooks, Roy L., ed. *When Sorry Isn't Enough: The Controversy over Apologies and Reparations for Human Injustice*. New York: New York University Press, 1999.

Burke, Kenneth. *The Rhetoric of Motives*. Berkeley: University of California Press, 1970.

Goffman, Erving. *Interaction Ritual: Essays on Face-to-Face Behavior*. New York: Anchor Books, 1967.

_____. *The Presentation of Self in Everyday Life*. New York: Anchor Books, 1959.

_____. *Relations in Public: Microstudies of the Public Order*. New York: Basic Books, 1971.

Grice, H. Paul. "Logic and Conversation." In *Speech Acts*. Edited by Peter Cole and Jerry L. Morgan. New York: Academic Press, 1975.

Grinnell, Frank W. "Obscuring American History: Reversing the Salem Witchcraft Convictions." *ABA Journal*. November 1957, 997–999.

Hearit, Keith, *Crisis Management by Apology*. Mahwah, NJ: Lawrence Erlbaum, 2005.

Holmes, Janet. *Men, Women and Politeness*. London: Longman, 1995.

Lakoff, Robin Tolmach. *Language and Power*. Berkeley: University of California Press, 2001.

_____. *Talking Power*. New York: Basic Books, 1990.

Lazare, Aaron. *On Apology*, New York: Oxford University Press, 2004.

Lind, Jennifer. *Sorry States: Apologies in International Politics*. Ithaca, NY: Cornell University Press, 2008.

Maga, Timothy P. "Ronald Reagan and Redress for Japanese-American Internment, 1983–88." *Presidential Studies Quarterly* 28 (1998): 606–619.

Naotsuka, R., Sakamoto, N., Hirose, T., Hagihara, H., Ohta, J., Maeda, S., and Hara, T. *Mutual Understanding of Different Cultures.* Tokyo: Science Education Institute, 1981.

Schumann, Karina, and Michael Ross. "Why Women Apologize More than Men: Gender Differences in Thresholds for Offensive Behavior." *Psychological Science* 21 (2010): 1649–1655.

Searle, John R. "Indirect Speech Acts." In *Syntax and Semantics, 3: Speech Acts.* Edited by Peter Cole and Jerry L. Morgan. New York: Academic Press, 1975, 59–82.

_____. *Speech Acts: An Essay in the Philosophy of Language.* Cambridge: Cambridge University Press, 1969.

_____. "A Taxonomy of Illocutionary Acts." In *Language, Mind and Knowledge.* Edited by Keith Gunderson. Minneapolis: University of Minnesota Press, 1975, 344–369.

Smith, Nick. *I Was Wrong: On the Meanings of Apologies.* Cambridge & New York: Cambridge University Press, 2008.

Strassfeld, Robert N. "Robert McNamara and the Art and Law of Confession: 'A Simple Desultory Philippic (Or How I Was Robert McNamara'd into Submission).'" *Duke Law Journal* 47, no. 491. 1997.

Sugimoto, Naomi, ed. *Japanese Apology across Disciplines.* Hauppauge, NY: Nova Publishers, 1999.

Tannen, Deborah. *Working 9 to 5: Men and Women at Work.* New York: HarperCollins, 1994.

Tavuchis, Nicholas. *Mea Culpa: A Sociology of Apology and Reconciliation.* Stanford, CA: Stanford University Press, 1991.

Tell, David. "Jimmy Swaggart's Secular Confession." *Rhetoric Society Quarterly* 39 no. 2. April 2009, 124–146.

Thomas, Jenny. *Meaning in Interaction.* London: Longman, 1995.

Trilling, Lionel. *Sincerity and Authenticity.* Cambridge, MA: Harvard University Press, 1972.

Ware, B. L., and Wil A. Linkugel. "They Spoke in Defense of Themselves: On the Generic Criticism of Apologia." *Quarterly Journal of Speech* 59 (1973): 273–283.

Weiner, Brian. *Sins of the Parents: The Politics of National Apologies.* Philadelphia: Temple University Press, 2005.

Index